File Your Own Divorce (+CD-ROM)

Sixth Edition

Edward A. Haman

Attorney at Law

SPHINX® PUBLISHING
AN IMPRINT OF SOURCEBOOKS, INC.®
NAPERVILLE, ILLINOIS
www.SphinxLegal.com

Sixth Edition: 2005
Second Printing: May, 2006

Published by: **Sphinx® Publishing, A Imprint of Sourcebooks, Inc.®**

Naperville Office
P.O. Box 4410
Naperville, Illinois 60567-4410
(630) 961-3900
Fax: 630-961-2168
www.sourcebooks.com
www.SphinxLegal.com

This publication is designed to provide accurate and authoritative information in regard to the subject matter covered. It is sold with the understanding that the publisher is not engaged in rendering legal, accounting, or other professional service. If legal advice or other expert assistance is required, the services of a competent professional person should be sought.

From a Declaration of Principles Jointly Adopted by a Committee of the American Bar Association and a Committee of Publishers and Associations

This product is not a substitute for legal advice.

Disclaimer required by Texas statutes.

Library of Congress Cataloging-in-Publication Data
Haman, Edward A.
File your own divorce / Edward A. Haman.-- 6th ed.
    p. cm.
 Includes index.
 ISBN 1-57248-517-5 (pbk. : alk. paper)
 1. Divorce--Law and legislation--United States--Popular works. 2. Divorce--Law and legislation--United States--Forms. I. Title.

KF535.Z9H35 2005
346.7301'66--dc22   2005014268

Printed and bound in the United States of America.
CHG — 10 9 8 7 6 5 4 3 2

Contents

DISCARD

How to Use the CD-ROM vii

Using Self-Help Law Books xi

Introduction xv

Chapter 1: Marriage Ins and Outs 1
    Marriage
    Divorce
    Annulment
    Legal Separation
    Deciding if You Really Want a Divorce
    Preliminary Matters

Chapter 2: The Legal System 11
    Theory vs. Reality
    Divorce Law and Procedure
    Legal Research

Chapter 3: Lawyers.............................19
Do You Want a Lawyer?
Selecting a Lawyer
Working with a Lawyer

Chapter 4: Types of Divorce Procedures..........29
Proving Grounds for Divorce
Consent Divorce
Uncontested Divorce
Contested Divorce
Military Considerations

Chapter 5: Property and Debts 35
Gathering Information
Property
Debts
Tax Considerations

Chapter 6: Alimony.............................47
Types of Alimony
Qualifications for Obtaining Alimony
Duration of Alimony
Calculating Alimony
Tax Considerations

Chapter 7: Child Custody and Visitation..........55
Custody
Child Custody and Visitation
Visitation

Chapter 8: Child Support 63
Gathering Information
Calculating Child Support
Tax Considerations

Chapter 9: Filing for Divorce...................69
The Complaint or Petition
Supporting Documents

Marital Settlement Agreement
Negotiating
Filing with the Clerk
Counseling, Mediation, and Parenting Classes
Collecting Information about Your Spouse

Chapter 10: Emergency Procedures..............95
Protecting Yourself
Protecting Your Children
Protecting Your Property
Temporary Alimony, Child Support, and Custody

Chapter 11: Notifying Your Spouse..............101
Notice of Filing the Complaint
Certificate of Service
Notice of Hearing
When You Cannot Find Your Spouse
How Your Spouse Responds

Chapter 12: Answering a Complaint for Divorce.......................109

Chapter 13: Contested Divorce 115
Procedural Differences between a Contested Divorce and an
    Uncontested Divorce
Property and Debts
Alimony
Child Support
Child Custody and Visitation

Chapter 14: The Court Hearing..................125
Setting a Court Date
Witnesses
Courtroom Manners
Your Hearing Presentation
The Judgment or Decree

Chapter 15: The Future.......................137

Glossary **139**

Appendix A: State Law Information **145**

**Appendix B: Sample Case with
            Completed Forms** **201**

Appendix C: Worksheets **229**

Appendix D: Blank Forms **243**

Index **281**

How to Use
the CD-ROM

Thank you for purchasing *File Your Own Divorce*. In this book, we have worked hard to compile exactly what you need to file your own divorce. Whether a settlement agreement or a financial statement, we have gathered the most important forms and documents you need to protect yourself, your children, and your assets. To make this material even more useful, we have included every document in the book on the CD-ROM that is attached to the inside back cover of the book.

You can use these forms just as you would the forms in the book. Print them out, fill them in, and use them however you need. You can also fill in the forms directly on your computer. Just identify the form you need, open it, click on the space where the information should go, and input your information. Customize each form for your particular needs. Use them over and over again.

The CD-ROM is compatible with both PC and Mac operating systems. (While it should work with either operating system, we cannot guarantee that it will work with your particular system and we cannot provide technical assistance.) To use the forms on your computer, you will need to use Adobe Reader. The CD-ROM does not contain this program. You can download this program from Adobe's website at

www.adobe.com. Click on the "Get Adobe Reader" icon to begin the download process and follow the instructions.

Once you have Adobe Reader installed, insert the CD-ROM into your computer. Double click on the icon representing the disc on your desktop or go through your hard drive to identify the drive that contains the disc and click on it.

Once opened, you will see the files contained on the CD-ROM listed as "Form #: [Form Title]." Open the file you need through Adobe Reader. You may print the form to fill it out manually at this point, or your can use the "Hand Tool" and click on the appropriate line to fill it in using your computer.

Any time you see bracketed information [ ] on the form, you can click on it and delete the bracketed information from your final form. This information is only a reference guide to assist you in filling in the forms and should be removed from your final version. Once all your information is filled in, you can print your filled-in form.

NOTE: *Adobe Reader does not allow you to save the PDF with the boxes filled in.*

• • • • •

Purchasers of this book are granted a license to use the forms contained in it for their own personal use. By purchasing this book, you have also purchased a limited license to use all forms on the accompanying CD-ROM. The license limits you to personal use only and all other copyright laws must be adhered. No claim of copyright is made in any government form reproduced in the book or on the CD-ROM. You are free to modify the forms and tailor them to your specific situation.

The author and publisher have attempted to provide the most current and up-to-date information available. However, the courts, Congress, and your state's legislatures review, modify, and change laws on an ongoing basis, as well as create new laws from time to time. By the very nature of the information and due to the continual changes in our legal system, to be sure that you have the current and best information for your situation, you should consult a local attorney or research the current laws yourself.

• • • • •

This publication is designed to provide accurate and authoritative information in regard to the subject matter covered. It is sold with the understanding that the publisher is not engaged in rendering legal, accounting, or other professional service. If legal advice or other expert assistance is required, the services of a competent professional person should be sought.

> —*From a Declaration of Principles Jointly Adopted by a Committee of the American Bar Association and a Committee of Publishers and Associations*

This product is not a substitute for legal advice.

> —*Disclaimer required by Texas statutes*

Using Self-Help Law Books

Before using a self-help law book, you should realize the advantages and disadvantages of doing your own legal work and understand the challenges and diligence that this requires.

The Growing Trend

Rest assured that you will not be the first or only person handling your own legal matter. For example, in some states, more than 75% of the people in divorces and other cases represent themselves. Because of the high cost of legal services, this is a major trend and many courts are struggling to make it easier for people to represent themselves. However, some courts are not happy with people who do not use attorneys and refuse to help them in any way. For some, the attitude is, "Go to the law library and figure it out for yourself."

We write and publish self-help law books to give people an alternative to the often complicated and confusing legal books found in most law libraries. We have made the explanations of the law as simple and easy to understand as possible. Of course, unlike an attorney advising an individual client, we cannot cover every conceivable possibility.

Cost/Value Analysis

Whenever you shop for a product or service, you are faced with various levels of quality and price. In deciding what product or service to buy, you make a cost/value analysis on the basis of your willingness to pay and the quality you desire.

When buying a car, you decide whether you want transportation, comfort, status, or sex appeal. Accordingly, you decide among such choices as a Neon, a Lincoln, a Rolls Royce, or a Porsche. Before making a decision, you usually weigh the merits of each option against the cost.

When you get a headache, you can take a pain reliever (such as aspirin) or visit a medical specialist for a neurological examination. Given this choice, most people, of course, take a pain reliever, since it costs only pennies; whereas a medical examination costs hundreds of dollars and takes a lot of time. This is usually a logical choice because it is rare to need anything more than a pain reliever for a headache. But in some cases, a headache may indicate a brain tumor and failing to see a specialist right away can result in complications. Should everyone with a headache go to a specialist? Of course not, but people treating their own illnesses must realize that they are betting on the basis of their cost/value analysis of the situation. They are taking the most logical option.

The same cost/value analysis must be made when deciding to do one's own legal work. Many legal situations are very straight forward, requiring a simple form and no complicated analysis. Anyone with a little intelligence and a book of instructions can handle the matter without outside help.

But there is always the chance that complications are involved that only an attorney would notice. To simplify the law into a book like this, several legal cases often must be condensed into a single sentence or paragraph. Otherwise, the book would be several hundred pages long and too complicated for most people. However, this simplification necessarily leaves out many details and nuances that would apply to special or unusual situations. Also, there are many ways to interpret most legal questions. Your case may come before a judge who disagrees with the analysis of our authors.

Therefore, in deciding to use a self-help law book and to do your own legal work, you must realize that you are making a cost/value analysis. You have decided that the money you will save in doing it yourself outweighs the chance that your case will not turn out to your satisfaction. Most people handling their own simple legal matters never have a problem, but occasionally people find that it ended up costing them more to have an attorney straighten out the situation than it would have if they had hired an attorney in the beginning. Keep this in mind while handling your case, and be sure to consult an attorney if you feel you might need further guidance.

Local Rules   The next thing to remember is that a book which covers the law for the entire nation, or even for an entire state, cannot possibly include every procedural difference of every jurisdiction. Whenever possible, we provide the exact form needed; however, in some areas, each county, or even each judge, may require unique forms and procedures. In our state books, our forms usually cover the majority of counties in the state, or provide examples of the type of form which will be required. In our national books, our forms are sometimes even more general in nature but are designed to give a good idea of the type of form that will be needed in most locations. Nonetheless, keep in mind that your state, county, or judge may have a requirement or use a form that is not included in this book.

You should not necessarily expect to be able to get all of the information and resources you need solely from within the pages of this book. This book will serve as your guide, giving you specific information whenever possible and helping you to find out what else you will need to know. This is just like if you decided to build your own backyard deck. You might purchase a book on how to build decks. However, such a book would not include the building codes and permit requirements of every city, town, county, and township in the nation; nor would it include the lumber, nails, saws, hammers, and other materials and tools you would need to actually build the deck. You would use the book as your guide, and then do some work and research involving such matters as whether you need a permit of some kind, what type and grade of wood are available in your area, whether to use hand tools or power tools, and how to use those tools.

Before using the forms in a book like this, you should check with your court clerk to see if there are any local rules of which you should be aware, or local forms you will need to use. Often, such forms will require the same information as the forms in the book but are merely laid out differently or use slightly different language. They will some-times require additional information.

Changes in the Law

Besides being subject to local rules and practices, the law is subject to change at any time. The courts and the legislatures of all fifty states are constantly revising the laws. It is possible that while you are reading this book, some aspect of the law is being changed.

In most cases, the change will be of minimal significance. A form will be redesigned, additional information will be required, or a waiting period will be extended. As a result, you might need to revise a form, file an extra form, or wait out a longer time period; these types of changes will not usually affect the outcome of your case. On the other hand, sometimes a major part of the law is changed, the entire law in a particular area is rewritten, or a case that was the basis of a central legal point is overruled. In such instances, your entire ability to pursue your case may be impaired.

To help you with local requirements and changes in the law, be sure to read the section in Chapter 2 on "Legal Research."

Again, you should weigh the value of your case against the cost of an attorney and make a decision as to what you believe is in your best interest.

Introduction

Going through a divorce is probably one of the most common and most traumatic encounters with the legal system. Paying a divorce lawyer can be expensive, and it comes at a time when you are least likely to have extra funds. In a contested divorce case, it is not uncommon for the parties to run up legal bills of over $10,000. At the same time, horror stories abound of lawyers charging substantial fees with little progress to show for them. This book is designed to enable you to obtain a divorce without hiring a lawyer. If you do hire a lawyer, this book will help you work with him or her more effectively, also helping to reduce your legal fees.

This book gives you a summary of the law and the legal system; helps you decide if you want an attorney; helps you evaluate your situation; and, guides you in filling out forms and following procedures. However, this is not a law school course, but rather a practical guide to get you through *the system* as easily as possible.

Legal jargon has nearly been eliminated. For ease of understanding, this book uses the term *spouse* to refer to your husband or wife (whichever applies). The terms *child* and *children* are used interchangeably. A glossary is included for other terms that have special meaning in a divorce setting.

The difficulty in covering any area of law on a national scale is that the law is different in each state. However, the general information required in the forms to be filed is very similar in each state. Appendix A of this book gives you some information about the specific laws and procedures in your state. It is still important for you to do further checking into these laws and procedures to be sure you get it right. Appendix B contains sample completed forms for an imaginary divorce case, which may also be helpful to you in completing your forms.

Appendix C contains several worksheets to help you prepare for filing for divorce, and to help you keep track of your case. Appendix D provides you with some blank forms, which need to be modified for your particular state. Some states (and even different judges and courts within a state) have their own required forms and procedures, so be sure to check with your court clerk to find out if any forms are required. Court clerks cannot give legal advice, but they can tell you what their court and judges require.

The old saying that *knowledge is power* is especially true with the law. Lawyers have worked hard for many years to make the law complicated, so that only they have the knowledge and the power. This book gives you a fair amount of knowledge so you can take back some of the power. By reading this book, you will know as much (or more) about divorce law and procedure as most recent law school graduates.

The more you know, the better your chances of favorable results. By deciding to become your own lawyer, you are becoming responsible for your own future. If you want the easy way out, you can pay a lawyer big bucks to do the job. But if you want to save money, you should go beyond the information in this book and do a little additional reading and research.

Read this entire book (including the listing for your state in Appendix A) before you prepare or file any papers. This will give you the information you need to decide which forms you need and how to fill them out. You may also need to visit your court clerk's office or local law library to get more information. Chapter 2 helps you find the information you need.

To complete the necessary forms, use the general instructions in the main part of this book and consult the listing for your state in Appendix A for detailed information. Also use the information from any additional reading and research you do. Once your forms are completed, follow the instructions in this book for filing your forms, notifying your spouse, and handling your court appearance. If you need to refer to this book for answers to specific questions, use the table of contents, glossary, and index to help locate the answers you need.

– Caution –

The information and forms in this book are of a general nature. You will need to learn more about the specifics of how things are done in your state. Before preparing or filing any court papers, be sure to read the information about your state in Appendix A. You should also read the actual statute or code sections for your state. More information about finding your state's requirements and procedures can be found in the section on "Legal Research" in Chapter 2.

Marriage Ins and Outs

Several years (or maybe only months) ago, you made a decision to get married. This chapter discusses, in a very general way, what you got yourself into and how you can get yourself out.

MARRIAGE

Marriage is frequently referred to as a contract. Under the law, it is a legal contract. Financial and property rights and obligations have been created that cannot be broken without a legal proceeding.

The focus at the wedding ceremony is on the emotional and romantic (and often the religious) aspects of a relationship. For many, it is also a religious contract. This book deals only with the legal contract.

Marriage gives each of the parties certain rights in property and creates certain obligations with respect to the support of any children the parties have (or adopt) together. Unfortunately, most people do not fully realize that these rights and obligations are being created until it comes time for a divorce. Depending upon the state you live in, you and your spouse may even have rights to property each of you had before you were married.

DIVORCE

A divorce is the most common method of terminating or breaking the marriage contract. (Some states refer to divorce as *dissolution of marriage*.) In a divorce, a court declares the marriage contract broken, divides the parties' property and debts, decides if either party should receive alimony, and determines the custody, support, and visitation with respect to any children the parties may have. Traditionally, a divorce could only be granted under very specific circumstances, such as for adultery or mental cruelty. Today, many states allow a divorce simply because one or both of the parties want one. This is referred to as a *no-fault* divorce. Typically, the complaint or petition only needs to state that the marriage is "irretrievably broken," "irreparably broken," or some similar words. What a divorce procedure is called in your state and what words are used for no-fault divorce can be found in the listing for your state in Appendix A of this book.

Before you can file your divorce case in any court, you must meet the residency requirement of that court. Although all states claim to have no-fault divorce laws, certain states try to make divorce difficult by requiring the parties to separate long before filing or by long residency requirements.

A list of those states that require relatively long periods of separation, with information about which nearby states may allow a quicker divorce, is on the following page. The separation period is in brackets, "[ ]," following the name of the state. The nearby states are listed next, with their residency requirements in parentheses, "( )." For example, if you live in Arkansas, you and your spouse must be separated for eighteen months before you can file for divorce. If you move to Kansas, you could file after sixty days (or after six months in Oklahoma or Texas, or after 180 days in Kentucky).

Of course, you would need to move to the other state for the required period of residency before filing. Also, the other state's divorce laws may favor your spouse, or may cause other problems that would make it better for you to stay where you are and wait out the separation period for your state. If you are interested in relocating for a quicker divorce, you should consult a lawyer in the other state, or at least one who is licensed in *both* states.

The information provided below is only a summary. The phrase *unless both agree* means that the separation period is not required if you and your spouse agree on the divorce and have settled the issues of property division, alimony, child support, and child custody. Refer to Appendix A for more information on the separation and residency requirements of various states.

Residency Requirements

State of Current Residence	Nearby State
Arkansas [18 months]	Kansas (60 days) Oklahoma or Texas (6 months) Kentucky (180 days)
District of Columbia [1 year, unless both agree]	Delaware (6 months)
Illinois [2 years, unless both agree]	Indiana or Wisconsin (6 months) Kentucky (180 days)
Maryland [1–2 years]	Delaware (6 months)
Mississippi [No-fault is only available if both parties agree. Otherwise, one of the traditional grounds must be used. Mississippi also has issues with its property division laws]	Alabama, Georgia, Florida, Texas, or Oklahoma (6 months) Kentucky (180 days)
Missouri [24 months]	Kansas (60 days) Kentucky (180 days)
Montana [180 days, unless both agree]	Idaho (6 weeks) South Dakota (60 days after filing) Washington (90 days after filing)
New Jersey [18 months]	Delaware (6 months)
New York [1 year]	Delaware (6 months)
North Carolina [1 year]	Georgia (6 months) Kentucky (180 days)
Ohio [1 year if spouse denies no-fault grounds]	Kentucky or Michigan (180 days)
Pennsylvania [2 years, unless both agree]	Delaware (6 months) Kentucky or Michigan (180 days)
South Carolina [1 year]	Georgia or Florida (6 months)
Tennessee [2 years, unless both agree]	Alabama or Georgia (6 months) Kentucky (180 days)
Vermont [6 months]	No nearby state where quicker divorce is available
Virginia [1 year; 6 months if no children]	Delaware (6 months) Kentucky (180 days)
West Virginia [1 year, unless both agree]	Delaware (6 months) Kentucky (180 days)

ANNULMENT

Although annulments are not covered in this book, it may be helpful to your situation if you are aware of this possible alternative to divorce. While a divorce can be viewed as breaking a valid marriage, an annulment is a determination that there never was a valid marriage. This is more difficult and often more complicated to prove, so it is not used very often.

Annulments are only possible in a few circumstances, usually when one of the parties was: too young to get married; mentally incompetent at the time of the wedding; induced to marry by fraud or duress; already married to someone else (bigamy); or, if the parties are too closely related by blood (incest). You should consult an attorney if you decide that you want an annulment.

If you are seeking an annulment for religious reasons and need to go through a church procedure (rather than a legal procedure), you should consult your priest or minister.

LEGAL SEPARATION

Legal separation is the procedure used to divide the property and provide for alimony, child custody, and support in cases in which the husband and wife live separately, but remain married. This was traditionally used to break the financial rights and obligations of a couple whose religion did not permit divorce. It is also sometimes used to prepare for an eventual divorce, by allowing you and your spouse to live apart for whatever period may be required by your state to get a no-fault divorce. Some states refer to this procedure as *divorce from bed and board*. Legal separation is not available in all states.

DECIDING IF YOU REALLY WANT A DIVORCE

Getting a divorce is one of the most emotionally stressful events in a person's life. Only the death of a loved one creates more stress than a divorce. It will also have an impact on several aspects of your life and can change your entire lifestyle.

Before you begin the process of getting a divorce, you need to take some time to think about how it will affect your life. This chapter helps you examine these things and offers alternatives in the event you want to try to save your relationship. Even if you feel absolutely sure that you want a divorce, read this chapter so you are prepared for what may follow.

Legal Divorce

Emotionally, breaking the legal bonds is the easiest part of divorce. It is simply the termination of your marriage contract and partnership.

The stress here is caused by going through a court system procedure and having to deal with your spouse as you go through it. The legal divorce can be the most confrontational and emotionally explosive stage. However, when compared to the other aspects of divorce, the stress from the legal divorce does not last as long.

There are generally three matters to be resolved through the legal divorce:

1. the divorce of two people, giving each person the legal right to marry someone else;

2. the division of their property (and responsibility for debts); and,

3. the care and custody of their children.

Although it is theoretically possible for the legal divorce to be concluded within a few months, the legalities most often continue for years. This is mostly caused by the emotional aspects leading to battles over children.

Social and Emotional Divorce

Divorce will have a tremendous impact on your social and emotional lives, which will continue long after you are legally divorced. These impacts include a lack of companionship, a sense of loss, and ultimately, returning to the dating scene.

Lack of companionship. Even if your relationship is stormy, you are probably still accustomed to having your spouse around. You may, at times, be able to temporarily put aside your problems and support each other in times of mutual adversity (such as when dealing with a death in the family, the illness of a child, or severe storm damage to your home). You may also feel a little more secure at night, not being alone in the house. Even if your marriage is miserable, you will still notice at least some emptiness, loneliness, or solitude after the divorce. You may simply miss having another person around.

Grief. Divorce may be viewed as the death of a marriage, or at least, the funeral ceremony for the death of a marriage. Like the death of anyone or anything you have been close to, you will feel a sense of loss. This aspect can take you through all of the normal feelings associated with grief, such as guilt, anger, denial, and acceptance.

You will get angry and frustrated over the years you have wasted. You will feel guilty because you failed to make the marriage work. You will find yourself saying, "I can't believe this is happening to me."

For months or even years, you will spend time thinking about your marriage. It can be extremely difficult to put it all behind you and get on with your life.

The single's scene—dating. After divorce, your social life will change. If you want to avoid solitary evenings watching TV, you will find yourself trying to get back into the single's scene. This will probably involve a change in friends, as well as a change in lifestyle. First, you may find that your current friends, who might all be married, no longer find that you, as a single person, fit in with their circle. Gradually, or even quickly, you are dropped from their guest list. Now you have to start making an effort to meet single people at work, going out on the town, and even dating. This experience can be very frightening, tiring, and frustrating after years of being away from this lifestyle. It can also be very difficult if you have custody of your children. On the other hand, it can be an exciting adventure.

Financial Divorce

Divorce has a significant financial impact in just about every case. Many married couples are just able to make ends meet. After getting divorced, there are suddenly two rent payments, two electric bills, and so on. For the spouse without custody, there is also child support to be paid. For at least one spouse—and often for both—money becomes even tighter than it was before the divorce. Also, consider that once you have divided your property, each will need to replace the items the other person kept. If she got the bedroom furniture and the pots and pans, he will need to buy his own. If he got the TV and the sofa, she will need to buy her own TV and sofa.

Children and Divorce

The effect upon your children and your relationship with them can often be the most painful and long-lasting aspect of divorce. Your family life will be permanently changed, because the *family* will no longer exist. Even if you remarry, stepparents rarely bring back the original feeling of a family. Your relationship with your children may become strained as they work through their feelings of blame, guilt, disappointment, and anger. This strain may continue for many years. Your children may even need professional counseling. Also, as long as there is child support and visitation involved, you will be forced to have at least some contact with your ex-spouse.

Alternatives to Divorce

By the time you have purchased this book and read this far, you have probably already decided that you want a divorce. However, if what you have just read and thought about has changed your mind, or you want to make a last effort to save your marriage, there are a few things you can try. These are only very basic suggestions. Details and other suggestions can be offered by professional marriage counselors.

Talk to your spouse. Choose the right time to talk to your spouse about your problems. Do not start the conversation when he or she is trying to unwind after a day at work or is trying to quiet a screaming baby. Try to establish a few ground rules for the discussion, such as:

- talk about how you feel instead of making accusations that may start an argument;

- each person listens while the other speaks (no interrupting); and,

- each person must say something that he or she likes about the other and about the relationship.

As you talk, you may want to discuss things such as where you would like your relationship to go, how it has changed since you got married, and what can be done to bring you closer together.

Change your thinking. Many people get divorced because they will not change something about their outlook or their lifestyle. Then, once divorced, many find they have made the change they resisted for so long.

Example:

George and Wendy were unhappy in their marriage. They did not seem to share the same lifestyle. George felt overburdened with responsibility and bored. He wanted Wendy to be more independent and outgoing, meet new people, handle the household budget, and go out with him more often. But Wendy was more shy and reserved, was not confident in her ability to find a job and succeed in the business world, and preferred to stay at home. Wendy wanted George to give up some of his frequent nights out with the guys, help with the cooking and laundry, stop leaving messes for her to clean up, and stop bothering her about going out all the time. But neither would try to change, and eventually all of the little things built up into a divorce.

After the divorce, Wendy was forced to get a job to support herself. Now she has made friends at work, goes out with them two or three nights a week, is successful and happy at her job, and is competent at managing her own budget. George now has his own apartment, cooks his own meals (something he finds he enjoys), and does his own laundry. He has also found it necessary to clean up his own messes and keep the place neat, especially if he is going to entertain guests.

Both George and Wendy have changed in exactly the way the other had wanted. It is too bad they did not make these changes *before* they got divorced! If you think some changes may help, give them a try. You can always go back to a divorce if things do not work out.

Counseling. Counseling is not the same as giving advice. A counselor should not be telling you what to do. A counselor's job is to assist you in figuring out what you really want to do, mostly by asking questions that will get you thinking.

Just talking things out with your spouse is a form of self-counseling. The only problem is how difficult it can be to remain objective and nonjudgmental. You both need to be able to calmly analyze what the problems are and discuss possible solutions.

Very few couples seem to be able to do this successfully, which is why there are professional marriage counselors. As with doctors and lawyers, good marriage counselors are best discovered by word of mouth. You may have friends who can direct you to someone who helped them. You can also check with your family doctor or your clergyman for a referral, or even check the telephone Yellow Pages under "Marriage and Family Counselors," or a similar category. You can see a counselor either alone or with your spouse.

Another form of individual counseling is talking to a close friend. Just remember the difference between counseling and advice-giving. Do not let your friend tell you what you should do.

Trial separation. Before going to the time and trouble of getting a divorce, you and your spouse may want to try getting away from each other for a while. A trial separation can be as simple as taking separate vacations, or as complex as separating into separate households for an indefinite period of time. This trial separation may give each of you a chance to think about how you will like living alone, how important or trivial your problems are, and how you really feel about each other.

PRELIMINARY MATTERS

Unless you and your spouse have already agreed to a divorce, you probably do not want your spouse to know that your are thinking of filing for divorce. This is a defense tactic, although it may not seem that way at first. If your spouse suspects you are filing a divorce, he or she may do things to prevent you from obtaining a fair result. This may include withdrawing money from bank accounts, hiding information about income, and hiding assets. For purposes of protecting your assets, you should at least be sure you have documentation of what you and your spouse own. (See Chapter 5 for more about what documentation you need to obtain.) There may also be other potential problems, such as domestic violence, or your spouse taking your child. Be sure to read Chapter 10 for more information about dealing with these and other problems.

The Legal System

This chapter gives you a general introduction to the legal system and divorce law. There are things you need to know in order to obtain a divorce (or help your lawyer get the job done), and to get through any encounter with the legal system with minimal stress. This chapter also discusses how the system is supposed to work (in theory), as well as some of the realities of our system. If you do not learn to accept these realities, you will experience a great deal of stress and frustration.

THEORY VS. REALITY

Our legal system is a system of rules. There are basically three types of rules.

1. *Rules of Law:* provide the basic substance of the law, such as a law telling a judge how to go about dividing your property.

2. *Rules of Procedure:* tell how matters are to be handled in the courts, such as requiring court papers to be in a certain form or filed within a certain time.

3. *Rules of Evidence:* require facts to be proven in a certain way.

Theory   The theory is that these rules allow each side to present evidence most favorable to that side, and an independent person or persons (the judge or jury) will be able to figure out the truth. Then, certain legal principles will be applied to that truth that will give a fair resolution of the dispute between the parties. These legal principles are supposed to be relatively unchanging, so we can all know what will happen in any given situation and can plan our lives accordingly. This will provide order and predictability to our society. Any change in legal principle is supposed to occur slowly, so the expected behavior in our society is not confused from day to day.

Reality   Unfortunately, the system does not really work this way. The following are only some of the problems in the legal system.

The system is not perfect. Our efforts to find fairness and justice have resulted in a complex set of rules. Contrary to how it may seem, the rules are not made just to complicate the system and confuse everyone. They are attempts to make the system as fair and just as possible. They have been developed over several hundred years, and in most cases, they do make sense. The rules are designed to apply to all people, in all cases. Unfortunately, following the rules does not seem to give a fair result in some situations.

Judges do not always follow the rules. It is a shocking discovery to find that the judges do not always pay any attention to legal theories and the law. Many judges make a decision simply on what they think seems fair under the circumstances. Unfortunately, what seems fair to a particular judge may depend upon his or her personal ideas and philosophy. For example, there is nothing in the divorce laws of many states that gives one parent priority in child custody. However, a majority of judges believe that a young child is generally better off with his or her mother. All other things being equal, these judges will find a way to justify awarding custody to the mother, even if it means twisting the law or the facts.

The system is often slow. Even lawyers get frustrated at how long it can take to get a case completed (especially if they do not get paid until it is done). Whatever your situation, things will take longer than you expect. Patience is required to get through the system with a minimum amount of stress. Do not let your impatience or frustration show. No matter what happens, keep calm, and be courteous and polite to the judge, the court clerks, any lawyers involved, and even your spouse (at least while you are in court).

No two cases are alike. Just because your friend's case went a certain way does not mean yours will have the same result. The judge can make a difference, and more often the circumstances will make the difference. Just because your coworker makes the same income as you and has the same number of children does not mean you can assume you will be ordered to pay the same amount of child support. There are usually other circumstances your coworker does not tell you about and possibly does not understand.

Half of the people lose. The legal system is designed to produce a winner and a loser. This usually precludes a win-win situation that might be possible (and more fair) with some other type of system. Remember, there are two sides to every legal issue, and there is only one winner. Do not expect to have every detail go your way. If you leave anything to the judge to decide, you can expect to have some things go your spouse's way.

DIVORCE LAW AND PROCEDURE

This section gives some general information about the typical laws and procedures in many states. Be sure to read the next two sections, which will help you find the specific laws for your state that you need to know.

The basic divorce law in most states is actually very simple. You will need to show the following four things.

1. That your marriage is broken. (This is done simply by stating this fact, which means that your marriage relationship is broken and cannot be saved.)

2. How you and your spouse should divide your property.

3. Who should have custody of your children and how should they be supported.

4. If one of you should receive alimony, and if so, how much and for how long.

The divorce procedure is also simple. There are basically three steps.

1. File a petition with the court clerk.

2. Notify your spouse.

3. Go to the hearing and present the information required.

(These matters are discussed in more detail in later chapters of this book.)

The Players

The law and the legal system are often compared to games, and just like in games, it is important to know the players.

The judge. The judge has the power to decide whether you can get divorced, how your property will be divided, who will get custody of the children, and how much the other will pay for child support. The judge is the last person you want to make angry. Judges have large caseloads, and like it best when your case can be concluded quickly and without hassle. The more you and your spouse can agree upon, and the more complete your paperwork is, the more you will please the judge.

The judge's secretary. The judge's secretary sets the hearings for the judge, and can frequently answer many of your questions about the procedure and what the judge prefers or requires. You do not want to make an enemy of the secretary. This means do not call often and do not ask too many questions (but a few questions are okay). You may want to start off saying that you just want to make sure you have everything in order for the judge. Be friendly and courteous, even if the secretary is rude. The secretary has a large case load just like the judge and may be suffering from stress, or he or she may just be a nasty person. You will get farther by being pleasant than by arguing or complaining.

The court clerk. While the secretary usually only works for one judge, the court clerk works with all of the judges. The clerk's office is the central place where all of the court files are kept. The clerk files your court papers and keeps the official records of your divorce.

Most people who work in the clerk's office are friendly and helpful. While they cannot give you legal advice (such as telling you what to say in your court papers), they can help explain the system and the procedures (such as telling you what type of papers must be filed).

The clerk has the power to accept or reject your papers, so you do not want to anger the clerk. If the clerk tells you to change something in your papers, change it. Do not argue or complain.

Lawyers. Lawyers serve as guides through the legal system and as modern-day hired guns. They try to guide their own client while trying to confuse, manipulate, or out-maneuver their opponent. Chapter 3 discusses lawyers in more detail.

The Law in Your State

You first need to refer to the listing for your state in Appendix A of this book, which gives you some basic information about the law in your state. More information about how to use Appendix A is found in later chapters. Also, call or visit the clerk of the court where you will be filing for divorce. The clerk will be able to tell you if there are any required forms you will need, how much filing fees are, where the nearest law library is located, and can give you some guidance about court procedures. However, the clerk cannot give you legal advice. It is also strongly suggested that you visit a law library. The next section of this chapter will give you more information about using the law library.

LEGAL RESEARCH

In order to be certain you are doing things correctly, you need to do some research into the divorce law in your state. Appendix A of this book provides some information regarding the law in each state and gives you a starting point for looking further.

After reading this book, you will want to visit your local law library. One can usually be found in or near your county courthouse. If you live near a law school, you can also find a library there. Do not hesitate to ask the law librarian to help you find what you need. The librarian cannot give you legal advice, but can show you where to find your state's laws and other books on divorce. Some typical sources are discussed in the following sections.

Statutes or Code

The main source of information will be the set of volumes that contain the laws passed by your state legislature. Depending upon your state, these will be referred to as either the *statutes* or the *code* of your state (for example, *Florida Statutes* or *Mississippi Code*). The actual title of the books may also include words such as *revised* or *annotated* (for example, *Annotated California Code, Illinois Statutes Annotated, Kentucky Revised Statutes,* or *Maine Revised Statutes Annotated*). *Revised* simply means updated, and *annotated* means that the books contain summaries of court decisions, as well as other information, that explain and interpret the laws.

In some states, the titles will also include the name of the publisher, such as *West's Colorado Revised Statutes Annotated, Vernon's Annotated Missouri Statutes,* or *Purdon's Pennsylvania Consolidated Statutes Annotated*. The listing for your state in Appendix A gives the title of the set of laws for your state after the words "The Law."

A few states have more than one set of laws, by various publishers. For example, Florida has both *Florida Statutes* (published by the State) and *Florida Statutes Annotated* (published by a private company). Each state's listing in Appendix A gives the name of the set of books used by the author. Ask the law librarian for help if you have any problems in locating your state's divorce laws.

Each year, the state legislatures meet and change the law. Therefore, it is important to be sure you have the most current version. Once you locate the set of books at the library, you will find that they are updated in one of three ways. The most common way to update laws is with a soft-cover supplement, which will be found in the back of each volume. There will be a date on the cover of the supplement to tell you when it was published (such as "2006 Cumulative Supplement"). If it is more than one year old, ask the librarian if it is the most current supplement.

Another way laws are updated is with a supplement volume, which will be found at the end of the regular set of volumes. This will also have a date or year on it.

A few states also use a loose-leaf binder in which pages are removed and replaced—or a supplement section is added—as the law changes.

Practice Manuals At the law library, you will also be able to find books containing detailed information about divorce law in your state, including sample forms for all different situations. Some of these books are written in connection with seminars for lawyers, and they can be very helpful in answering your questions about very specific situations.

Court Rules Court rules are the rules of procedure that are applied in the courts of your state. They may also contain some approved forms. You probably will not need to use the court rules much, but they may be helpful if the court clerk or judge tells you that you have not done something right. In such a case, you may need to read the rule to find out how to correct the problem.

Case Law You probably will not need to do any more research than to look up the divorce law provisions in your state's statutes or code, and look at some of the forms in a form and procedure book. The following information is provided just in case you need (or want) to go further with your research. In addition to the laws passed by the legislature, law is also made by the decisions of the judges in various cases each year. To find this *case law* you will need to go to a law library. In addition to annotated codes or statutes, there are several types of books used to find case law.

Digests. A *digest* is a set of volumes that gives short summaries of appeals court cases, and directs you to where you can find the court's full written opinion. The information in the digest is arranged alphabetically by subject. First, try to find a digest for your state (such as *New York Digest*). There is a digest that covers the entire United States, but it will be easier to find your state's laws in a state digest. Look for the chapter on "Divorce" or "Dissolution of Marriage," then look through the headings for the subject you want. If you cannot find a chapter titled "Divorce," look in the index under "Divorce" to find out what chapter title you should use.

Case reporters. The *case reporters* are where the appeals courts publish their written opinions on the cases they hear. There may be a specific reporter for your state, or you may need to use a regional reporter that contains cases from several states in your area. Your librarian can help you locate the reporter you need.

There may be two *series* of the regional reporter, and in some places, three or four. The second and subsequent series are newer than the first. If you found a case in a digest, or otherwise have a citation to a case you want to read, you can find it in a case reporter. For example, if the digest tells you that the case of *Smith v. Smith* is located at *149 So.2d 721,* you can find the case by going to Volume 149 of the Southern Reporter 2d Series, and turning to page 721. In its *opinion*, the court discusses what the case was about, what questions of law were presented for consideration, and what the court decided and why.

Legal Encyclopedia   A legal encyclopedia is similar to a regular encyclopedia. You simply look up the subject you want (such as "Divorce"), in alphabetical order, and it gives you a summary of the law on that subject. It will also refer to specific court cases, which can then be found in a reporter. On a national level, the two main sets are *American Jurisprudence* (abbreviated *Am. Jur.*) and *Corpus Juris Secundum* (C.J.S.). You may also find a set for your state, such as *Florida Jurisprudence* or *Texas Jurisprudence*.

Online Research   The statutes of most states and other legal information can be accessed online at:

www.findlaw.com

Once you get to the site, click on "Search Cases & Codes," then scroll down to "U.S. State Laws–Cases, Codes, Statutes and Regulations." Finally, click on the name of the state you want.

Findlaw will also give you links to state and federal court opinions, as well as numerous legal resources. If you want to skip navigating through the Findlaw site, you can go straight to your state's website, which is listed in Appendix A.

Lawyers

Whether or not you need an attorney depends upon many factors, such as how comfortable you feel handling the matter yourself; whether your situation is more complicated than usual; and, how much opposition you get from your spouse or from your spouse's attorney. It may also be advisable to hire an attorney if you encounter a judge with a hostile attitude. A very general rule is that you should consider hiring an attorney whenever you reach a point where you no longer feel comfortable representing yourself. This point varies greatly with each person, so there is no easy way to be more definite. (Other special situations in which you might need an attorney are discussed in later chapters of this book.)

DO YOU WANT A LAWYER?

One of the first questions you will want to consider—and most likely the reason you are reading this book—is: *How much will an attorney cost?* Attorneys come in all ages, shapes, sizes, sexes, racial, and ethnic groups—and price ranges. For a very rough estimate, you can expect an attorney to charge anywhere from $150 to $1,000 for an uncontested divorce, and from $800 and up for a contested divorce.

Lawyers usually charge an hourly rate for contested divorces, ranging from about $75 to $300 per hour. Of course, these fees may vary from state to state. Most new (and therefore, less expensive) attorneys would be quite capable of handling a simple divorce, but if your situation became more complicated, you would probably prefer a more experienced lawyer.

Advantages to Hiring an Attorney

There are several situations when using an attorney will be to your advantage. Some of those situations would include the following.

✪ Judges and other attorneys may take you more seriously. Most judges prefer both parties to have attorneys. They feel this helps the case move in a more orderly fashion, because both sides will know the procedures and relevant issues. People representing themselves very often waste time on matters that have absolutely no bearing on the outcome of the case.

✪ Attorneys prefer to deal with other attorneys for the same reasons judges do.

✪ A lawyer will serve as a buffer between you and your ex-spouse. This can lead to a quicker passage through the system by reducing the chance for emotions to take control and confuse the issues.

✪ You can let your lawyer worry about all of the details. By having an attorney, you only need to become generally familiar with the contents of this book. It will be your attorney's job to file the proper papers in the correct form, and to deal with the court clerks, the judge, the process server, your ex-spouse, and your ex-spouse's attorney.

✪ Lawyers provide professional assistance with problems. It is an advantage to have an attorney in the event your case is complicated or suddenly becomes complicated. It can also be comforting to have a lawyer to turn to for advice or to answer your questions.

Advantages to Representing Yourself

There are, however, situations in which representing yourself will have distinct advantages. Some of those situations include the following.

- ✪ You save the cost of a lawyer.

- ✪ Sometimes judges feel more sympathetic toward a person not represented by an attorney. Sometimes this results in the unrepresented person being allowed a certain amount of leeway with the procedural rules.

- ✪ The procedure may be faster. Two of the most frequent complaints about lawyers received by bar associations involve delay in completing the case and failure to return phone calls. Most lawyers have a heavy caseload that sometimes results in cases being neglected for various periods of time. If you are following the progress of your own case, you will be able to diligently push it through the system.

- ✪ Selecting an attorney is not easy. As the next section shows, it is hard to know whether you are selecting an attorney you will be happy with.

Middle Ground

You may want to look for an attorney who is willing to accept an hourly fee to answer your questions and give you help as you need it. This way, you save some legal costs, but still get some professional assistance. Just be aware that lawyers tend to find fault with anything they did not personally prepare. For example, you can show a lawyer a document he prepared, and if he does not remember he prepared it, he will find things to change. A lawyer may tell you that you have done everything wrong and try to persuade you let him or her handle your case entirely. Therefore, you may want to resort to seeing a lawyer only if you have encountered a problem at the clerk's office or with the judge.

SELECTING A LAWYER

Selecting a lawyer is a two-step process. First, you need to decide which attorney to make an appointment with. Then, you need to decide if you want to hire that attorney.

Finding Possible Lawyers

There are many ways to find an attorney. Some of the ways may give you a little more confidence in your selection as you go to evaluate the lawyer, while others may provide a quick list to choose from with no other information. The following are some of the most common ways to find an attorney.

Ask a friend. A common—and frequently the best—way to find a lawyer is to ask someone you know to recommend one. This is especially helpful if the lawyer represented your friend in a divorce or other family law matter.

Attorney referral service. An attorney referral service is a service, usually operated by a bar association, that is designed to match a client with an attorney handling cases in the area of law the client needs. The referral service does not guarantee the quality of work, the level of experience, or the ability of the attorney. Finding a lawyer this way will at least connect you with one who is interested in divorce and family law matters, and probably has some experience in this area. You can find one by looking in the Yellow Pages phone directory under "Attorney Referral Services" or "Attorneys."

Yellow Pages. In addition to attorney referral services, you can check the Yellow Pages under the heading for "Attorneys." Many of the lawyers and law firms will place display ads here indicating their areas of practice and educational backgrounds. Look for ads for firms or lawyers that indicate they practice in areas such as divorce, family law, or domestic relations.

Ask another lawyer. If you have used the services of an attorney in the past for some other matter (for example, a real estate closing, traffic ticket, or a will), you may want to call and ask if he or she handles divorces, or could refer you to an attorney whose ability in the area of family law is respected.

Evaluating a Lawyer

After putting together a list of potential attorneys, should select three to five lawyers worthy of further consideration. Your first step will be to call each attorney's office, explain that you are interested in seeking a divorce, and ask the following questions.

✪   Does the attorney (or firm) handle divorces?

✪   How much can you expect it to cost?

✪   How soon can you get an appointment?

If you like the answers you get, ask if you can speak to the attorney. Some offices will permit this, but others will require you to make an appointment. Make the appointment if that is what is required. Once you contact the attorney (either on the phone or at the appointment), ask the following questions.

✪   How long has the attorney been in practice?

✪   How long has the attorney been in practice in your state?

✪   What percentage of the attorney's cases involve divorce cases or other family law matters? (Do not expect an exact answer, but you should get a rough estimate that is at least 20%.)

✪   How long will it take? (Do not expect an exact answer, but the attorney should be able to give you an average range and discuss things that may make a difference.)

✪   How much will it cost? (Do not expect an exact answer, but the attorney should be able to give you a range of costs and what could affect overall costs.)

If you get acceptable answers to these questions, it is time to ask yourself the following questions about the lawyer.

✪   Do you feel comfortable talking to the lawyer?

✪   Is the lawyer friendly toward you?

✪   Does the lawyer seem confident in him- or herself?

✪   Does the lawyer seem to be straightforward with you and able to explain things so you understand?

If you get satisfactory answers to all of these questions, you probably have a lawyer you will be able to work with. Most clients are happiest with an attorney they feel comfortable with.

WORKING WITH A LAWYER

Once you hire your attorney, let your lawyer do his or her job. For example, it is your lawyer's job to communicate with your spouse or with your spouse's lawyer. Many lawyers have had clients lose or damage their cases when the client decides to say or do something on his or her own.

You will work best with your attorney if you listen to his or her instruction and keep an open, honest, and friendly attitude. You should also consider the following suggestions.

Ask Questions

If you want to know something, or if you do not understand something, ask your attorney. If you do not understand the answer, tell your attorney and ask that it be explained again. There are many points of law that even lawyers do not fully understand, so you should not be embarrassed to ask questions. Many people who say they had a bad experience with a lawyer either did not ask enough questions or had a lawyer who would not take the time to explain things to them. If your lawyer is not taking the time to explain what he or she is doing, it may be time to look for a new lawyer.

Give Complete Information

Anything you tell your attorney is confidential. An attorney can lose his or her license to practice if he or she reveals information without your permission, so do not hold back. Tell your lawyer everything, even if it does not seem important to you. There are many things that can change the outcome of a case, but seem unimportant to the average person.

Do not hold something back because you are afraid it will hurt your case. It will definitely hurt your case if your lawyer does not find out about it until hearing it from your spouse's attorney. Knowing information in advance can eliminate or reduce the damage to your case.

Accept Reality   Listen to what your lawyer tells you about the law and the system, and accept it. It will do you no good to argue because the law or the system does not work the way you think it should. For example, if your lawyer tells you that the judge cannot hear your case for two weeks, do not try demanding that a hearing be set for tomorrow. By refusing to accept reality, you are only setting yourself up for disappointment. Remember—it is not your attorney's fault that the system is not perfect, or that the law does not say what you would like it to say.

Be Patient   Be patient with the system (which is often slow), as well as with your attorney. Do not expect your lawyer to return your phone call within an hour. He or she may not be able to return it the same day, either. Most lawyers are very busy and overworked. It is rare that an attorney can maintain a full caseload and still make each client feel like the only client.

Talk to the Secretary   Your lawyer's secretary can be a valuable source of information. Be friendly and get to know him or her. Often, he or she will be able to answer your questions, and you will not get a bill for the time you talk to him or her.

Be on Time   This applies to appointments with your lawyer and to court hearings.

Keep Your Case Moving   Many lawyers operate on the old principle of *the squeaking wheel gets the oil*. Work on a case tends to get put off until a deadline is near, an emergency develops, or the client calls. There is a reason for this. Many lawyers take more cases than can be effectively handled in order to increase their income. Your task is to become a squeaking wheel that does not squeak too much. Whenever you talk to your lawyer, ask the following questions.

  ✪   What is the next step?

  ✪   When do you expect it to be done?

  ✪   When should I talk to you next?

If you do not hear from the lawyer when you expect, call him or her the following day. Do not remind your lawyer that he or she did not call; just ask how things are going.

Avoid Excess Fees

Of course you do not want to spend unnecessary money for an attorney. The following are a few things you can do to avoid excess legal fees.

- ✪ Do not make unnecessary phone calls to your lawyer.

- ✪ Give information to the secretary whenever possible.

- ✪ Direct your question to the secretary first. The secretary will refer it to the attorney if he or she cannot answer it.

- ✪ Plan your phone calls so you can get to the point and take less of your attorney's time.

- ✪ Do some of the leg work yourself. Pick up and deliver papers yourself, for example. Ask your attorney what you can do to assist with your case.

- ✪ Be prepared for appointments. Have all related papers with you and plan your visit to get to the point. Make an outline of what you want to discuss and what questions you want to ask.

Pay Your Bill

No client gets prompt attention like a client who pays his or her lawyer on time. However, you are entitled to an itemized bill, showing what the attorney did and how much time it took. Review your bill carefully. There are numerous stories of people paying an attorney money in advance (a retainer), only to have the attorney make a few phone calls to the spouse's lawyer, then ask for more money. If your attorney asks for $500 or $1,000 in advance, be sure that you and the lawyer agree on what is to be done for this fee. For $500, you should at least expect to have a petition prepared, filed with the court, and served on your spouse (although the filing and service fees will probably be extra).

Many attorneys will have you sign an agreement that states how you will be charged, what is included in the hourly fee, and what is extra. Many states also require signed agreements regarding fees for divorce cases, so do not be surprised if your lawyer asks you to sign a fee agreement.

Firing Your Lawyer

If you find that you can no longer work with your lawyer or do not trust your lawyer, it is time to either continue alone or get a new attorney. You will need to send your lawyer a letter stating that you no longer desire his or her services, and are discharging him or her from your case.

Also state that you will be coming by his or her office the following day to pick up your file. The attorney does not have to give you his or her own notes, or other work he or she has in progress, but he or she must give you the essential contents of your file (such as copies of papers already filed or prepared and billed for, any documents you provided). If he or she refuses to give you your file for any reason, contact your state's bar association about filing a complaint or grievance against the lawyer.

You will need to settle any remaining fees charged. Realize that until a new attorney is accepted by the court, you are now responsible to make sure your case is proceeding according to what the judge has ordered.

Types of Divorce Procedures

Traditionally, it was not easy to get a divorce. The law usually required certain circumstances to exist before a divorce could be granted, and these circumstances did not include that the parties simply no longer wanted to be married. The reasons for a divorce are called *grounds* for divorce. Traditional grounds for divorce were adultery, physical or mental cruelty, insanity, desertion or abandonment, imprisonment, alcoholism, and impotence. If you could not prove one of these situations, the divorce was denied.

Today, however, all states have what is commonly referred to as no-fault divorce. No-fault divorce laws generally allow you to get a divorce just because you and your spouse no longer want to be married. This is most commonly phrased as *irreconcilable differences* or *irretrievable breakdown* of the marriage. Some states use *incompatibility, irrevocable breakdown,* or *irremediable breakdown*. Texas uses more complicated language:

> *The marriage of the parties has become insupportable because of discord or conflict of personalities that has destroyed the legitimate ends of the marriage relationship and prevents any reasonable expectation of reconciliation.*

A few states require you and your spouse to live apart for a certain length of time before you can file for divorce. These states will use language similar to that of New Jersey, which requires:

The parties have been living separate and apart for eighteen months, and there is no reasonable prospect of reconciliation.

The listing for your state in Appendix A, under the section titled "Grounds," gives you the exact language to use in your petition or complaint. If there is a separation period, the traditional grounds are listed in Appendix A. If any of them apply to you, you can file right away (without waiting for the separation period). However, you will need to prove these traditional grounds. For all states, a reference is given to the law that contains the grounds for divorce. Refer to the section on "Separation and Residency Requirements" in Chapter 1 for more information.

PROVING GROUNDS FOR DIVORCE

The following is a brief discussion of how you would usually prove certain grounds for divorce at the final hearing.

No-Fault   For a no-fault divorce, you need to testify that your marriage is irretrievably broken (or use whatever language is used in your state), and briefly tell the judge why you do not want to be married any longer. In some states and in some types of consent procedures, your spouse may also need to say the same thing. If there is a separation period required, you may also need to bring a friend to testify that you and your spouse have been living apart for the required period.

Adultery   To prove the ground of adultery, you need testimony from someone who has good, first-hand knowledge of your spouse's affair. This can be you, a friend, a neighbor, or even a private investigator you hired to investigate your spouse. It will have to be someone who has seen your spouse with the other person in a situation strongly indicating adultery, such as engaging in a sexual act, coming and going from a hotel room, etc. It will not do to have someone testify that they heard your spouse was seen with the other person or is having an affair. Of course, you can also use any admission your spouse might make to you or another person.

Cruelty, Desertion, Alcoholism, Drug Abuse, or Impotence

The grounds of cruelty, desertion, alcoholism, drug abuse, or impotence can generally be proven by your testimony alone. It is helpful for you to have another person testify as well in order to verify what you say. Also helpful is the testimony of a doctor or other professional who has treated your spouse for alcoholism, drug abuse, or impotence. A court order for treatment of alcoholism or drug abuse, or other documented evidence could also be used.

Insanity

To prove the ground of insanity, you need the testimony of a mental health professional (psychiatrist, psychologist, etc.) who has examined your spouse; someone with official records documenting the insanity; or, a certified copy of a court order committing your spouse to a mental institution. It will not be enough for you and your friends to go to court and say, "He's crazy." Some states have specific laws about what circumstances need to exist, which procedures must be followed, and what needs to be proven if insanity grounds are used.

Imprisonment

To prove the ground of imprisonment, you need a certified copy of the court's judgment of conviction and sentencing order. Some states only allow divorce for felony convictions or for prison sentences of more than a certain length of time. Just be sure the papers you have show whatever information is required by the divorce laws in your state.

CONSENT DIVORCE

Technically, there are generally two different divorce procedures. However, in practice, the procedures can be broken down into three. They are *consent divorce*, *uncontested divorce*, and *contested divorce*. A *consent divorce* is when you and your spouse both agree to the divorce and can work out the matters of property division, alimony, child custody, and support. This may be referred to by other names, such as *simplified* divorce, but it is not available in all states. Look under the listing for your state in Appendix A, and check with your court clerk to find out if there is a special consent divorce procedure in your state. In this situation, getting a divorce is merely a matter of filing certain forms with the court and getting the judge to approve your agreement. If special consent procedures are not available in your state, you can get the same result with an uncontested divorce procedure.

UNCONTESTED DIVORCE

The *uncontested* procedure is mainly used in the following situations:

- ✪ by those who are in agreement (or can reach an agreement);

- ✪ if your spouse fails to respond to the petition or complaint; or,

- ✪ if you cannot locate your spouse.

If you reach an agreement, you will file a copy of the agreement with the clerk. Your spouse may also need to file an *answer* or *response*, which is a written response to the petition or complaint. In this case, your spouse's answer would say that he or she agrees with your petition or complaint.

If your spouse does not respond to your petition or complaint, or cannot be found, you can continue to the final hearing and get a divorce by default. In most states you will still need to testify and present your proof. Very few states will grant a divorce without any testimony or proof.

CONTESTED DIVORCE

The *contested* procedure will be necessary if you and your spouse are arguing over some matter and cannot resolve it. This may be the result of disagreement over custody of the children, the payment of child support or alimony, the division of your property, or any combination of these items. (Chapter 13 of this book discusses the contested divorce in more detail.)

MILITARY CONSIDERATIONS

If either you or your spouse are in the military, any type of divorce will be more complicated. Various federal laws must be considered, primarily concerning: notice to the other party; alimony and child support; the distribution of retirement and other benefits; what information must be included in any final judgment; and, what forms must be submitted to the military. For the spouse of the service person, this will also require some negotiation to compensate for the loss of certain benefits, including the *Survivor Benefit Plan*. This applies if either or both parties are on active duty, in the reserve, or retired from, any of the following.

- ✪ U.S. Air Force

- ✪ U.S. Army

- ✪ U.S. Marine Corps

- ✪ U.S. Navy

- ✪ U.S. Coast Guard

- ✪ U.S. Public Health Service

- ✪ National Oceanographic and Atmospheric Administration

In such a situation, it is strongly suggested that you find a lawyer who is familiar with the special problems encountered when one or both parties are in the military. All branches of the service offer some form of legal assistance (such as the JAG office), but you may also wish to check with your local bar association referral service for an attorney who has experience with divorces in military families.

The two federal laws that have an impact are the *Servicemembers Civil Relief Act* (SCRA) and the *Uniformed Services Former Spouse's Protection Act* (USFSPA). Each of these will be discussed briefly, but they are extensive sets of laws with a complexity that requires an experienced lawyer to fully evaluate.

SCRA   The Servicemembers Civil Relief Act (SCRA) was signed into law in 2003, making substantial changes to the *Soldier's and Sailor's Civil Relief Act* (SSCRA) of 1940. The general purpose of this act is to protect active duty members and their dependents from suffering legal disadvantages as a result of being in the service. The SCRA applies to all types of civil legal and administrative proceedings. As it relates to divorces, the more significant provisions require that a court appoint an attorney for an active duty member before a judgment can be entered, that the proceeding can be delayed for a minimum of ninety days in certain circumstances, and that certain forms be filed to show the court whether the defendant or respondent is in the military. Although the use of videotaped testimony, the required granting of leave, and the availability of pay records may make a delay of proceedings unnecessary, there are still legal procedural steps that must be followed, which are best handled by a knowledgeable attorney.

USFSPA   The *Uniformed Services Former Spouse's Protection Act* (USFSPA) allows for the distribution of military retirement pay to a divorced spouse. The calculation of the amount the spouse is to receive can be complicated, and the law is not applied uniformly from state to state (or from court to court). The law also provides for limits on the awards of alimony, child support, and retirement benefits, as well as for methods of enforcing court orders. All of this requires an experienced attorney to protect the rights of both parties.

Property and Debts

This chapter will discuss the division of property and debts. You will initially use this chapter to get an idea of what to expect in your situation, and will refer back to this chapter when preparing your paperwork and proceeding with your case. **WORKSHEET 1** will help you gather the **PERSONAL INFORMATION** you will need about yourself, your spouse, and your children. It will be helpful to have this information all in one place when completing the various court forms.

GATHERING INFORMATION

It is extremely important that you collect all of the financial information you can get. Make copies of as many of these papers as possible and keep them in a safe and private place (where your spouse will not find them). Make copies of new papers as they come in, especially as you get close to filing court papers and as you get close to a court hearing. This may be needed for proof if your case becomes contested or your spouse will not provide any information. This information should include the following, or as much as you can get.

✪   Your most recent income tax return and W-2 tax forms for you and your spouse

✪   Any other income documents (such as interest, stock dividends, etc.)

✪   Your spouse's most recent paystub, hopefully showing year-to-date earnings (otherwise, try to get copies of all paystubs since the beginning of the year)

✪   Deeds to real estate

✪   Titles to cars, boats, or other vehicles

✪   Your will and your spouse's will

✪   Life insurance policies

✪   Stocks, bonds, or other investment papers

✪   Pension or retirement fund papers and statements

✪   Health insurance cards and papers

✪   Bank account or credit union statements

✪   Your spouse's Social Security number and driver's license number

✪   Names, addresses, and phone numbers of your spouse's employer, close friends, and family members

✪   Credit card statements, mortgage documents, and other debt papers

✪   Copies of bills or receipts for regular expenses, such as electric, gas, car insurance, etc.

✪   Copies of bills, receipts, insurance forms, or medical records for any unusual medical expenses (including for recurring or continuous medical conditions) for yourself, your spouse, or your children

✪   Any other papers showing what you and your spouse earn, own, or owe

You should collect papers to show what you (and your spouse) earn, spend, own, and owe. **WORKSHEET 2** is a **DOCUMENT CHECKLIST** to help you collect these documents, however, it is not necessarily a complete list of all possible items. Space is provided for you to add items to the list.

Use the **DOCUMENT CHECKLIST** to check off the documents as you obtain the originals or copies. This will help you keep track of what you have, and what you need to obtain.

PROPERTY

The two basic legal terms you will see for property division are *community property* and *equitable distribution*. All states have adopted one of these terms or concepts. Both are ways of dividing property, and include consideration of when the property was acquired and under what circumstances. As a practical matter, which term is used is not as important as the specific factors found in each state's laws.

Generally, all of the property you and your spouse acquired during your marriage is owned by both of you together (or *jointly*). This is commonly called *marital property*. Most states divide property into *marital* and *nonmarital* (sometimes called *separate* or *sole*) property. Basically, nonmarital property is property considered to be owned by each party separately. This is usually property that each party owned before getting married. It may also include gifts and inheritances during the marriage and any property acquired during the marriage by exchanging nonmarital property. (For example, a car you owned before you got married would be nonmarital property. If you traded it for another car after you got married, the new car would still be nonmarital property.)

States vary as to whether income generated from the nonmarital property is considered nonmarital property. States also vary as to whether an increase in the value of nonmarital property is nonmarital property. The answer for your state may depend upon whether the spouse had anything to do with causing the income or increase in value.

Each party will keep his or her nonmarital property, and the court will apply various factors to divide the marital property. Refer to your state's listing in Appendix A to determine what property is nonmarital in your state and what factors are used to divide the marital property.

You will need to refer to your state's listing in Appendix A to see how property is divided. Look under the heading titled "Property." The following information will help you understand the information listed for your state.

⬥   The first thing stated is whether your state uses *community property* or *equitable distribution* as its legal theory. This is for your general information only, in the event the judge or someone else mentions it. These concepts have subtle legal differences, but these are generally not significant.

⬥   Next is a statement as to whether *fault* is considered in dividing property. If fault is a factor, one party may be entitled to more than half of the property if the spouse caused the breakup of the marriage (such as adultery, cruelty, etc.). In order to get additional property, it is necessary to prove the other person was at fault, even if you are using the no-fault grounds.

⬥   Next is a list of the types of property that are considered *separate, nonmarital,* or *sole* property in your state. This is property that each party is allowed to keep, free from any claims of the other. All other property is *marital property*, and is subject to division between you and your spouse. Some states do not make a distinction between marital and nonmarital property, but consider when and how the property was acquired as a factor in determining how to divide the property. Any exceptions or conditions are noted.

⬥   Any factors used in your state to divide property is listed next.

❖ You will also find references to your state's statute or code sections dealing with property division. It is a good idea for you to look up the actual law at your law library. This reference tells you where to find it.

Property Inventory

The following information will assist you in completing the **PROPERTY INVENTORY**. (see worksheet 3, p.233.) This worksheet is a list of all of your property and key information about that property. You will notice that it is divided into nine columns, designated as follows.

❖ Column (1): If your state divides property into marital and nonmarital property, put an "H" or "W" in the box in this column to indicate the husband's or wife's nonmarital property.

❖ Column (2): In this column, you will describe the property. (A discussion regarding what information should go in this column follows.)

❖ Column (3): This column is used to write in the serial number, account number, or other number that will help clearly identify that piece of property.

❖ Column (4): This is for the current market value of the property.

❖ Column (5): This shows how much money is owed on the property, if any.

❖ Column (6): Subtract the balance owed from the value. This will show how much the property is worth to you (your equity).

❖ Column (7): This column shows who is the current legal owner of the property. "H" designates the husband, "W" the wife, and "J" is for jointly owned property.

NOTE: *Make your list by first completing columns (1) through (7), then go back and fill in columns (8) and (9).*

◈ Column (8): This column will be checked for those pieces of property the husband will probably keep.

◈ Column (9): This column is for the property the wife will probably keep.

The following types of property should be included in your list.

Cash. List the name of the bank, credit union, etc., and the account number for each account. This includes savings and checking accounts, as well as certificates of deposit (CDs). The balance of each account should be listed in the column entitled EQUITY. (Leave the VALUE and BALANCE OWED columns blank.)

Real estate. List each piece of property you and your spouse own. The description might include a street address for the property, a subdivision name and lot number, or anything that lets you know what piece of property you are referring to. Real estate may be in both of your names, in your spouse's name alone, or in your name alone. The only way to know for sure is to look at the deed to the property. (If you cannot find a copy of the deed, try to find mortgage papers or payment coupons, homeowners insurance papers, or a property tax assessment notice.)

The owners of property are usually referred to on the deed as the *grantees*. In assigning a value to the property, consider the market value, which is how much you could probably sell the property for. This might be what similar houses in your neighborhood have sold for recently. You might also consider how much you paid for the property, or how much the property is insured for. Do *not* use the tax assessment value, as this is usually considerably lower than the market value.

Vehicles. This category includes cars, trucks, motor homes, recreational vehicles (RVs), motorcycles, boats, trailers, airplanes, and any other means of transportation for which the state requires a title and registration. You should include the make, model, year, and serial number or vehicle identification number (VIN). To determine value, you can go to the public library and ask to look at the blue book for cars, trucks, or whatever it is you are looking for. A *blue book* (which may be any color) gives the average values for used vehicles. Your librarian can help you find what you need. You can also find this information online through any number of websites containing valuations for vehicles. Type "blue book" into any search engine, such as Google, and you will get a selection of resources to choose from.

Another source is to look in the classified advertising section of a newspaper to see what similar vehicles are selling for. You might also try calling a dealer to see if he can give you an idea of the value. Be sure you consider the condition of the vehicle.

Appliances, electronic equipment, and yard machines. This category includes items such as televisions, VCRs, refrigerators, lawn mowers, and power tools. Do not worry about assigning a value to these items unless you are familiar enough with them to simply know what they are worth.

Furniture. List all furniture as specifically as possible. You should include the type of piece (such as sofa, coffee table, etc.), the color, and if you know it, the manufacturer, line name, or the style. Furniture usually will not have a serial number, although if you find one be sure to write it on the list. Once again, do not worry about a value unless you know what it is worth.

Jewelry and other valuables. You do not need to list inexpensive or costume jewelry. You can plan on keeping your own personal watches, rings, etc. However, if you own an expensive piece you should include it in your list, along with an estimated value. Be sure to include silverware, furs, original art, gold, coin collections, and so on. Again, be as detailed and specific as possible.

Stocks and bonds. All stocks, bonds, or other *paper investments* should be listed. Write down the number of shares and the name of the company or other organization that issued them. Copy any notation, such as *common* or *preferred* stock or shares. This information can be obtained from the stock certificate itself or from a statement from the stock broker.

Other big ticket items. This is simply a general reference to anything of significant value that does not fit in one of the categories already discussed. Examples might be a portable spa, an above-ground swimming pool, golf clubs, guns, pool tables, camping or fishing equipment, farm animals, or machinery.

What not to list. You will not need to list your clothing and other personal effects. Pots and pans, dishes, and cooking utensils ordinarily do not need to be listed, unless they have some unusually high value.

Once you have completed your list, go back through it and try to determine who should end up with each item. The ideal situation is for both you and your spouse to go through the list together and divide things fairly. However, if this is not possible, you will need to offer a reasonable settlement to the judge. Consider each item, then make a checkmark in either column (8) or (9) to designate whether that item should go to the husband or wife. You may make the following assumptions:

- ✪ your nonmarital property will go to you;

- ✪ your spouse's nonmarital property will go to your spouse;

- ✪ you should get the items that only you use;

- ✪ your spouse should get the items only used by your spouse; and,

- ✪ the remaining items should be divided to equalize each party's share, taking into consideration who would really want each item.

To somewhat equally divide your property, first you need to know the total value of your property. Do not count the value of the nonmarital items (unless the information for your state in Appendix A indicates it should be included). Add the remaining amounts in the EQUITY column of the **PROPERTY INVENTORY**. (see worksheet 3, p.233.) This will give you an approximate value of all marital property.

When it comes time for the hearing, you and your spouse may be arguing over some or all of the items on your list. This is when you will be glad that you made copies of the documents relating to the property on your list. Arguments over the value of property may need to be resolved by hiring appraisers to set a value; however, you will have to pay the appraiser a fee. Dividing your property is discussed further in later chapters.

Pensions and military benefits. The division of pensions and military and retirement benefits can be a complicated matter. Whenever these types of benefits are involved, you will need to consult an attorney or a CPA to determine the value of the benefits and how they should be divided.

DEBTS

Although there are cases in which one spouse gets a piece of property but the other spouse must make payments for it, the general rule is whoever gets the property also gets the debt owed on that property. This seems to be a fair arrangement in most cases.

Debt Inventory On the **DEBT INVENTORY** you will list each debt owed by you or your spouse. (see worksheet 4, p.234.) If your state provides for marital and nonmarital property, marital and nonmarital debt needs to be considered regarding property distribution.

Any debt incurred before you were married is yours alone. The **DEBT INVENTORY** contains a column for N-M debts. Mark each nonmarital debt with an "H" or "W" to show the husband's and wife's nonmarital debts. You will be responsible for your nonmarital debt and your spouse will be responsible for his or hers. For each debt, fill in worksheet 4 as follows.

◈ Column (1): Write in "H" or "W" to show each of your nonmarital debts.

◈ Column (2): Write in the name and address of the creditor (the bank, company, or person the debt is owed to).

◈ Column (3): Write in the account, loan, or mortgage number.

◈ Column (4): Write in any notes to help identify what the loan was for (such as "Christmas gifts," "Vacation," etc.).

◈ Column (5): Write in the amount of the monthly payment.

◈ Column (6): Write in the balance still owed on the loan.

◈ Column (7): Write in the date (approximately) when the loan was made.

◈ Column (8): Note whether the account is in the husband's name (H), the wife's name (W), or jointly in both names (J).

◈ Columns (9) & (10): These columns note who will be responsible for the debt after the divorce.

As with your property, each of you will keep your nonmarital debts and the remainder should be divided fairly equal—taking into consideration who will keep the property the loan was for.

TAX CONSIDERATIONS

As you know, the United States income tax code is extremely complicated and ever-changing. For this reason, it is impossible to give detailed legal advice with respect to taxes in a book such as this. Any information could easily be out of date by the time of publication. Therefore, it is strongly recommended that you consult a tax expert about the consequences of a divorce. The following gives you a general idea of the tax considerations that relate to property division.

You and your spouse may be exchanging title to property as a result of your divorce. Generally, there will *not* be any tax to pay as the result of such a transfer. However, whoever gets a piece of property will be responsible to pay any tax that may become due upon sale (such as capital gains tax).

The Internal Revenue Service has issued numerous rulings about how property is to be treated in divorce situations. One issue commonly raised is whether a certain divorce settlement arrangement is really alimony or property division (this is discussed more in the following chapter on alimony). You also need to be especially careful if you are transferring any tax shelters or other complicated financial arrangements.

Cost of Getting a Divorce

You cannot deduct legal fees and court costs for getting a divorce. But you may be able to deduct legal fees paid for tax advice in connection with a divorce and legal fees to get alimony. In addition, you may be able to deduct fees you pay to appraisers, actuaries, and accountants for services in determining your correct tax or in helping to get alimony.

The attorney's fees you pay may include charges that are deductible and charges that are not deductible. You should request that your attorney's fee billing statement include a breakdown showing the amount charged for each service performed.

You must itemize your deductions on Form 1040—Schedule A to claim deductible fees. They are claimed as miscellaneous itemized deductions subject to the 2%-of-adjusted-gross-income limit.

Fees for getting alimony. Because you must include alimony you receive in your gross income, you can deduct fees you pay to get or collect alimony.

Example:

You pay your attorney a fee for handling your divorce and an additional fee that is for services in getting and collecting alimony. You can deduct the fee for getting and collecting alimony, subject to the 2% limit, if it is separately stated on your attorney's bill.

Nondeductible expenses. You cannot deduct the costs of personal advice, counseling, or legal action in a divorce. These costs are not deductible, even if they are paid, in part, to arrive at a financial settlement or to protect income-producing property. However, you can add certain legal fees you pay specifically for a property settlement to the basis of the property you receive. For example, you can add the cost of preparing and filing a deed to put title to your house in your name alone to the basis of the house. You cannot deduct fees you pay for your spouse or former spouse, unless your payments qualify as alimony.

Alimony

This chapter discusses alimony. You will initially use this chapter to get an idea of what to expect in your situation, and may refer back to it when preparing your paperwork and proceeding with your case.

The term alimony is increasingly being considered outdated. In many states, the term has been replaced by *support*, *spousal support*, *maintenance*, *spousal maintenance*, or *spousal support and maintenance*. For simplicity, the word alimony is used in this book. If neither you nor your spouse are seeking alimony, you may disregard this chapter.

Your primary source of information about the alimony laws in your state is the listing for your state in Appendix A. The following discussion explains some of the common aspects of alimony and the common variations among the states. This provides you with a good base for understanding the alimony laws of your state. You will eventually need to find out what is required in your particular state, and Appendix A will be your starting point.

TYPES OF ALIMONY

Traditionally, only the wife could obtain alimony from her husband. Today, most state laws provide that alimony may be granted to either the husband or the wife. In reality, however, there are few cases in which a wife will be ordered to pay alimony to her husband. There are two types of alimony—*rehabilitative* and *permanent*. You may also hear of what is commonly called *lump sum* alimony, which is when there is a one-time payment by one spouse to the other. A lump sum alimony payment can easily cause problems with the IRS, as it could be construed as part of your property settlement, and cause undesired tax consequences.

Rehabilitative Alimony

Rehabilitative alimony is for a limited period of time, and is to enable one of the spouses to get the education or training necessary to find a job. This is usually awarded when one of the parties has not been working during the marriage.

Permanent Alimony

Permanent alimony continues for a long period of time, possibly until the death of the party receiving the alimony. This is typically awarded when one of the spouses is unable to work due to a physical or mental condition.

QUALIFICATIONS FOR OBTAINING ALIMONY

There are often three questions to be answered regarding alimony.

1. Is the person entitled to alimony?

2. If so, how long is the person entitled to receive alimony?

3. If so, how much alimony should the person receive?

Not everyone is entitled to alimony; therefore, the first step is to determine whether alimony is available in your situation. The circumstances necessary to qualify for alimony vary from state to state. The most common considerations in determining eligibility for alimony include:

✪   the duration of the marriage;

✪   whether the person seeking alimony lacks sufficient income or property for support (or to maintain the standard of living established during the marriage); and,

✪   whether the other spouse has sufficient income to pay alimony.

In some states, the person seeking alimony must prove that the divorce is the fault of the other party. The listing for your state in Appendix A gives you the specific requirements for your state.

DURATION OF ALIMONY

Once it is determined that alimony is appropriate, the next step is to determine the period of time alimony should be paid. In most states, the duration will be for a temporary period of time, making rehabilitative alimony more common than permanent alimony.

Generally, alimony is awarded for whatever period of time is agreed upon by the parties, or whatever period of time the judge determines is reasonable so the person seeking alimony can get the education and training needed to become employable. An exception may be made for a custodial parent (most often the mother) who must stay at home to care for a very young child. Any provisions applicable to you can be found in your state's listing in Appendix A.

CALCULATING ALIMONY

Calculating the amount of alimony varies greatly from state to state. Many states list numerous factors, but they all come down to an attempt to be more specific about the two factors historically used to determine alimony:

1. the financial needs of the spouse seeking alimony and

2. the ability of the spouse who will be paying alimony to pay.

Some states do not have any guidance in their laws, and leave it up to judges to determine with guidance from decisions of the state appellate courts. Other states have laws that list the factors judges must consider. Unlike child support, no state has yet established tables or formulas for determining the amount of alimony. The factors to be considered in your case are found in your state's listing in Appendix A.

If your state does not have any factors in its laws, you can still get a good idea of what the court is likely to consider by looking at the factors used by other states. These factors typically include such things as the following.

- *The length of the marriage.* Often, no alimony will be awarded if the marriage was of short duration, such as less than five years. The longer the marriage, the more likely alimony will be awarded.

- *The standard of living established during the marriage.* Generally, the spouse seeking alimony will be entitled (to whatever extent possible considering the income of the other) alimony sufficient to maintain this standard of living.

- *The age, and physical and emotional health of the parties.*

- *The educational level of the parties.* This may compare their educational level at the time of marriage and at the present.

- *The present income of both parties.*

- *The earning capacity of the spouse seeking alimony.*

- *The time and expense needed for the party seeking alimony to acquire the education or training necessary to find appropriate employment.*

✪ *The child custody responsibilities of the spouse seeking alimony.* Generally, a custodial parent who needs to stay at home to raise a young child will not be required to seek employment outside the home until the child is of school age. Also, if a child has a serious medical condition, the custodial parent may not be required to seek outside employment.

✪ *Either party's contribution to the education, training, increased earning capacity, or career of the other.*

✪ *The decisions of the parties regarding employment, career, economics, education, and parenting arrangements.* This relates to any decisions for one parent to stay at home to care for children, instead of pursuing education and career.

✪ *The property division.*

✪ *The tax consequences of an alimony award.*

✪ *The legal obligations of each spouse to support any others* (such as alimony or child support from a previous marriage).

✪ *The cost of health care and insurance.*

Most states that list factors also include "any other relevant factor," which is a catch-all for anything that the judge may decide to consider that is not listed elsewhere.

A primary variation from state to state is how the issue of fault is treated. In some states, if the break up of the marriage is determined to be the fault of one spouse, that may be a factor as to both whether alimony is awarded and the amount of alimony. The law of other states says that fault is not to be considered. Whether fault is an issue is stated in the listing for each state in Appendix A.

Some states also have provisions for what will terminate alimony. Generally, the remarriage of the spouse receiving alimony will terminate alimony. Some states will also terminate alimony if the spouse receiving it cohabitates with a nonrelative member of the opposite sex.

TAX CONSIDERATIONS

As you know, the United States income tax code is extremely complicated and ever-changing. For this reason, it is impossible to give detailed legal advice with respect to taxes in a book such as this. Any information could easily be out of date by the time of publication. Therefore, it is strongly recommended that you consult a tax expert about the consequences of a divorce. The following gives you a general idea of the tax considerations that relate to alimony.

Alimony

Alimony can cause the most tax problems of any aspect of divorce. The IRS is always making new rulings on whether an agreement is really alimony or property division. The basic rule is that alimony is treated as income to the person receiving it and as a deduction for the person paying it. Therefore, in order to manipulate the tax consequences, many couples try to show something as part of the property settlement instead of as alimony—or the reverse. As the IRS becomes aware of these tax games it issues rulings on how it will view a certain arrangement. If you are simply talking about the regular, periodic payment of cash, the IRS will probably not question that it is alimony. (But if you try to call it a property settlement, you may run into problems.) The important thing is to consult a tax expert if you are considering any unusual or creative property settlement or alimony arrangements.

Alimony or Property Division

Whether you should try to settle things with alimony or property division (or a combination of the two) is determined by your particular financial and tax situation. Generally, alimony is taxable income to the person receiving it and is a tax deduction for the person paying it.

There are various things that the IRS and state courts consider to determine whether a payment is alimony or property division. This is not determined by how it is called in the divorce judgment. Generally, a payment to or for a spouse under a divorce or separation instrument is alimony if the spouses do not file a joint return with each other and all the following requirements are met.

✪ ***The payment is in cash.*** Only cash payments, including checks and money orders, qualify as alimony.

✪ *The instrument does not designate the payment as not alimony.* You and your spouse can designate that otherwise qualifying payments are not alimony. You do this by including a provision in your divorce or separation instrument that states the payments are not deductible as alimony by you and are excludable from your spouse's income.

✪ *The spouses are not members of the same household at the time the payments are made.* This requirement applies only if the spouses are legally separated under a decree of divorce or separate maintenance. Payments to your spouse while you are members of the same household are not alimony if you are legally separated under a decree of divorce or separate mainte-nance. A home you formerly shared is considered one household, even if you physically separate yourselves in the home. There is an exception—if you are not legally separated under a decree of divorce or separate maintenance, a payment under a written sep-aration agreement, support decree, or other court order may qualify as alimony even if you are members of the same house-hold when the payment is made.

✪ *There is no liability to make any payment (in cash or prop-erty) after the death of the recipient spouse.* If you must continue to make payments for any period after your spouse's death, the part of the payment that would continue is not alimony whether made before or after the death. If all of the pay-ment would continue, then none of the payments made before or after the death are alimony.

✪ *The payment is not treated as child support.* A payment that is specifically designated as child support or treated as specifi-cally designated as child support under your divorce or separation instrument is not alimony. The designated amount or part may vary from time to time. Child support payments are neither deductible by the payer nor taxable to the payee.

There can also be tax complications if the payments are front-loaded in excess of certain permissible amounts. (For details, the IRS rules governing this issue are found in Sections 71 and 215 of the Internal Revenue Code.)

If you would be paying alimony, the alimony would be tax deductible, but you would be running the risk that your spouse could get the alimony amount or duration increased if circumstances change. Therefore, if you could persuade your spouse to take a greater share of the property instead of an alimony award, you would prevent your spouse from getting any more later—but you would sacrifice the alimony tax deduction.

If you would be receiving alimony, you would be able to ask the court for an increase in the amount or duration of the alimony if circumstances changed, but you would have to pay taxes on the alimony you receive. Therefore, if you accepted more of the property instead of alimony, you would avoid paying some taxes by sacrificing your ability to seek an increase later if you need one.

Cost of Getting a Divorce

You cannot deduct legal fees and court costs for getting a divorce. But you may be able to deduct legal fees paid for tax advice in connection with a divorce and legal fees to get alimony. In addition, you may be able to deduct fees you pay to appraisers, actuaries, and accountants for services in determining your correct tax or in helping to get alimony.

The attorney's fees you pay may include charges that are deductible and charges that are not deductible. You should request that your attorney's fee billing statement include a breakdown showing the amount charged for each service performed.

You must itemize your deductions on Form 1040—Schedule A to claim deductible fees. They are claimed as miscellaneous itemized deductions subject to the 2%-of-adjusted-gross-income limit.

Fees for getting alimony. Because you must include alimony you receive in your gross income, you can deduct fees you pay to get or collect alimony.

Example:

You pay your attorney a fee for handling your divorce and an additional fee that is for services in getting and collecting alimony. You can deduct the fee for getting and collecting alimony, subject to the 2% limit, if it is separately stated on your attorney's bill.

Child Custody and Visitation

This chapter discusses child custody and visitation. You will initially use this chapter to get an idea of what to expect in your situation, and will refer back to this chapter when preparing your paperwork and proceeding with your case.

As with just about everything else in divorce law, many states are coming up with new terminology for *custody* and *visitation*. Therefore, you may see terms like *shared custody* and *sole custody*; *legal custody* and *physical placement*; *shared parenting*; *primary custodian* and *secondary custodian*; or *managing conservatorship* (in Texas). For simplicity, the words *custody* and *visitation*, and *custodial parent* and *noncustodial parent* are used in this book.

CUSTODY

In general, the parent who has custody is the parent with whom the child lives a majority of the time. The custodial parent is also the one making most of the day-to-day decisions concerning the child (such as what time the child must be in the house in the evening and what time the child goes to bed). When the child is visiting with the noncustodial parent, the noncustodial parent makes these day-to-day decisions. In most states, unless the judge orders otherwise, both parents are entitled to have a say in major decisions affecting the child's welfare (such as medical treatment). In the event the parents cannot agree on such major matters, either the divorce judgment will give the custodial parent final say, or the matter will be brought before the judge for a decision.

CHILD CUSTODY AND VISITATION

As with everything else in divorce, things are ideal when both parties can agree on the question of custody of the children. Generally, the judge will accept any agreement you reach, provided it does not appear that your agreement will cause harm to your children.

In spite of a modern philosophy voiced in most states that there is no preference between the mother and father for custody, you will find that most judges are from the old school of thought and believe that (all things being equal) a young child is better off with the mother. Because of these statements in the law, the judge may go to great lengths to find that all things are not equal, in order to justify his decision to award custody to the mother. It happens day after day in courts throughout the country, and it is a reality you may have to deal with. If you and your spouse cannot agree on how these matters will be handled, you will be leaving this important decision to the judge. The judge cannot possibly know your child as well as you and your spouse. So it makes sense for you to work this out yourselves. Otherwise, you are leaving the decision to a stranger.

It is difficult to predict the outcome of a custody battle because there are too many factors and individual circumstances. The only exception is where one parent is clearly unfit and the other can prove it. Drug abuse and child abuse are probably the most common charges against a spouse, but unless there has been an arrest and conviction, it is difficult to prove to a judge. In general, do not charge your spouse with being unfit unless you can prove it. Judges are not impressed with unfounded allegations, and they can do more harm than good for your case.

Custody Factors   Usually, the judge will go along with any custody agreement made by the parties. When the parties cannot agree, most states have laws that set forth the factors the judge must consider when determining custody. A few states do not have any factors in their laws, and leave it up to judges to determine custody (with guidance from decisions of the state appellate courts). These appellate court decisions usually end up discussing the same factors that are found in the laws of the other states.

All of these state laws and court decisions can be traced back to the concept that a custody decision should be based upon what is in the best interests of the child. The factors used by courts today are simply attempts to explain how a judge should determine what is in the child's best interest.

In making a decision:

- ✪ which parent is more likely to allow the other to visit with the child;

- ✪ the love, affection, and other emotional ties existing between the child and the parent;

- ✪ the ability and willingness of each parent to provide the child with food, clothing, medical care, and other material needs;

- ✪ the length of time the child has lived with either parent in a stable environment;

- ✪ the permanence, as a family unit, of the proposed custodial home;

- ✪ the moral fitness of each parent;

- ✪ the mental and physical health of each parent;

- ✪ the home, school, and community record of the child;

- ✪ the preference of the child, providing the child is of sufficient intelligence and understanding; and,

- ✪ any other factor the judge decides is relevant.

The special needs child. If your child has special needs, the ability of you and the other party to meet those needs may also be considered. Special needs involve the gifted child who had special educational needs, as well as the child with physical or emotional problems and handicaps. This will probably involve expert testimony to verify the child's condition and needs, and show which parent is best able to meet those needs. This does not mean the financial ability to meet the needs, because that can be taken care of by child support. But if the child needs daily in-home physical therapy, the judge may grant custody to the parent who works fewer hours and therefore has more time for therapy.

Refer to the listing for your state in Appendix A. Look under the heading "Child Custody." This lists the factors to be considered according to the law of your state, note any other considerations specific to your state, and gives a reference to the sections of your state's statutes or code relating to custody.

Counseling, Mediation, and Parenting Classes

There is a trend to attempt to resolve custody and visitation disputes outside the courtroom, and to minimize the effects of divorce on children. Some states now require parents to attend some type of counseling, or go through mediation. Only if this is not successful can the matter be presented to the judge. There is frequently a cost associated with counseling and mediation, which must be paid by the parties. Some states also require the parents to attend parenting classes before a divorce will be granted. The main purpose of this is to make the parents aware of the effect of the divorce on their children, and help them deal with these effects. Your court clerk should be able to tell you if counseling, mediation, or parenting classes are required.

Paternity Issues

In most cases, the paternity of the child is not in dispute. However, if a question of paternity arises in your case, it is strongly suggested that you hire a lawyer. Some states do not allow a father to challenge paternity if the child was born during the marriage. The legal principle is that a child born during a marriage is presumed to be a child of that marriage. The law seeks to prevent such a child from being deemed illegitimate. If such a challenge is allowed, it will probably be necessary to obtain a court order for DNA testing. This is not a simple matter that can be handled without a lawyer.

There are several types of scientific tests available to assist in determining paternity. There are four types of testing commonly used.

○ **ABO Test.** This is the most basic blood type testing. Blood samples are taken from both parties and the child. These samples are tested to determine each person's blood type— A, B, AB, or O. The presumed father may be excluded from such a test.

However, statistics show that a man who is not the father will only be excluded in 10%–13% of cases. This is because of the probability that the real father would have the same blood type as the man who is not the father.

Example:

If the mother has Type A blood and the presumed father has Type B blood, a child of their would have either Type A or Type B. If the child turns out to have Type O, the child must have inherited it from a man with Type O. Therefore, the presumed father could not be the child's father.

○ **Red Cell Series.** This is an ABO test that adds a test for the Rh factor. This further narrows the matter, but still allows for a man who is not the father to be excluded in only 50% of the cases.

○ **HLA (Human Leukocite Antigen) Test.** This test requires blood samples from both parties and the child. This tests more unique factors in blood. With the HLA test, a man who is not the father will be excluded in about 90% of the cases.

○ **DNA.** One nice feature about DNA testing is that it can be done with samples from only the presumed father and the child. Therefore, it can be done if the mother is uncooperative. It is commonly done by taking saliva sampled, so needles are not involved. DNA testing is about 99.9% accurate.

Before the days of HLA and DNA testing, blood tests were used to try to rule out a person as the father, or to support other evidence of paternity. They were not conclusive proof of paternity or nonpaternity. At best, the tests indicated that the man was, or was not, the father. When HLA testing came about, much more significance was placed on the test results. HLA testing results usually indicated whether the husband was the father with better than 90% accuracy.

Courts tended to rely on the HLA test, so that a positive HLA test would prove paternity unless the presumed father came up with some very convincing evidence to the contrary (such as that he was out of the state when conception occurred, or was sterile). Now, with the high degree of accuracy of DNA testing, the results leave very little room for doubt either way.

If you seek to challenge paternity, it is likely that your spouse will not be willing to submit a scientific test, and may do everything possible to stand in the way of having even a simple saliva sample taken from the child. Therefore, it may be necessary for you to file a motion asking the judge to issue an order that the child (and your spouse) be tested. Regardless of whether you are the husband or the wife, after the test results are released, you may desire to challenge the results. All of this is best left up to a knowledgeable attorney.

Tax Considerations

As you know, the United States income tax code is extremely complicated and ever-changing. For this reason, it is impossible to give detailed legal advice with respect to taxes in a book such as this. Any information could easily be out of date by the time of publication. Therefore, it is strongly recommended that you consult a tax expert about the consequences of a divorce. The following gives you a general idea of the tax considerations that relate to child support.

✪   Whoever has custody gets to claim the children on his or her tax return (unless both parents file a special IRS form agreeing to a different arrangement each year).

✪   The parent receiving child support does not report it as income.

✪   The parent paying child support cannot deduct it.

If you are sharing physical custody, the parent with whom the child lives for the most time during the year is entitled to claim the child as a dependent. Form 8332, *Release of Claim to Exemption for Child of Divorced or Separated Parents,* is the IRS form that must be used to reverse this. It must be filed each year. Therefore, if you and your spouse have agreed that you will get to claim the children (even though you do not have custody), you should get your spouse to sign an open-ended form that you can file each year, so that you do not have to worry about it each year. A phone call to the IRS can help you get answers to questions on this topic.

VISITATION

The term *visitation* typically refers to the time allotted for the non-custodial parent to spend with the child. There is no limit to the variations of visitation schedules. Many divorce judgments simply state that the noncustodial parent is entitled to *reasonable visitation* or *liberal visitation*, leaving it up to the parents to work it out. While this gives the parents the most flexibility, it more often leads to conflict and disagreements. In most cases, it is best for the judgment to clearly spell out a visitation schedule.

Visitation Factors

Very few states have any guidelines for visitation orders. This leaves it up to the judge to determine visitation on a case-by-case basis. The types of factors judges consider include how far apart the parties will live after the divorce, the age of the child, the child's activities, and the time the parents have available considering their work schedules. For example, granting a noncustodial parent visitation on alternating weekends might not be appropriate if the noncustodial parent lives 200 miles away from the custodial parent.

Visitation may also change over time, as problems arise between the parents, as the child grows older, or as the parents' situations change. The visitation order is usually the easiest part of a judgment to modify.

Grandparents and Visitation

Traditionally, grandparents and other relatives had no visitation rights. For example, if the child's father died, was imprisoned, or ran off, the mother could refuse to allow the paternal grandparents to see the child. This potential problem became publicized and started a trend in state legislatures to pass laws giving grandparents the right to seek visitation through the courts. Some parents, afraid that they could be forced to allow their children to visit with undesirable (or even abusive) grandparents, challenged these laws. Eventually, the question made its way to the United States Supreme Court. In the case of *Troxel v. Granville*, the Supreme Court decided that parents have the right to raise their children as they see fit, and states cannot force them to allow grandparent visitation. At this point, the best bet for a grandparent is to try to maintain a good relationship with both parents of their grandchild.

If you are concerned that your parents may be denied access to your children if you were no longer around, you may wish to try to negotiate with your spouse for a provision in your divorce judgment that would guarantee that your parents could see the children. While a court may not be able to order grandparent visitation, a court may enforce such an agreement if made between you and your spouse. To get your spouse to agree, you may offer a similar agreement with respect to your spouse's parents.

Child Support

This chapter explains child support. You will initially use this chapter to get an idea of what to expect in your situation, and will refer back to this chapter when preparing your paperwork and proceeding with your case.

GATHERING INFORMATION

Child support is about finances. It is generally determined by the income of one or both parents, and the financial needs of the child. Most states have schedules, tables, or formulas that figure out the basic needs of the child based upon the income of the parents. Therefore, the basic information that will need to be gathered to determine child support is the income and expenses of the parties. If there are any unusual financial needs of the child, those will need to be documented.

CALCULATING CHILD SUPPORT

The exact child support calculation method varies from state to state. However, all states use one of two models—a percentage of the non-custodial parent's income (the *percentage of income method*) or an apportioned share of the child's needs based on the combined income of both parents (the *apportionment method*). Each of these is generally explained in the following section. More details about the calculation of child support in your state can be found in your particular state's listing in Appendix A.

Percentage of Income Method

With the *percentage of income method*, child support is set at a certain percentage of the noncustodial parent's income, based upon the number of children to be supported. This is the simpler method and the one that has been in the longest. In some states, the gross income is used; but in other states, certain deductions are allowed and net income is used.

Example

In Illinois, gross income is used. If the noncustodial parent has one child, he or she pays 20% of his or her gross income. For additional children, the percentages are 25% for two children, 32% for three children, 40% for four children, 45% for five children, and 50% for six or more children. The law of Illinois, as with many other states, provides for adjustments for special needs and circumstances.

Worksheet 5: Child Support Worksheet—Percentage of Income Method. **WORKSHEET 5** is a basic child support calculation worksheet for people who are filing for divorce in a state that uses the percentage of income method. If you states uses the combined income method, use **WORKSHEET 6** instead. (See the next section regarding using the combined income method). See the listing for your state in Appendix A to determine which method is used by your state.

The calculation of child support is often a complicated procedure, and varies greatly from state to state. Therefore, this form is very general in nature. It includes information that is common to many states, however, any given income, deduction, or other item may or may not be used in your state. Be sure to refer to Appendix A of this book, as well as any other source you consult, for information about how your state calculates child support, to determine whether a particular item on this form applies to you. For example, some states use gross income, while others allow deductions for such things as income taxes and FICA.

Alimony is generally only considered income if the person is actually receiving it on a regular basis. Deductions for alimony and child support are only allowed if the alimony and child support is actually being paid on a regular basis.

A few states only use gross income. If you are in one of those states, you will not need to complete the portion of **WORKSHEET 5** relating to "Deduction from Income." Instead, your "Total Gross Income" and "Total Net Income" will be the same. Once you arrive at your "Total Net Income," you will multiply it by the percentage of income from your state's law, based upon the number of children to be supported. For example, if your "Total Net Income" is $2,500 per month, you have two children, and your state law says two children are entitled to 20%; the child support amount would be $500 per month ($2,500 x .2 = $500).

Combined Income Method

The *combined income method* (also referred to as the apportionment method) involves a little more calculating, and can be summarized in five steps.

1. Determine the income of each parent (gross or net, depending upon the state).

2. Add the incomes together to get the *combined income*.

3. Read the chart provided in your state's statutes to obtain the basic needs for the child or children (based on the number of children and the combined income).

4. Calculate the noncustodial parent's percentage of the combined income (divide the noncustodial parent's income by the combined income).

5. Multiply the child's needs (from the chart) by the noncustodial parent's percentage, which results in the noncustodial parent's apportioned share of the child's needs.

Worksheet 6: Child Support Worksheet—Combined Income Method. WORKSHEET 6 is a basic child support calculation worksheet for people who are filing for divorce in a state that uses the combined income method. If you state uses the percentage of income method, use WORKSHEET 5 instead (see prior section). See the listing for your state in Appendix A to determine which method is used by your state.

The calculation of child support is often a complicated procedure, and varies greatly from state to state. Therefore, this form is very general in nature. It includes information that is common to many states, however, any given income, deduction, or other item may or may not be used in your state. Be sure to refer to Appendix A of this book, as well as any other source you consult, for information about how your state calculates child support, to determine whether a particular item on this form applies to you. For example, some states only allow deductions for income taxed and FICA, while other states allow one or more of the additional deductions listed in WORKSHEET 6.

Alimony is generally only considered income if the person is actually receiving it on a regular basis. Deductions for alimony and child support are usually only allowed if the alimony and child support are actually being paid on a regular basis. Item 6 is for any other adjustments that may be called for. Various states allow for adjustments for such things as child care costs, a child's health insurance costs, and the amount of time the child spends with each parent. You will need to consult your state's laws to determine whether any such adjustments are allowed, and if so, how the adjustment is to be calculated.

TAX CONSIDERATIONS

As you know, the United States income tax code is extremely complicated and ever-changing. For this reason, it is impossible to give detailed legal advice with respect to taxes in a book such as this. Any information could easily be out of date by the time of publication. Therefore, it is strongly recommended that you consult a tax expert about the consequences of a divorce. As previously stated in Chapter 7 regarding child custody, the following gives you a general idea of the tax considerations that relate to child support.

✪   Whoever has custody gets to claim the children on his or her tax return (unless both parents file a special IRS form agreeing to a different arrangement each year).

✪   The parent receiving child support does not report it as income.

✪   The parent paying child support cannot deduct it.

Filing for Divorce

If you decide to file for divorce, there are many legal forms that you will need to complete. There is nothing magical about legal forms. They are simply a way of communicating information to the court. Appendix D contains various typical legal forms for you to use. However, these forms may need to be changed to meet the requirements of your court. You will need to compare the forms in Appendix D with the forms used in your court to be sure the format is acceptable. The best way to do this is to visit the court clerk's office. Tell the clerk that you would like to see a divorce file. These files are usually open to the public and you should be allowed to look at one. (Better still, ask to see two or three.) You will want to copy the format of the papers in these files as closely as possible. Any time you are not sure how to prepare a form, take a look at someone else's file at the clerk's office. In preparing the forms in Appendix D, an attempt has been made to use simple English, keeping legal jargon to a minimum.

Appendix B contains examples of completed forms for a fictional case. They are just examples to give you some idea of how the forms might be completed. This is not the only way to complete the forms, and changes will probably need to be made for your particular state.

You will need to keep copies of court papers, correspondence, and other documents. These papers are best kept in some type of file folder, or perhaps in a 3-ring binder. **WORKSHEET 7** is a **DIVORCE FILE COVER SHEET**, which is designed to provide you with quick references to important information about your divorce case. It is suggested that you place it inside the front cover of your file folder, or as the first sheet in a 3-ring binder. **WORKSHEET 7** will be useful whenever you need your case number, or the name, address, phone number, or other contact information for the judge, court clerk, your spouse, or your spouse's attorney.

It is also important to keep copies of all court documents in chronological order, so that you may quickly locate them. Most attorneys keep court papers in a file folder, with the most recent one on top and a numbered tab on the first page of each document. Stick-on tabs can be purchased at any office supply store, or you can use Post-It Notes. **WORKSHEET 8** can be used as an index for these papers, and placed as the top page in your file folder or 3-ring binder. In the first column, write in the number of the document that corresponds to the number on that document's tab. Typically, the divorce complaint or petition will be document number one. In the second column, write in the title of the document, and in the third column write in the date the document is dated or filed with the court. Below is an example.

Doc. #	Document Title	Date
1	Summons and Petition for Divorce	3/07/06
2	Sheriff's Certificate of Service	3/16/06
3	Motion for Default	4/07/06

Paper Size The forms in this book are on letter-sized paper, which measures 8½" x 11". Traditionally, courts used longer legal-sized paper, which measures 8½" x 14". However, many states have changed to letter-sized in recent years. Check with your court clerk to find out whether letter-sized paper is acceptable. If you must use legal-sized paper, you will need to prepare your forms on the longer paper or copy any of the forms you use from Appendix D on to legal-sized paper.

Case Style Legal forms begin with the identification of the court and the names of the parties. This part of the form is called the *caption* or *case style*. Look at how case styles have been set up in the divorce files you review at the court clerk's office as each court may have slight variations to this style.

Once your case is assigned a case number by the court clerk, the case number will also become part of the case style. The information for your state in Appendix A will help you figure out the proper case style. Including how the court and the parties are designated. Below is an example of a case style for a fictional state:

```
                     STATE OF SUPERIOR
      IN THE CIRCUIT COURT OF THE FOURTH JUDICIAL
             CIRCUIT, IN AND FOR MONROE COUNTY


      In Re the Marriage of:     Case No._____


      Dorothy Johnson,
                Petitioner,
                and
      James Gordon Johnson,
                Respondent.
```

As mentioned, the case style will vary slightly, depending upon which state you live in. The title for the court will be different in each state. For example, in California, the court is "SUPERIOR COURT OF CALIFORNIA, COUNTY OF _____ " (you will need to fill in the name of the county where you are filing your case). Refer to the listing for your state in Appendix A, and look under the heading "Case Style/Parties." This will tell you how the courts are named in your state.

Any blank spaces will need to be filled in with the proper county or judicial circuit number (or both). If a circuit number needs to be filled in, it should be written out instead of using a numeral ("FOURTH," not "4th"). A few states also call the court by a different name depending upon the county. For example, in Maine, some counties handle divorce cases in *District Court* and other counties handle them in *Superior Court*.

Do not forget to go to your court clerk's office and ask to see the divorce file of someone else. Look in the file, notice how the case style is arranged, then copy the same format in your papers. If you have any questions about the proper case style, ask the court clerk.

Parties. Different states also refer to the parties in various ways. The *parties* are the people involved in the divorce case (you and your spouse). Below the name of the court in the "Case Style/Parties" listing in Appendix A, you will find how the parties are referred to in your state. The two most common ways of referring to the parties in a divorce case are as the *plaintiff* and *defendant*, or the *petitioner* and *respondent*.

In states that allow the parties to file a joint petition for divorce (usually when they both want a divorce and are in agreement about all of the issues), they are referred to as *copetitioners*. Other variations are used in Florida, Louisiana, and Mississippi. Again, do not forget to look at someone else's file at the court clerk's office to check the format.

Once you determine the proper case style for your court, you will use the same case style in all of the papers you file. Space is left at the top of the forms in Appendix D so that you can fill in the case style. If your state's case style does not fit on the forms in Appendix D, you will need to use a blank sheet of paper and type your own form using those in Appendix D for guidance.

It may not be absolutely necessary that you use a typewriter to fill in the forms, although typing is preferred by judges and gives a much more professional appearance than handwriting. If you do not own a typewriter, borrow one from a friend, rent one for a day, or ask if one is available at your local library or court clerk's office. If typing is not possible, print the information and be sure that your writing can be easily read. See Appendix B for examples of some completed forms.

THE COMPLAINT OR PETITION

The *complaint* or *petition* is the basic paper you will file to begin the divorce process. The most common names for this paper are *Complaint for Divorce, Petition for Dissolution of Marriage,* and *Petition for Divorce.* It is called a *Complaint for Dissolution of Marriage* in Connecticut, a *Bill for Divorce* in Maryland, and a *Bill of Complaint for Divorce* in Mississippi. If you refer to the listing for your state in Appendix A, under the heading "Complaint Title" you will find the name used in your state. A small number of states have different types of divorce procedures, and use different names depending upon which procedure is used. For convenience, the word *complaint* will be used to describe this document. Just be sure to use the correct name for your state when you prepare your papers. (see Appendix A.)

A **COMPLAINT FOR DIVORCE** is found in Appendix D. (see form 2, p.247.) You may need to modify this form to comply with the requirements of your state or your particular court. Before using the form in this book, either call or visit your court clerk's office and ask the clerk if there are any official forms you must use. If so, get the official forms and use them. Also, ask to see one or more divorce files for other people. These files are usually open to the public, and looking at files allows you to see how local attorneys prepared the complaint. Modify the form in this book to fit the format commonly used in the court where you will be filing for divorce.

NOTE: *Be sure to refer to your state's listing in Appendix A when filling in the information in form 2.*

To complete a **COMPLAINT FOR DIVORCE**, you need to do the following.

◈ Complete the case style according to the instructions in the first section of this chapter.

◈ Refer to your state's listing in Appendix A, under the heading for "Complaint Title," to find out how to title the document (such as "Complaint for Divorce" or "Petition for Dissolution of Marriage"). This title will go on the line in the center of the form, below the case style.

◈ In the first (unnumbered) paragraph, type in the word "Plaintiff" or "Petitioner" (whichever is used in your state) in the first blank, and the word "Husband" or "Wife" in the second blank (whichever describes you). The complaint title used in your state (from Appendix A) goes in the third blank. Type the word "Defendant" or "Respondent" (whichever is used in your state) in the fourth blank, and "Husband" or "Wife" (whichever describes your spouse) in the last blank.

◈   Paragraph 1: Check the box for "Husband" or "Wife," whichever meets the residency requirements for your state. Type the name of your state in the first blank, the date residency began in the second blank, the name of the county in the third blank, and date in the fourth blank.

◈   Paragraphs 2 and 3: Fill in the information, or as much of it as you know, about you and your spouse. If you do not know certain information, type in the word "unknown" in the blank.

◈   Paragraph 4: Type in the date you and your spouse were married; the name of the city and state where you were married; and, the name of the city, county, and state where your marriage is registered (which will probably be the same as where you were married).

◈   Paragraph 5: Type in the date you and your spouse separated. The "Grounds" section in your state's listing in Appendix A will tell you if you must be separated in order to get divorced. Some states allow you to live in the same house as long as you are not having sexual relations, some states require you to live in separate housing, and other states do not have any requirement that you be separated at all. If you are in a state that does not require a separation of any kind and you are not separated, simply type in "Not Applicable." However, if your state does require a separation, be sure to include the date of your separation, and be sure you have been separated for the time required as indicated in Appendix A.

◈   Paragraph 6: Check the box or boxes that apply to your situation. A minor child is one under the age of majority (adulthood) in your state. This age is usually 18, but it may be different in your state. A *dependent* child is one who is over the age of majority, but is still dependent upon you for support, usually due to some physical or mental handicap (such as from illness, injury, or birth defect). It generally does not include a normal, healthy adult child who is simply still living with you. In Item D, the column marked "Current Custody" indicates with whom the child is now living. This may be either "Husband" or "Wife" if you have separated, "Husband and Wife" if you are still living in the same home, or with a third party who should be designated by name and relationship to the child, such as "aunt" or "family friend." If you do have children, your state may require you to file a **UNIFORM CHILD CUSTODY JURISDICTION ACT AFFIDAVIT**. (see form 5, p.259.) You would then check the box in Item 6E and complete form 2 from Appendix D. (See p.73 for instructions on completing form 2.) The blank in Item 6E should be completed by typing in the word "complaint," "petition," or whatever complaint title is used in your state. For example, if your state calls it a *Petition for Divorce*, you should type in the word "petition."

◈ Paragraph 7: Check the box that applies to you, then type in either "divorce" or "dissolution or marriage" (whichever is used in your state) in the blank. In the space below the words "on the following grounds," type in the grounds for divorce you are using. For no-fault cases, you may use the grounds exactly as stated in your state's listing in Appendix A. If you wish to use any of the traditional grounds for your state, you will need to look up the law and use language as close to the statute or code as possible. You will also need to do further research to be sure you are including all of the information you need. (See the section in Chapter 2 regarding legal research.) Some states want you to give facts to show why the ground is justified, while other states prohibit you from doing this. Refer to Appendix A for more information.

◈ Paragraph 8: If you and your spouse have signed a **MARITAL SETTLEMENT AGREEMENT** (see form 4, p.255), check this box. Also check the box for each matter settled in your agreement. If there is no agreement, leave this paragraph alone.

◈ Paragraph 9: First, check the box to indicate whether you *do* or *do not* have property that needs to be divided. The ideal situation is for you and your spouse to agree about what each of you will get, divide your property, and move your property to where each of you is living. Then you can check the box for Item A and not worry further about property. However, this is not usually possible unless you and your spouse are able to work well together with a divorce pending. If you have a **MARITAL**

Settlement Agreement (see form 4, p.255), check the box for Item 9B. You will then need to complete and file form 4 along with your complaint. (See p.86 for instructions for completing form 4.) If there is no agreement on property, check the box for Item C, and type in the name of the complaint as you did in Paragraph 6E of this form. If your state recognizes separate or nonmarital property (check Appendix A), check the boxes for Items D and E, and list under each the assets and debts you believe should be separate for you and your spouse.

✧ Paragraph 10: If you desire to have your name changed along with your divorce, check the box that applies to you and type in the new name you wish to have. Check Appendix A to find out what name changes are allowed in your state. Some states allow either party to change their name, and some only allow the wife to change her name. Some allow a change to any name, some only to a maiden name, and some only to a maiden or other former name.

✧ Paragraph 11: You do not need to do anything with this paragraph.

✧ Paragraph 12: This is where you indicate what *relief* you are requesting, which is a legal way of describing what you want the court to do. First, check the box for "Husband" or "Wife" (whichever applies to you). Then, check the other boxes that apply (after referring to your state's listing in Appendix A, under the heading "Complaint Title," for what must be included in your decree or judgment). When completing this, considering the following.

> ***Item A.*** Check the box for the name used in your state for divorce actions. This will either be "divorce from the bonds of marriage" or "dissolution of marriage." Use the first phrase if your complaint or petition uses the word "divorce" and the second phrase if your complaint or petition uses the phrase "dissolution of marriage."

> ***Item B.*** Check the first box if this paragraph applies to your situation. *Legal custody* refers to who makes major

decisions concerning your child. This can be either you, your spouse, or both of you jointly. Be sure to check Appendix A for any special requirements in your state for joint custody.

Item C. Check the first box if this paragraph applies to your situation. *Physical custody* refers to where the child's primary residence will be.

Item D. Check the first box if this paragraph applies to your situation. Checking the box for *reasonable* visitation leaves it up to you and your spouse to agree on a schedule. This provides the most flexibility to arrange visitation around your schedules, but it can also create problems if there is anger between you and your spouse.

Unless you can cooperate fairly well, you should probably check the box for *scheduled* visitation and attach a sheet of paper describing a schedule to be followed. A typical schedule might be: *Alternate weekends from 6:00 PM Friday to 6:00 PM Sunday; alternate holidays consisting of New Years Day, Easter, Memorial Day, Fourth of July, Labor Day, Thanksgiving, Christmas Eve, and Christmas Day; alternate birthdays of the child; and, two weeks during summer vacation from school.* Only check the box for "Restricted or Supervised" if there is some reason you can prove that your spouse poses some danger to the child (such as a history of child abuse or neglect).

Items E, F, and G. Check the appropriate boxes.

Item H. Check this box if you are requesting alimony, and check "Husband" or "Wife" (whichever applies to you).

Item I. Check this box if property needs to be divided. The only time you would not check this box is if you have already divided your property and have checked the box for Paragraph 9, Item A.

Item J. If you want your name changed, check this box and type in the new name you want. Modify it as necessary if you are in one of the few states that allow the husband to change his name. (see Appendix A.)

Item K. This simply allows you to ask for other temporary orders if necessary.

Item L. This is a space for you to indicate any special relief you want from the court. An attempt has been made to cover the most common matters, but if something has been left out, you can check this box and type it in here.

⟐ Take this form to a notary public. Fill in the date and sign your name on the two lines designated "Signature" before the notary. You may type in your name, address, and telephone number on the lines below the first signature line before you go to the notary, but DO NOT sign on either line until you are before the notary. The notary will complete the form, and it is then ready for filing.

Simplified Procedures

If you and your spouse are in agreement on all matters, look in Appendix A or check with your court clerk to see if you can use a simplified procedure or file a joint complaint or petition. If this is not possible, you can still simplify things by having your spouse file an **ANSWER AND WAIVER** (see form 6, p.261), which will be discussed in Chapter 12. Without modification, form 6 may not satisfy the requirements in your state and county, and definitely will not satisfy the requirements of the following states.

- Alaska (simplified procedure)

- California (summary dissolution procedure)

- Delaware

- Iowa

- Montana (summary procedure)

- ✪   Nebraska

- ✪   Nevada (summary procedure)

- ✪   Oregon (summary procedure)

- ✪   Tennessee

- ✪   Texas

- ✪   Wisconsin

Be sure to read the information found in Appendix A for these states to see what changes or additions are needed.

SUPPORTING DOCUMENTS

Some states require certain papers to be filed along with the complaint. These typically consist of a financial statement and an affidavit to comply with the *Uniform Child Custody Jurisdiction Act*. To find out what—if any—supporting documents must be filed, first check the listing for your state in Appendix A. Next, check with the court clerk, and be sure to ask if there are any official mandatory forms you need to use.

Financial Statement

If a financial statement is required but there is no official mandatory form, you may use the sample **FINANCIAL STATEMENT**. (see form 3, p.251.) The **FINANCIAL STATEMENT** is designed to show information on a monthly basis. If you are paid weekly or every two weeks, you will need to convert your income to a monthly figure. The same conversion will be required for any of your expenses that are not paid monthly. To convert weekly amounts to monthly amounts, just take the weekly figure and multiply it by 4.3. (There are roughly 4.3 weeks to a month.) To convert from every two weeks, divide by 2 and then multiply by 4.3.

Fill in all of the blank spaces on the **FINANCIAL STATEMENT**, then take it to a notary public before you sign it. Most of the blanks in the financial affidavit clearly indicate what information is to be filled in. However, the following may answer some questions.

◈ Complete the case style according to the instructions in the first section of this chapter.

◈ After the words STATE OF, type in the name of your state. After the words COUNTY OF, type in the county in which the Financial Statement will be signed.

◈ Type your name in the blank in the first paragraph.

◈ Complete the information called for in ITEM 1 for your occupation, employer's name and address, Social Security number, pay period, and rate of pay.

"RATE OF PAY" refers to your hourly rate, or weekly, monthly, or yearly salary, whichever applies to your situation.

"PAY PERIOD" refers to how often you receive your paycheck, such as weekly, every two weeks, twice a month, and so on.

"AVERAGE GROSS MONTHLY INCOME" refers to your total income before any deductions for taxes or other items. The items listed on the form are commonly included as income items. A more detailed definition of gross income may be found in your state's child support law. (see Appendix A.) Add these items (if any) to your AVERAGE GROSS MONTHLY INCOME and type in the total on the line for TOTAL MONTHLY GROSS INCOME.

DEDUCTIONS refers to allowable deductions from gross income. The items listed on the form are commonly allowed deductions, but a more detailed list may be found in your state's child support laws. (see Appendix A.)

To get the TOTAL NET INCOME figure, subtract the TOTAL DEDUCTIONS from the TOTAL GROSS MONTHLY INCOME.

◈ ITEM 2 refers to AVERAGE MONTHLY EXPENSES. Simply refer to each item listed and estimate as best you can the amount you spend on that item in a month. If a particular item is an annual expense, such as auto insurance, convert it to a monthly amount. Under the section for OTHER EXPENSES, list anything not covered elsewhere in the financial statement, then total these other expenses. The section for PAYMENTS TO CREDITORS is for listing what you owe for money borrowed or otherwise owed. This will usually be credit cards or other monthly installment payments. Total the monthly payments to creditors. Next, add all of your monthly expenses, other expenses, and monthly payments to creditors. Type in this total on the line marked TOTAL MONTHLY EXPENSES.

◈ To complete ITEM 3 on ASSETS, refer to the list you made on the **Property Inventory**. (see worksheet 3.)

◈ To complete ITEM 4 on LIABILITIES, refer to the list you made on the **Debt Inventory**. (see worksheet 4.)

◈ Take the form to a notary and sign it before the notary on the line designated "Affiant." The notary will complete the part of the form directly below your signature.

◈ Under the heading CERTIFICATE OF SERVICE, you will need to fill in the date when you mail a copy of this form to your spouse and sign your name again above the line marked "Signature."

Uniform Child Custody Jurisdiction Act Affidavit

All states have adopted the *Uniform Child Custody Jurisdiction Act,* which is designed to eliminate the problems that arose when one parent took the children out of state and tried to get custody in the new state. To assure that there are no violations of this Act, many courts require you to file a form providing information about your children. A sample **Uniform Child Custody Jurisdiction Act Affidavit** (see form B, p.210) may be found in Appendix B. Even if your state does not require this form, it will not hurt to file it anyway if you have minor children.

Complete the **UNIFORM CHILD CUSTODY JURISDICTION ACT AFFIDAVIT** as follows.

◈   Complete the case style according to the instructions in the first section of this chapter.

◈   Paragraph 1: Type in the name and present address of each of your children.

◈   Paragraph 2: Type in the addresses where each child has lived during the past five years. If a child is not yet five years old, type in the places the child has lived since birth.

◈   Paragraph 3: Type in the names and current addresses of persons with whom each child has lived during the past five years. If the child has only lived with you and your spouse, type in "With the Husband and Wife for past five years at," then type in the addresses where you have lived during this period.

◈   Paragraph 4: This requires you to tell whether you have been involved in any other court cases involving the custody of, or visitation with, your children. Similarly, Paragraph 5 requires you to tell if you know of any court case involving custody of, or visitation with, the children (even if you were not involved in the case). If there are no such cases, type in the word "None" below Paragraphs 4 and 5. If there are such cases, you need to check the appropriate box to indicate whether the other case is continuing or has been *stayed* (temporarily stopped) by the other court. Also check whether you want the judge in your divorce case to take some action to protect the children from abuse or neglect (usually this will not be necessary in an uncontested case).

◈   Paragraph 6: If there is any person other than you or your spouse who has custody of a child, or who claims custody or visitation rights, type in that person's name and address. If there is no such third person, type in the word "None."

⟡ Paragraph 7: Type in the child's (or children's) *home state* on the line. Read the definition of home state in Paragraph 7 of the form.

⟡ Type in your name, address, and phone number on the appropriate lines at the bottom of the form.

⟡ Take the form to a notary and sign it on the "Signature" line before the notary, then file it with the clerk along with your **COMPLAINT FOR DIVORCE**.

Answer and Waiver

If you and your spouse can agree on everything, and both of you sign and file a **MARITAL SETTLEMENT AGREEMENT**, you do not need to complete an **ANSWER AND WAIVER**. (see form 6, p.261.) If your spouse is in full agreement about the divorce, but does not want to sign a settlement agreement, you can simplify and speed up the case by having your spouse sign an **ANSWER AND WAIVER** before a notary public. If this form is used, you will not need to go through the procedure in Chapter 11 regarding notifying your spouse, and you will not need to complete the **AFFIDAVIT OF NONMILITARY SERVICE**. (see form 7, p.263.)

To complete the **ANSWER AND WAIVER**, you need to do the following.

⟡ Complete the case style according to the instructions in the first section of this chapter.

⟡ In the first (unnumbered) paragraph, type in the word "Defendant" or "Respondent," (whichever term is used in your state) in the first blank; your spouse's name in the second blank; and, the complaint title used in your state ("Complaint for Divorce," "Petition for Dissolution of Marriage," and so on) in the third blank.

⟡ Paragraph 1: Type in the word "Defendant" or "Respondent," whichever term is used in your state, in the first blank. Type in the word "Complaint" or "Petition" (or whatever complaint title is used in your state).

⟡ Paragraphs 2 and 3: In the blanks, type in the word "Defendant" or "Respondent," whichever term is used in your state.

❖ Below the "Signature" line, type in your spouse's name, address, and phone number.

❖ Have your spouse sign on the "Signature" line before a notary public.

Affidavit of Nonmilitary Service

If your spouse is not in the military service, and will not sign either a **MARITAL SETTLEMENT AGREEMENT** (see form 4, p.255) or an **ANSWER AND WAIVER** (see form 6, p.261), you will need to complete the **AFFIDAVIT OF NONMILITARY SERVICE**. (see form 7, p.263.) To complete the **AFFIDAVIT OF NONMILITARY SERVICE**, you need to do the following.

❖ Complete the case style according to the instructions in the first section of this chapter.

❖ Type your name in the blank space in the first (unnumbered) paragraph.

❖ Check either Paragraph 1 or 2, whichever applies. Type in the word "Defendant" or "Respondent" (whichever term is used in your state) in the blanks in Paragraphs 1 or 2 (depending upon which paragraph applies to your situation).

❖ Type in your name, address, and phone number below the signature line.

❖ Sign before a notary public on the line above the word AFFIANT.

Call the court clerk to ask when the **AFFIDAVIT OF NONMILITARY SERVICE** needs to be filed. Some courts require that it not be signed too far in advance, because they want the information to be reasonably current. Some courts require that the notary public's date on the **AFFIDAVIT OF NONMILITARY SERVICE** be within a certain number of days before filing a **MOTION TO ENTER DEFAULT** (see form 10, p.269), or before the final hearing. File the **AFFIDAVIT OF NONMILITARY SERVICE** with the clerk.

If your spouse is not willing to file an **ANSWER AND WAIVER**, or a **MARITAL SETTLEMENT AGREEMENT**, and is in the military, you do not need to complete this form and should consult a lawyer. Federal laws

designed to protect service personnel while overseas can create special problems in these situations.

**Request for
Certificate of
Military Status**

If you do not know if your spouse is in the military service, you will
need to complete the **REQUEST FOR CERTIFICATE OF MILITARY STATUS** (see
form 8, p.265) before you can complete form 7. Complete the **REQUEST
FOR CERTIFICATE OF MILITARY STATUS** as follows.

◈   Complete the case style according to the instructions in the
first section of this chapter.

◈   Type in your spouse's name and Social Security number on the
lines marked "Party" and "Soc. Sec. #."

◈   Type in the date on the line indicated, and your name, address,
and telephone number under the heading "Requesting Party."

◈   Sign the form on the line marked "Signature."

You will then need to make seven copies of this form. Mail one to each
of the six addresses listed on the form (one to each branch of the U.S.
Government considered military service), file the original with the
court clerk, and keep a copy for yourself. Be sure to enclose a self-
addressed, stamped envelope with each copy sent to a service branch.
Each service branch will then check its records and mail you a notice
as to whether your spouse is in that branch (these notices may then
be filed with the court clerk).

If your spouse is in one of the service branches, his or her address will
be provided. You can then send your spouse notice of the divorce, and
see if some agreement can be reached so you can use the uncontested
procedure. If your spouse is in the service and cannot be contacted or
will not cooperate (by either filing an *answer*, a *financial affidavit*, or
a *settlement agreement*), you should contact an attorney. If your
spouse is not in the service, complete form 7.

MARITAL SETTLEMENT AGREEMENT

The **MARITAL SETTLEMENT AGREEMENT** includes provisions for agreements on property division, child support and custody, alimony, and attorney's fees. (see form 4, p.255.) Whether you and your spouse agreed on everything from the start or you have gone through extensive negotiations to reach an agreement, you need to put your agreement in writing. This is done through a **MARITAL SETTLEMENT AGREEMENT**. Even if you do not agree on everything, you should put what you do agree on into a written agreement. This form cannot possibly cover every possible agreement or situation, but it should serve as a guide to help you create an agreement to fit your specific circumstances.

To complete the **MARITAL SETTLEMENT AGREEMENT** you need to do the following.

◈ Complete the case style according to the instructions in the first section of this chapter.

◈ Type in your name and your spouse's name in the blanks in the first paragraph. Type in the date you were married.

◈ In each section, there are boxes for you to check the provision that applies to your situation. Read through each one and look for places where you need to mark a box or type in information to fit your situation.

◈ You will type in the names of your children in the CHILD CUSTODY section. Physical custody refers to whom each child will live with as the child's permanent residence. Any special arrangements you wish to include in this section can be typed in by the last box in this section.

◈ The section on CHILD SUPPORT will require you to type in an amount and a period, such as "$500.00" per "month." You will also need to check the box for either "Husband" or "Wife" in the sections on child support and health insurance. Many states require that provisions for health insurance be in every divorce judgment. (see Appendix A.)

⬥ Refer to the instructions in Chapter 5 regarding how to complete the sections on the division of property and debts.

⬥ There are three possible boxes to check in the alimony section. Check the first box if no alimony is to be paid by either you or your spouse. The second box is to be checked if you and your spouse have agreed to alimony. If so, you will also need to check the appropriate box for who is to pay the alimony and fill in the amount, when that amount is to be paid (weekly, monthly, etc.), and for how long. For *rehabilitative alimony*, this time will be until a specific date. For *permanent alimony*, just cross out the words "for a period of." The last box is to check if there are any special agreements regarding alimony.

⬥ Each of you should sign and date the form (before a notary) where indicated at the bottom, then file it with the court clerk.

NEGOTIATING

It is beyond the scope and ability of this book to fully present a course in negotiation techniques. However, a few basic rules may be of some help.

Ask for More than You Want

Asking for more than you want always gives you room to compromise. By giving up a few things, you will end up with close to what you really want. With property division, this means you will review your **PROPERTY INVENTORY** (see worksheet 3, p.233) and decide which items you really want, would like to have, and do not care much about. Also try to figure out which items your spouse really wants, would like to have, and does not care much about.

At the beginning, you will say that you want certain things. Your list will include: everything you really want; almost everything you would like to have; some of the things you do not care about; and, some of the things you think your spouse really wants or would like to have. Once you find out what is on your spouse's list, you begin trading items. Generally, you try to give your spouse things they really want and that you do not care about, in return for your spouse giving you the items you really care about and would like to have.

Child Custody

If you will be receiving child support, you should first work out what you think the judge will order based upon the child support guidelines used in your state. Then you should ask for more and negotiate down to what the guidelines call for. If your spouse will not settle for something very close to the guidelines, give up trying to work it out and let the judge decide. Most states will not allow parents to compromise about their child's welfare and the judge will insist on following the guidelines.

Generally, child custody tends to be something that cannot be negotiated. It is more often used as a threat by one of the parties in order to get something else, such as more of the property or lower child support. If the real issue is one of these other matters, do not be concerned by a threat of a custody fight. In these cases, the other party probably does not really want custody and will not fight for it. If the real issue is custody, you will not be able to negotiate for it and will end up letting the judge decide anyway.

Let Your Spouse Start the Bidding

In negotiating, it is believed that the first person to mention a dollar figure loses. Whether it is a child support figure or the value of a piece of property, try to get your spouse to name the amount he or she thinks first. If your spouse starts with a figure almost what you had in mind, it will be much easier to get to your figure. If your spouse begins with a figure far from yours, you know how far in the other direction to begin your bid.

Give Your Spouse Time to Think and Worry

Your spouse is probably just as afraid as you about the possibility of losing to the judge's decision, and would probably like to settle. Do not be afraid to state your *final offer*, then walk away. Give your spouse a day or two to think it over. Maybe he or she will call back and make a better offer. If not, you can always *reconsider* and make a different offer in a few days, but do not be too willing to do this or your spouse may think you will give in even more.

Know Your Bottom Line

Before you begin negotiating, you should try to set a point that you will not go beyond. If you have decided that there are four items of property that you absolutely must have, and your spouse is only willing to agree to let you have three, it is time to end the bargaining session and go home.

By the time you have read this far, you should be aware of two things:

1. the judge will roughly divide your property equally and

2. the judge will probably follow the child support guidelines.

This awareness should give you an approximate idea of how things will turn out if the judge is asked to decide these issues, which should help you to set your bottom line on them.

FILING WITH THE CLERK

Always, make at least four copies of your complaint and any of the other papers you prepared. This will give you one copy to file with the clerk (the original), one for your spouse, one for yourself, and one extra copy just in case the clerk asks for two copies or you decide to hire an attorney and need a copy for him or her. Filing is about as simple as making a bank deposit, although the following information will help things go more smoothly.

Call the court clerk's office. You can probably find the phone number under the county government section of your phone directory. Ask the clerk the following questions (along with any other questions that come to mind, such as where the clerk's office is located and what their hours are).

✪   How much is the filing fee for a divorce case?

✪   Does the court have any special forms that need to be filed with the petition? (If there are special forms, you will need to go down to the clerk's office and pick them up.)

✪   How many copies of the complaint and other forms do you need to file with the clerk?

Next, take your complaint and any other papers to be filed to the clerk's office. The clerk handles many different types of cases, so be sure to look for signs telling you which office or window to go to. You should be looking for signs that say such things as "Family Court,"

"Family Division," or "Filing." If it is too confusing, ask someone where you file a divorce case.

Once you have found the right place, simply hand the papers to the clerk and say, "I'd like to file this." The clerk will examine the papers, then do one of two things—say "Thank you" (and collect the filing fee or direct you to where to pay it) or tell you that something is not correct. If you are told something is wrong, ask the clerk to explain to you what is wrong and how to correct the problem. Although clerks are not permitted to give legal advice, the types of problems they spot are usually very minor things that they can tell you how to correct. It is often possible to figure out how to correct it from the way the clerk explains what is wrong.

Filing Fees   When you file your initial court papers, you will usually need to pay a filing fee. You will also need to pay a fee to the sheriff or other process server to have the papers delivered to your spouse. The service fee may be left with the clerk when you file your papers, or may need to be given directly to the sheriff. Most, if not all, states have procedures for waiving these fees if you do not have the financial means to pay. This usually means that your financial situation is such that you would qualify for public assistance or fall below some specific low-income standards. If this is your situation, ask the court clerk what you need to do to qualify for a waiver of these court costs. This will usually involve filling out a few forms to formally ask for a waiver and to explain your financial situation to allow the courts to determine if you qualify. The information required, and the way the information is presented, varies from state to state.

COUNSELING, MEDIATION, AND PARENTING CLASSES

There is a trend to attempt to resolve property division, alimony, and child support, custody, and visitation disputes outside of the courtroom. Some states require parties in divorce cases to go through mediation. Only if this is not successful can the matter be presented to the judge. Unfortunately, this may be a requirement even if your spouse is so difficult that you know with certainty he or she will never reach an agreement through mediation. In some states it may be possible to file a motion to dispense with mediation, but this would require the assistance of an attorney, and may be just as costly as going through mediation.

Some states also require the parents to attend parenting classes before a divorce will be granted. The main purpose of this is to make the parents aware of the effect of the divorce on their children, and help them deal with those effects. Some states also allow the judge to order the parties to attend marriage counseling, if the judge thinks it may be possible for the parties to resolve the differences and avoid a divorce.

There is frequently a cost associated with counseling, mediation, and other programs, which must be paid by the parties. Your court clerk should be able to tell you if mediation or parenting classes are required. As for court-ordered marriage counseling, you will have to wait to see if the judge orders it.

COLLECTING INFORMATION ABOUT YOUR SPOUSE

In many states the judge will require that you and your spouse provide some kind of financial information. If you cannot find a particular form used in your state, use the **FINANCIAL STATEMENT** (see form 3, p.251,) from Appendix D.

If your spouse has indicated that he or she will not cooperate at all and will not provide a **FINANCIAL STATEMENT**, you may have to try to get the information yourself. You can go to the hearing and tell the judge that your spouse will not cooperate, but the judge may just issue an order requiring your spouse to provide information (or be held in contempt of court), and continue the hearing to another date. It may help speed things up if you are able to get the information yourself and have it available at the hearing. This will require you to get subpoenas issued.

In some states, before you send a subpoena to your spouse's employer (or bank or accountant), you need to let your spouse know what you are about to do. The thought that you are about to get these other people involved in your divorce may be enough to get your spouse to cooperate. If your spouse calls and says, "I'll give you the information," give him or her a few days to follow through. Ask when you can expect to receive the **FINANCIAL STATEMENT**, and offer to send your spouse another blank copy if he or she needs one. If your spouse sends a completed **FINANCIAL STATEMENT** as promised, do not send the subpoena. If your spouse does not follow through, go ahead with the subpoena.

The procedure and forms for subpoenas vary for each state. Look at a divorce file at your court clerk's office, or check at your local law library to see which forms and procedures are used in your state or county. An example of a typical subpoena form is included in Appendix _. You can send out subpoenas to as many people or organizations as you need, but you will need to use the following procedure for each subpoena.

To determine where to send subpoenas, look at the **FINANCIAL STATEMENT** and see what type of information is asked for. If you were able to do a good job making copies of important papers while preparing to file for divorce, you should have the information you need to figure out where you need to send subpoenas. Your spouse's income information can be obtained from his or her employer. Stock and bond information can be obtained from his or her stock broker, bank account balances from the bank, auto loan balances from the lender, and so on. You can have subpoenas issued to any or all of these places, but do not overdo it. Concentrate on income information (especially if you are asking for child support or expect to pay child support) and information on the major property items. Be sure that your subpoena accurately and precisely describes what information is being requested.

It may not be necessary to send out subpoenas if you have recent copies of the papers relating to these items. You can always show the judge the copies of your spouse's paystubs, W-2 tax statements, or other papers at the hearing.

NOTE: *Many states do not allow you to have such a subpoena served until your spouse has had a specific number of days to file a written objection. Be sure to check your state's laws before sending such a subpoena.*

The general procedure is to mail a copy of a notice form (called a *Notice of Production from Non-Party* in some states), along with a copy of the subpoena to your spouse. Make sure that you actually mail it on the date you indicated on the *Notice of Production from Non-Party*. If your spouse does not file a **FINANCIAL STATEMENT** (or provide you with adequate income information) or send you a written objection to the subpoena within the time permitted in your state, you will proceed with getting the subpoena issued by the clerk. If your spouse does send you a written objection, you will either need to get your spouse to agree to give you the information, or you will have to file a *Motion to Issue Subpoena* and get a hearing date from the judge's secretary. The judge will then decide if you can send out the subpoena.

Next, have the sheriff personally serve the subpoena to the person or place named in the subpoena. The sheriff will need at least one extra copy of the subpoena and a check for the service fee. The employer, bank, etc., should send you the requested information. If the employer calls you and says you must pay for copies, ask him or her how much they will cost and send a check or money order (if the amount is not too high and you do not already have some fairly recent income information). If the employer does not provide the information, you can try sending a letter to the employer with a statement that:

> *unless you provide the information requested in the subpoena in seven days, a motion for contempt will be filed with the circuit court.*

This may scare the employer into sending you the information. The sheriff will have also filed an affidavit verifying when the subpoena was served.

There are more procedures you could go through to force the employer to give you the information, but it is probably not worth the hassle and you would probably need an attorney to help you with this process. At the final hearing, you can tell the judge that your spouse refused to provide income information and the subpoena was not honored by the employer. The judge may do something to help you, or he or she may advise you to see a lawyer.

Interrogatories

There is also a procedure where you send written questions to your spouse that he or she must answer in writing and under oath. These written questions are called *interrogatories*. However, if your spouse did not file a **FINANCIAL STATEMENT**, he or she probably will not answer the interrogatories, leaving you in the same situation with the subpoena.

Emergency Procedures

chapter 10

Some people have three special concerns when preparing to file for a divorce.

1. How to protect themselves and their children from their spouse.

2. How to be sure their spouse will not be able to take the marital property and hide it.

3. How they are going to support themselves and their children during the divorce proceedings.

There are additional legal papers you can file in these situations. If your spouse is resourceful and determined, there is no guaranteed way to prevent the problems discussed. All you can do is put as many obstacles in his or her way as possible, and prepare for him or her to suffer legal consequences for acting improperly (such as being put in jail for contempt of court). Since the requirements vary from state to state, forms are not provided for all of these situations. You will need to check with your court clerk or law library. (See the section on "Legal Research" in Chapter 2.)

PROTECTING YOURSELF

Most, if not all, states have laws setting up procedures to protect people from *family* or *domestic violence*. Check the listing for your state in Appendix A under the heading "Domestic Violence" to find the reference for laws for your state. These laws are usually fairly simple, and frequently even contain the forms to be used. You can also check with the court clerk. Many states require the court clerk to help people with the forms and procedures for protection from domestic violence.

You can also file a motion for a restraining order from domestic violence. This will be part of your divorce case, using the same case style. Look for forms in books on divorce at your law library or adapt the forms used in your state's laws on protection from domestic violence. One possible advantage to this procedure is that you may avoid a separate filing fee charged under some laws on protection from domestic violence.

Either procedure will typically result in the judge signing an order prohibiting your spouse from physically abusing or harassing you. If your spouse violates the order, he or she can then be arrested and charged with contempt of court. It is usually easier to get police officers to arrest an abusive or harassing spouse if you have a court order.

It is also possible to file a motion asking the judge to order your spouse to move out of your home. This usually requires you to show that your spouse is physically abusing you, in some other way harassing you, or intimidating you from proceeding with the divorce case. This is even more likely to be granted if you have temporary custody of your children and you can show that your spouse's actions are causing the children added mental stress.

These legal solutions will work with most spouses. However, they may not be enough to control a very irrational and violent spouse. In such cases, it may be necessary for you and your children to find somewhere else to live. This can be with a friend or relative (preferably where your spouse cannot find you), or in a center for abused spouses that are available in many cities. If you need to resort to this, it would probably be a good idea to see an attorney who can advise you on how to best protect yourself and take the necessary legal action.

PROTECTING YOUR CHILDREN

If you are worried that your spouse may try to kidnap your children, you should make sure that the day care center, baby-sitter, relative, or whomever you leave the children with at any time are all aware that you are in the process of a divorce, and that the children are only to be released to you personally (not to your spouse or to any other relative, friend, etc.).

To prevent your spouse from taking the children out of the United States, you can apply for a passport for each child. Once a passport is issued, the government will not issue another. Get their passport and lock it up in a safe deposit box. (This will not prevent them from being taken to Canada or Mexico, where passports are not required, but will prevent them from being taken overseas.) You can also file a motion for the court to deny passport privileges to your children. A copy of the judge's order is sent to the U.S. State Department, which will not issue a passport for your children.

PROTECTING YOUR PROPERTY

If you genuinely fear that your spouse will try to remove money from bank accounts and try to hide important papers showing what property you own, you may want to take some action to protect the assets before your spouse can take them. However, you can make a great deal of trouble for yourself with the judge if it appears that you are you trying to get the assets for yourself.

The best thing to do is only take one-half of the assets you believe to be in danger. For example, suppose you and your spouse have a joint bank account with a balance of $10,000. If you take the entire $10,000, it may appear that you intend to keep it all for yourself and are leaving nothing for your spouse to live on. Instead, take only $5,000 and put it in an account in your name alone. Keep a copy of the joint account statement showing the full $10,000, your withdrawal receipt for the $5,000, and your new account deposit receipt or first statement showing the deposit. This way, you can prove what the total amount was and that you only took half.

With a bank account, it is easy to obtain papers to prove what was there and what has been taken. With other types of assets, it may not be so easy to prove. You may need to take a witness with you, take photographs of the assets, make a written inventory of the items left and taken, or all of the above.

Be sure to make a complete list of any property you do take, and be sure to include these items in your **FINANCIAL STATEMENT**. (see form 3, p.251.) You may need to convince the judge that you only took these items temporarily, in order to preserve them until a final judgment is entered.

Do not spend any cash you take from a bank account or sell or give away any items of property you take. Of course, you may use money to pay for necessary expenses, such as rent, food, car payments or medical bills.

Any cash should be placed in a separate bank account, without your spouse's name on it, and kept separate from any other cash you have. Any papers—such as deeds, car titles, or stock or bond certificates— should be placed in a safe deposit box without your spouse's name on it.

The idea is not to take these things for yourself, but to get them in a safe place so your spouse cannot hide them and deny they ever existed. Do not do this unless it is absolutely necessary to protect the property.

You can also file a motion asking the judge to issue an order requiring your spouse to produce certain property, or restraining your spouse from hiding, disposing of, or destroying property. In a few states, there is an automatic restraining order imposed in all cases as soon as the complaint is filed.

TEMPORARY ALIMONY, CHILD SUPPORT, AND CUSTODY

If your spouse has left you with the children, the mortgage, and monthly bills, and is not helping you financially, you may want to consider asking the court to order the payment of support for you and the children during the divorce procedure. Of course, if you were the only person bringing in income and have been paying all the bills, do not expect to get any temporary support.

Try to find a sample motion for temporary alimony, child support and custody, and a sample order by checking other files at the clerk's office or at your local law library. Such a motion may also be called a *motion for temporary relief,* a *motion for relief pendente lite,* or some similar name. (*Pendente lite* is a Latin phrase meaning "pending the litigation".) If you are unable to find a sample, use the **Motion for Temporary Relief** (see form 12, p.275) and an **Order for Temporary Relief** (see form 13, p.277), found in Appendix D.

To complete the **Motion for Temporary Relief**, you need to the following.

◈   Complete the case style according to the instructions in Chapter 9.

◈   Check the box or boxes that apply to your situation.

◈   Spaces are available to type in any other relief you need, any special allegations required in your state, and to explain why you might want the matter decided without notifying your spouse in advance. In the interest of fairness, judges do not usually issue orders unless both parties are notified and have an opportunity to give their respective sides. However, in certain circumstances, judges do not require notice in advance. These circumstances are usually emergency situations, such as if there is a real danger your spouse will try to take your children. You will need to say why you could not notify your spouse, or what efforts you made to attempt to notify him or her. Also, some courts are more willing than others to issue temporary support and custody orders, depending upon the local practice.

◈   Type in the date, sign your name on the line marked "Signature," and type your name, address, and phone number below the line.

◈   Unless your spouse has already filed a **Financial Statement**, you may also want to attach copies of any of your spouse's paystubs, most recent tax forms, or other information showing your spouse's income. You should have already filed your financial affidavit that will show what your monthly expenses are, as well as your income.

This form needs to be presented to the judge, along with the **ORDER FOR TEMPORARY RELIEF**. (see form 13, p.277.) Call the judge's secretary and tell him or her that you would like to submit a "motion for temporary relief" in a divorce case to the judge, and ask him or her how you should do this. The secretary may tell you to come in with your papers at a certain time, to mail them to the judge, or to submit them to the court clerk's office. Just follow the secretary's instructions.

To complete the **ORDER FOR TEMPORARY RELIEF**, all you need to do is complete the top portion of the form. The judge should either fill in the rest or tell you how to fill it in. An extra box and space have been included in the **ORDER FOR TEMPORARY RELIEF** to be used if the judge wants you to put any additional things in the **ORDER**.

Once you have a signed copy of the **ORDER FOR TEMPORARY RELIEF**, mail or deliver a copy to your spouse. Then, complete a **CERTIFICATE OF SERVICE** (see the **CERTIFICATE OF SERVICE**) to show that you have served your spouse. (see form 1, p.245.) Instructions for completing form 3 are found in Chapter 11.

Notifying Your Spouse

If you are using a procedure for a joint petition allowed in your state, you do not need to worry about the information in this chapter (your spouse will have to sign the petition, so it will be obvious that he or she knows about the divorce). Also, you do not need to worry about this chapter if you and your spouse are in agreement about everything, but do not qualify for a joint petition procedure. Your spouse can simply file an **Answer and Waiver** (see form 6, p.261), or you can both sign and file a **Marital Settlement Agreement**. (see form 4, p.255.) However, in all other cases, you are required to notify your spouse that you have filed for divorce. This gives your spouse a chance to respond to your complaint or petition.

NOTICE OF FILING THE COMPLAINT

The usual way to notify your spouse that you filed for a divorce is called *personal service*, which is where the sheriff (or someone else designated by the judge) personally delivers the papers to your spouse. This is done using a *summons*. Be sure to check with the court clerk about the proper form for the summons, because this varies for each state. An example of a typical summons is found in Appendix B, but you will need to use the form used in your county. Look in a divorce file at the clerk's office or check at your local law library to find the proper summons form.

Once you have prepared the summons, take it to the clerk for signature. Then, call the county sheriff's office in the county where your spouse lives. Ask how much it will cost to have him or her served with divorce papers, and ask how many copies of the complaint and summons need to be provided to the sheriff's office. Deliver or mail the required copies of your complaint (together with any other papers you filed) and summons, and a check or money order for the service fee to the sheriff's office.

A sheriff's deputy will personally deliver the papers to your spouse. You must give the sheriff accurate information about where your spouse can be found. If there are several addresses where your spouse might be found (such as home, a relative's home, and work), enclose a letter to the sheriff with all of the addresses and any other information that may help the sheriff find your spouse (such as the hours your spouse works). Be sure you give the sheriff information that will be truly useful to get your spouse served, and do not just speculate where he or she *might* be found.

The deputy will fill out a form to verify that the papers were delivered (including the date and time they were delivered), and will file a copy of that form with the court clerk. The deputy should also send you a copy to let you know your spouse has been served, but you may need to check your court file in the clerk's office.

Once you know the date your spouse was served, you can count the number of days to find out when a response is due. Wait an additional five days to allow for mailing and any clerk's office filing delay, then go to the clerk's office and see if an answer is in your court file. A later section of this chapter will advise you on what to do depending upon how your spouse responds to being served.

CERTIFICATE OF SERVICE

Once your spouse has been served with the complaint, you may simply mail him or her copies of any papers you file later. All you need to do is sign a statement (called a *certificate of service*) indicating that you mailed copies to your spouse. Some of the forms in this book will have a certificate of service for you to complete. If any form you file does not contain one, you will need to complete the **CERTIFICATE OF SERVICE**. (see form 1, p.245.) Complete the **CERTIFICATE OF SERVICE** as follows.

- ◈ Complete the case style according to the instructions in Chapter 9.

- ◈ Type in the name or title of the papers being sent on the first blank in the main paragraph.

- ◈ Check the box for how the papers are being sent (mailed or hand delivered) and the date the papers are being sent.

- ◈ Type in the name, address, and telephone number of the person (or persons) to whom the papers are being sent (usually your spouse or your spouse's attorney).

- ◈ Sign your name on the line marked "Signature," and type in your name, address, and phone number where indicated below the signature line. This form is to be filed with the court clerk as your proof that you sent a copy.

NOTICE OF HEARING

Once you get a hearing date set with the judge, you will need to notify your spouse of when the hearing will be. This is done by preparing a **NOTICE OF HEARING**. (see form 9, p.267.) Before using form 9, look at a divorce file in the clerk's office or check at your local law library for the notice of hearing form used in your state or county. If you cannot find one, use form 9. To complete the **NOTICE OF HEARING**, you need to do the following.

⟡ Complete the case style according to the instructions in Chapter 9.

⟡ After the word "TO," type in your spouse's name and mailing address. If your spouse has an attorney, type in the attorney's name and address.

⟡ In the spaces in the main paragraph, type in the required information about when and where the hearing will be held. This includes the day of the week, the date, the time, the judge's name, and the location of the hearing, including room number (if available) and address of the courthouse. (See Appendix B for an example of a completed **NOTICE OF HEARING**.)

You will probably need at least four copies of the **NOTICE OF HEARING**, so you can mail one copy to your spouse, file the original with the court clerk, and keep two copies for yourself.

WHEN YOU CANNOT FIND YOUR SPOUSE

Your spouse has run off and you have no idea where he or she might be. So how do you have the sheriff deliver a copy of your **COMPLAINT** to your spouse? In this situation you cannot use the sheriff. Instead of personal service, you will use a method of giving notice called *service by publication*. This is one of the more complicated procedures in the legal system. The requirements, forms, and procedures for service by publication vary for each state. You will need to research your state's requirements at your local law library. Examples of typical forms used in service by publication are included in Appendix B. The information that follows gives you an idea of how service by publication works.

The Diligent Search   The court will only permit publication when you cannot locate your spouse. This also includes the situation in which the sheriff has tried several times to personally serve your spouse, but it appears that your spouse is hiding to avoid being served. First, you will have to show that you cannot locate your spouse by letting the court know what you have done to try to find him or her. In making this search, you should try the following.

- ✪ Check the phone book and directory assistance in the area where you live.

- ✪ Check directory assistance in the area where you last knew your spouse to be staying.

- ✪ Ask friends and relatives who might know where your spouse might be staying.

- ✪ Check with the post office where he or she last lived to see if there is a forwarding address. (You can ask by mail if it is too far away.)

- ✪ Check records of the property tax collector or property assessor to see if your spouse owns property.

- ✪ Write to your state's motor vehicle licensing and drivers' licensing offices to see if your spouse has a car registration or driver's license.

- ✪ Check with any other sources you know that may lead you to a current address (such as landlords, prior employers, and so on).

If you do come up with a current address, go back to personal service by the sheriff, but if not, continue with this procedure. Even if you find your spouse in another state, still have him or her personally served. To do this, call the sheriff in the county and state where your spouse lives, and arrange for personal service by the sheriff.

Preparing and Filing Court Papers

Once you have made your search, you need to notify the court. This is done by filing a *motion for service by publication*. All this form does is tell the court what you have done to try to locate your spouse, and asks for permission to publish your notice. An example of a typical *motion for service by publication* is included in Appendix B.

You will also prepare a *notice of action*. This is the notice that will be published in the newspaper. An example of a typical *notice of action* is included in Appendix B.

The Clerk's Job   Note that the *notice of action* is signed by the court clerk. The clerk will sign on the *notice of action* and probably return two copies to you. If the clerk finds any errors in your papers, he or she will notify you regarding what needs to be corrected. You should provide the clerk with a self-addressed, stamped envelope when you deliver or send him or her these papers.

Publishing   Your next step is to have a newspaper publish your *notice of action*. Check the Yellow Pages listings under "Newspapers" and call several of the smaller ones in your county (making sure it is in the same county as the court). Ask if they are *approved for legal announcements*. If they are, ask how much they charge to publish a *notice of action* in a divorce case. What you are searching for is the cheapest paper. Most areas have a paper that specializes in the publishing of legal announcements, at a much cheaper rate than the regular daily newspapers. If you look around the courthouse, you may be able to find a copy of this paper.

The *notice of action* will be published the number of times required in your state. Get a copy of the newspaper the first time it appears and check to be sure it was printed correctly. If you find an error, notify the newspaper immediately. The newspaper will send you a form certifying that the *notice of action* has been published the required number of times. File this form with the court clerk.

As indicated in the *notice of action*, your spouse has until a certain date to respond. If your spouse responds to the notice published in the newspaper, continue with the divorce procedure. If your spouse does not respond by the date indicated in the *notice of action*, proceed with the **MOTION TO ENTER DEFAULT**, as discussed in the next section of this chapter. (see form 10, p.269.)

HOW YOUR SPOUSE RESPONDS

Once you have done what is needed to notify your spouse, you must wait and see how your spouse responds. Based on the actions he or she takes, you will do one of the following.

Your Spouse Files an Answer

If your spouse files an *answer*, the first thing you should do is read it carefully. This will tell you what your spouse agrees to and what he or she disputes. For example, if you asked for custody of the children in your complaint and your spouse does not ask for custody in his or her answer, then you should get custody without having to argue for it at the hearing. If he or she does ask for custody, you know you will either have to negotiate or have the judge resolve the question. The answer will give you a good idea of what you will need to negotiate on or prove at the hearing.

An answer may also contain new claims that you will need to respond to. This will frequently be called a *counterclaim* or a *cross-claim*.

Example:

You did not ask for alimony and you designated your car as marital property in your complaint (or financial statement). However, in your spouse's answer, he or she asks that you pay alimony, and claims your car as his or her nonmarital property. These are new claims that you must respond to. You will do this by preparing an *answer to counterclaim* (or use whatever your spouse called his or her new claim). This will simply deny whatever new claims were made in your spouse's answer. (See Chapter 12 for more information on answering complaints.)

Once your spouse has filed an answer (and you have responded to any new claims from your spouse), you can have the case set for a final hearing. Just be sure that you have met any waiting period—as indicated in Appendix A—for your state. Many states do not allow a final hearing to be conducted or a judgment to be entered until a certain amount of time after the complaint is filed, or until your spouse is served. Of course, while you are waiting for the hearing date to arrive you can always try to negotiate a settlement with your spouse. (See Chapter 14 for more information about setting a hearing date.)

Your Spouse does Nothing

If your spouse does not file an answer or join you in a **MARITAL SETTLEMENT AGREEMENT** (see form 4, p.255) within the time allowed in your state after the sheriff delivers the complaint, your spouse is in *default*. You will need to notify the court clerk that your spouse has not filed an answer and ask the clerk to formally enter the default in your court file. To accomplish this, you need to complete a **MOTION TO ENTER DEFAULT** (see form 10, p.269), and deliver it to the clerk.

To complete the **MOTION TO ENTER DEFAULT**, you need to do the following.

◈ Complete the case style according to the instructions in Chapter 9.

◈ Fill in the date.

◈ Sign your name on the line at the end of the first paragraph, and type your name, address, and phone number below the line.

The clerk will complete the bottom portion of the form and return a copy to you. Once the default has been entered by the clerk, you are ready to set a hearing date.

chapter 12

Answering a Complaint for Divorce

If your spouse is willing to proceed to a final hearing, but does not want to sign a **MARITAL SETTLEMENT AGREEMENT** (see form 4, p.255), you can have your spouse file a simple **ANSWER**. A few states have forms available at the court clerk's office for this purpose, or you can use the **ANSWER AND WAIVER**. See Chapter 9, for information about completing form 6 in this situation.

If you are the one being served with divorce papers, you will need to file some type of written response. You will be told by the papers you receive (usually in the summons) how many days you have in which to file your response. This time period is twenty days in most states, but may be longer in some. Do not let this period pass. If you do not respond in the time allowed, your spouse may seek a default. (This procedure is explained in Chapter 11.) There may be several different ways to answer a complaint for divorce, including:

✪ *Answer* (called a *response* in some states);

✪ *Answer and Counterclaim*;

✪ *Motion to Dismiss*; and,

✪   *Motion for a More Definite Statement* (sometimes called a *Motion for Bill of Particulars*)

Answer   An answer is where you either admit or deny what is in your spouse's complaint. If you wish to file an answer, first check with your court clerk's office to see if a form is available. If not, you may use the **ANSWER** form in Appendix D. (see form 14, p.279.) To complete the Answer, you need to do the following.

⬦   Complete the case style according to the instructions in the first section of Chapter 9.

⬦   In the first (unnumbered) paragraph, type in the word "Defendant" or "Respondent" (whichever term is used in your state) in the first blank; your name in the second blank; and, the complaint title used in your state ("Complaint for Divorce," "Petition for Dissolution of Marriage," etc.) in the third blank.

⬦   Paragraph 1: This is for you to indicate which parts of the complaint you agree with, or *admit*. Type in the word "Defendant" or "Respondent" (as appropriate for your state) in the first blank space. In the second blank, referring to the complaint, fill in the number or numbers of each paragraph of the complaint with which you agree. In the third blank, type in the word "complaint" or "petition," as appropriate for your state.

NOTE: *It is not necessary to admit any paragraphs. If you wish to deny all of the paragraphs of the complaint, you may either leave this paragraph blank or cross it out.*

⬦   Paragraph 2: This is for you to indicate which parts of the complaint you disagree with, or *deny*. Type in the word "Defendant" or "Respondent" (as appropriate for your state) in the first blank space. In the second blank, referring to the complaint, fill in the number or numbers of each paragraph of the complaint with which you disagree. In the third blank, type in the word "complaint" or "petition," as appropriate for your state.

NOTE: *It is not necessary to deny any paragraphs. If you wish to admit all of the paragraphs of the complaint, you* *may either leave this paragraph blank or cross it out. You may use form 6 instead of form 14. (See Chapter 9 for instructions for form 6.)*

❖ Paragraph 3: This is for the situation in which you do not have enough information to either admit or deny an allegation in the complaint. For example, if the complaint states that your spouse has been a resident of a particular county for six months, and you do not know where he or she has been living for the past six months, you can use paragraph 3 to indicate your lack of knowledge. Type in the word "Defendant" or "Respondent" (as appropriate for your state) in the first blank space. In the second blank, referring to the complaint, fill in the number or numbers of each paragraph of the complaint with which you agree. In the third blank, type in the word "complaint" or "petition," as appropriate for your state.

NOTE: *It is not necessary to fill anything in for this paragraph. If you wish to either admit or deny all of the paragraphs of the complaint, you may either leave this paragraph blank or cross it out.*

❖ In paragraph 2, type in the words "divorce" or "dissolution of marriage," as appropriate for your state, in the first blank space. In the second blank, type in the word "complaint" or "petition," as appropriate for your state.

❖ After the word "WHEREFORE," type in the word "Defendant" or "Respondent," as appropriate for your state.

❖ In paragraph 2, after the phrase beginning "WHEREFORE," type in the name of the judgment or decree used in your state. (See the listing for your state in Appendix A.)

❖ Below the "Signature" line, type in your name, address, and phone number.

❖ Take the form to a notary public and sign on the "Signature" line before the notary.

Answer and Counterclaim

An *Answer and Counterclaim* is used when you want to either admit or deny what is in your spouse's complaint and add to it your own complaint for divorce. This would be used if your spouse's complaint left out some important matter or if you wanted to make a claim of your own, such as for child custody.

Motion to Dismiss

A Motion to Dismiss is used when you find there is a situation or some defect in the complaint that prevents your spouse from proceeding with the divorce. This will take the place of an Answer if it is filed within the response time. This will require a hearing, at which time the judge will either grant your motion to dismiss or deny the motion and tell you how many days you have to file an **ANSWER**.

There are two common reasons for a *motion to dismiss*. First, the complaint does not contain the information required by the law of your state. For example, many states require the complaint to state the age or date of birth of the children. If your spouse did not include this information in the complaint, the judge may dismiss the complaint. Your spouse is free to file a new complaint that does meet the legal requirements.

The second common reason is if neither you nor your spouse meet the residency requirements for your state. For example, in Michigan, a divorce may not be filed until one party has been a resident for 180 days. If you and your spouse just moved to Michigan twenty-six days ago, you spouse's complaint will have to be dismissed.

The information for your state in Appendix A will give you some ideas of what may be grounds for a dismissal. (See Chapter 2 on "Legal Research" if you would like to do more research about dismissals.)

Motion for a More Definite Statement

Most states do not want a complaint for divorce to include details of the parties' problems. This is why you will generally see the grounds for divorce stated simply as "the parties have irreconcilable differences" or "adultery" (if traditional fault-based grounds are used). If you want more details of the facts your spouse intends to use as justification for the divorce, you will need to file a **MOTION FOR A MORE DEFINITE STATEMENT**. This is sometimes called a *Motion for Bill of Particulars*. It simply asks your spouse to provide you with more detailed information to support something in the complaint that is not clear. You will need to specify what matters in the complaint require further details.

Again, be sure to review the information for your state in Appendix A. This will require a hearing, at which time the judge will either deny your motion and tell you when you need to file an **Answer**, or grant the motion and tell your spouse when to file a paper with detailed information and tell you when you must file an **Answer**. Your spouse will then file a *bill of particulars* or other such paper containing the additional details. You may then either file an **Answer** or one of the other possible responses.

Generally, any of the motions previously discussed will only result in a delay of the divorce. Therefore, you may want to just file an **Answer** and proceed with settlement negotiations or a final hearing.

Contested Divorce

This book cannot turn you into a trial lawyer. It can be very risky to try to handle a contested case yourself, although it has been done. There are several differences between a contested and an uncontested case.

PROCEDURAL DIFFERENCES BETWEEN A CONTESTED DIVORCE AND AN UNCONTESTED DIVORCE

In an *uncontested case*, the judge will usually agree with whatever you and your spouse have worked out. In a contested case, you need to prove that you are entitled to what you are asking for. This means you will need a longer time for the hearing, you will need to present papers as evidence, and you may need to have witnesses testify for you.

You may also have to do some extra work to get the evidence you need, such as by sending out subpoenas (discussed in Chapter 14) or even hiring a private investigator.

You will need to pay extra attention to assure that your spouse is properly notified of any court hearings, and that he or she is sent copies of any papers you file with the court clerk.

When it becomes apparent that you have a contested divorce, it is probably time to consider hiring an attorney—especially if the issue of child custody is involved. If you are truly ready to go to war over custody, it shows that this is an extremely important matter for you, and you may want to get professional assistance. You can expect a contested case when your spouse is seriously threatening to fight you every inch of the way, or when he or she hires an attorney.

On the other hand, you should not assume that you need an attorney just because your spouse has hired one. Sometimes it will be easier to deal with the attorney than with your spouse. The attorney is not as emotionally involved and may see your settlement proposal as reasonable. Discuss things with your spouse's attorney first and see if things can be worked out. You can always hire your own lawyer if your spouse's attorney is not reasonable. Just be very cautious about signing any papers until you are certain you understand them. You may want to have an attorney review any papers prepared by your spouse's lawyer before you sign them.

Aside from deciding if you want a lawyer, there are two main procedural differences between the uncontested and the contested divorce. First, you will need to be more prepared for the hearing. Second, you will not prepare the **FINAL JUDGMENT** (see form 11, p.271) until after the hearing with the judge. This is because you will not know what to put in the **FINAL JUDGMENT** until the judge decides the various matters in dispute.

The next sections discuss how to prepare for the issues to be argued at the hearing.

PROPERTY AND DEBTS

Generally, the judge will look at your property and debts and try to divide them *fairly*. This does not mean they will necessarily be divided 50-50. What you want to do is offer the judge a reasonable solution that looks fair. Check your state's listing in Appendix A to see what factors are used to divide property.

You may need to prove what items should be designated as your *separate* or *nonmarital* property. Generally, this will involve proving that you had the property before you were married (such as with dated sales receipts or deeds) or that you acquired the property by gift or inheritance (such as with a letter from the person making the gift, or with a will or probate court order).

It is time to review the **PROPERTY INVENTORY** (see worksheet 3, p.233) and the **DEBT INVENTORY** (see worksheet 4, p.234) you prepared earlier. For each item or property, note which of the following categories it fits into (it may fit into more than one):

- ✪ nonmarital property you or your spouse are entitled to keep;

- ✪ you really want;

- ✪ you would like to have;

- ✪ you do not care either way;

- ✪ your spouse really wants;

- ✪ your spouse would like to have; and,

- ✪ your spouse does not care either way.

Now, start a list of what each of you should end up with, using the categories listed. You will eventually end up with a list of things you can probably get with little difficulty (you really want and your spouse does not care), those that you will fight over (you both really want), and those that need to be divided but can probably be easily divided equally (you both do not really care).

At the hearing, the judge may try to get you to work out your disagreements, but he or she will not put up with arguing for very long. In the end, the items you cannot agree upon will arbitrarily be divided, or you may be ordered to sell those items and divide the money you get equally.

Concerning the few items that are really important to you, it may be necessary to try to prove why you should get them. In addition to using the factors applied in your state, it will help if you can convince the judge of one or more of the following.

- ✪   The item is nonmarital property or was acquired by you either before marriage or by gift or inheritance.

- ✪   You paid for the item out of your own earnings or funds.

- ✪   You are the one who primarily uses that item.

- ✪   You use the item in your employment, business, or hobby.

- ✪   You are willing to give up something else you really want in exchange for that item. (You will try to give up something from your "do not care" or your "like to have" list.)

- ✪   The item is needed for your children (assuming you will have custody).

The best thing you can do is make a list of how you think the property should be divided. Make it a reasonably fair and equal list, regardless of how angry you are at your spouse. Even if the judge changes some of it to appear fair to your spouse, you will most likely get more of what you want than if you do not offer a suggestion. (This is not an exception to the negotiating rule of letting your spouse make the first offer, because at this point you are no longer just negotiating with your spouse. You are now negotiating with the judge. You are trying to impress the judge with your fairness, not trying to convince your spouse.)

Special problems arise if a claim of nonmarital property becomes an issue. This may be in terms of your spouse trying to get your nonmarital property, or in terms of you trying to get property you feel your spouse is wrongly claiming to be nonmarital. It is also a good idea to have any papers that prove the property you claim to be nonmarital property is actually nonmarital property. These would be papers showing that:

- ✪ you bought the item before you were married (such as dated sales receipts);

- ✪ you received the item as a gift (this usually must be from someone other than your spouse);

- ✪ you inherited the item as your own property (such as certified copies of wills and probate court papers); or,

- ✪ you got the property by exchanging it for property you had before you got married, or for property you received as a gift or through an inheritance (such as a statement from the person you made the exchange with, or some kind of receipt showing what was exchanged).

You may want to dispute your spouse's claim that certain property is nonmarital. Check Appendix A to see what factors are used in determining whether property is marital or nonmarital. Various states use some of the following concepts in allowing you to claim an interest in what would otherwise be your spouse's nonmarital property.

- ✪ The value of the property increased during your marriage.

- ✪ You made financial contributions to the purchase, repair, maintenance, or improvement of the property.

- ✪ You made other nonfinancial contributions to the repair, maintenance, or improvement of the property (such as by making repairs or building an addition onto a home).

- ✪ You and your spouse treated the property as if it was marital property.

If you want to get to assets that your spouse is claiming are nonmarital, you will need to collect the following types of evidence.

✪   Papers showing that you helped pay for the asset (such as a check that you wrote or bank statements showing that your money went into the same account that was used to make payments on the asset). For example, suppose your spouse purchased a house before you got married. During your marriage, you made some of the mortgage payments with your own checking account (you will have cancelled checks, hopefully with the mortgage account number on them, to prove this). At other times, you deposited some of your paychecks into your spouse's checking account and your spouse wrote checks from that account to pay the mortgage (again, there should be some bank records and cancelled checks to show that this was done). Since you contributed to the purchase of the house, you can claim some of the value of the house as a marital asset.

✪   Papers showing that you paid for repairs of the asset. If you paid for repairs on the home or a car your spouse had before you were married, you may be able to claim part of the value.

✪   Papers showing that the asset was improved or increased in value during your marriage.

Example 1:

Your spouse owned the house before you were married. During your marriage, you and your spouse added a family room to the house. This will enable you to make a claim for some of the value of the house.

Example 2:

Your spouse owned the house before you were married. The day before you got married, the house was worth $85,000. Now the house is appraised at $115,000. You can claim part of the $30,000 of increased value.

During the hearing, the judge will announce who gets what items. Make a list as the judge tells you. Then, complete the **FINAL JUDGMENT** (see form 11, p.271) according to what the judge says. Once you have completed the **FINAL JUDGMENT**, make a copy and send it to your spouse. Send the original to the judge (not the court clerk), along with a completed **CERTIFICATE OF SERVICE** (see form 1, p.245) stapled to it showing the date you sent a copy to your spouse. If your spouse does not object to how you have prepared the **FINAL JUDGMENT**, the judge will sign the judgment and return a copy to you. You should send the judge the original and two copies of the **FINAL JUDGMENT**, along with two stamped envelopes (one addressed to yourself and the other addressed to your spouse).

ALIMONY

A dispute over alimony may require a lawyer, especially if there is a request for permanent alimony because of a disability. Such a claim may require the testimony of expert witnesses (such as doctors, accountants, and actuaries), which requires the special knowledge of an attorney.

A charge of adultery may also require a lawyer (and possibly a private investigator as well). You should determine what information (including papers and the testimony of witnesses) you will need to present to the judge to either support or refute the reasons alimony was requested. Be sure to refer to your state's listing in Appendix A for the factors used to determine whether a person is eligible for alimony, and how the amount and duration of alimony is determined.

For temporary (also called *rehabilitative*) alimony, the most common reason is that the person needs financial help until he or she can get training to enter the work force. The questions that will need to be answered are the following.

- ✪   What has the person been trained for in the past?

- ✪   What type of training is needed to become employable in that field?

- ✪   How long will this training take?

- ✪   What amount of income can be expected upon employment?

- ✪   How much money is required for the training?

Questions that may be asked in either a temporary or a permanent alimony situation include the following.

- ✪ What was the situation of the parties during their marriage that led to the person not working?

- ✪ What contribution to the marriage has that person made?

- ✪ What improper conduct on the part of the other party makes an award of alimony appropriate (if fault is a factor in your state)?

You should be prepared to present evidence regarding these questions.

CHILD SUPPORT

In many states, the question of child support is mostly a matter of a mathematical calculation. This is usually done in one of two ways:

1. by a percentage of the payor's gross or net income (the percentage increases with the number of children) or

2. through a two-step process in which the child's needs are determined by adding the incomes of you and your spouse, and reading a table provided by your state or its statutes. Then the payor's child support amount is determined by multiplying the needs of the child by the payor's percentage of the parties' total income.

Example:

Frank's income is $3,000 per month and Joan's income is $2,000 per month. This gives a total income of $5,000 per month. According to their state's table, this total income indicates the financial needs for their one child are $904.00. Joan will have custody, so Frank will be paying support. Frank's income is 60% of their total income, so he will pay 60% of the $904.00 needed by the child, or $542.40 per month (.60 x $904.00).

Getting a fair child support amount depends upon the accuracy of the income information presented to the judge. If you feel fairly sure that the information your spouse presents is accurate, or that you have obtained accurate information about his or her income, there is not much to argue about. The judge will simply take the income information provided, use the formula to calculate the amount to be paid, and order that amount to be paid.

In most cases, there will not be much room to argue about the amount of child support, so there usually is not a need to get an attorney. If you claim your spouse has not provided accurate income information, it will be up to you to prove this to the judge by showing the income information you have obtained from your spouse's employer or other source of income. (See Chapter 9 on obtaining this information.)

The only areas open for argument are whatever special needs are claimed by the party asking for child support. Most states will allow some deviation from the formula for children with special medical, educational, or other unusual needs. Once again, it will be necessary for that party to provide proof of the cost of these special needs by producing testimony of professionals, billing statements, receipts, or other papers to show the amount of these needs.

The judge's decision regarding child support will have to be put into the **FINAL JUDGMENT**. (see form 11, p.271.) Read Chapter 14 for instructions on preparing the **FINAL JUDGMENT**.

CHILD CUSTODY AND VISITATION

Generally, if you are the wife, the odds start out in favor of you getting custody—but do not depend upon the odds. Start out by reviewing the guidelines the judge will use to decide the custody question. These can be found in the listing for your state in Appendix A. For each item listed, write down an explanation of how that item applies to you. This will be your argument when you have your hearing with the judge.

Many custody battles revolve around the moral fitness of one or both of the parents. If you become involved in this type of custody fight, you should consult a lawyer. Charges of moral unfitness (such as illegal drug use, child abuse, or immoral sexual conduct) can require long court hearings involving the testimony of many witnesses, as well as possibly the employment of private investigators. For such a hearing you will require the help of an attorney who knows the law, what questions to ask witnesses, and the rules of evidence.

However, if the only question is whether you or your spouse have been the main caretaker of the child, you can always have friends, neighbors, and relatives come into the hearing (if they are willing to help you) to testify on your behalf. It may not be necessary for you to have an attorney, but if you need to subpoena unwilling witnesses to testify, you should have an attorney. (See the section on "Witnesses" in Chapter 14.)

The Court Hearing

You will need to set a time and date for the hearing. You may also decide that you want to have witnesses testify on your behalf. Contact these people *early* to determine whether they would be willing to testify during the proceeding. Both of these items need to be handled courteously and promptly.

SETTING A COURT DATE

You will need to set a hearing date for the final hearing or for any preliminary matters that require a hearing (such as a *Motion for Temporary Relief*). The court clerk may be able to give you a date, but you will probably have to get a date from the judge's secretary. (If you do not know which judge, call the court clerk, give the clerk your case number, and ask for the name and phone number of the judge assigned to your case.) You can then either call or go see that judge's secretary, and tell him or her you would like to set a final hearing date for a divorce (or for whatever preliminary motion needs a hearing). Usually, the judge's phone number can be found in the government section of your phone book.

Length of Time   The secretary may ask you how long the hearing will take. If you are using a simplified or *summary* procedure available in your state, tell the secretary, and he or she will probably know how much time to allow. If you are unable to use a simplified procedure, but you and your spouse have agreed on everything (an uncontested divorce), tell the secretary it is an uncontested divorce and ask for ten minutes (unless he or she advises you differently).

If you have a contested divorce, it could take anywhere from thirty minutes to several days, depending upon things such as what matters you disagree about and how many witnesses will testify. One rule of thumb is that the more time you need for a hearing, the longer it will take to get the hearing. Also, it is better to over-estimate the time required, rather than not schedule enough time and have to continue the hearing for several weeks. Judges do not go over the time scheduled.

The secretary will give you a date and time for the hearing, but you will also need to know where the hearing will be held. Ask the secretary for the location. You will need the street address of the courthouse, as well as the room number, floor, or other location within the building.

Notifying Your Spouse   Once you get a hearing date set with the judge, you will need to notify your spouse of when the hearing will be held. This is done by preparing a **NOTICE OF HEARING**. (see form 9, p.267.) Look at a divorce file at the clerk's office or check your local law library for the notice of hearing forms used in your state or county. An example of a typical **NOTICE OF HEARING** is included in Appendix B. A blank form is in Appendix D to use if you cannot find a specific form for your court. You will need four copies of the **NOTICE OF HEARING**. Mail one to your spouse, file the original with the court clerk, and keep two copies for yourself.

WITNESSES

The witnesses you choose to testify will depend upon what you are trying to prove at the hearing. For child custody and visitation issues, witnesses may include relatives, friends, neighbors, police officers, child abuse investigators, social workers, doctors, psychologists, school counselors, and teachers. For the financial issues (property division, alimony, and child support), witnesses may include employers, bank officials, appraisers, friends, neighbors, and relatives who can verify your financial situation and that of your spouse. You will need to decide who you think would be a witness to help your position and who your spouse might use to hurt your position.

First, make a list of each fact you want to prove at the hearing. Again, this will depend upon the issues in dispute. Beside each fact, write down the name of the witness or witnesses you believe will be able to testify to that fact. Next, make a list of potential witnesses, their addresses and telephone numbers, what facts they will prove for you, and what you expect each would say in court.

Your next step is to talk to each potential witness to be sure of what they would say at the hearing. Never assume you know what a witness will say at the hearing. Many cases have been lost by a witness giving surprise testimony at a hearing. A general rule is *never ask a question unless you know what the answer will be*.

For each witness you interview, you want to ask the specific questions you might ask at the hearing, and allow the witness to describe what he or she saw, heard, and *knows*. This will allow you to find out new information and will possibly lead you to other witnesses.

There is danger of a witness telling you one thing before the hearing, then changing his or her testimony at the hearing. The best way to reduce this danger is to take the witness' deposition. This is where you have the sheriff serve a notice on the witness to appear at a specific place and time to answer questions before a court reporter. Unfortunately, this can be very expensive. You will have to pay for the court reporter to show up and record the testimony, and then pay the reporter to type up a record, or *transcript*, of the deposition. You can expect to pay about $45 for the court reporter, plus at least $100 per hour of testimony transcribed. The advantage to having a transcript is that you can use it to contradict the witness if he or she says something different at the hearing. Most lawyers only take depositions of the witnesses for the opposing party. They extensively question their own witnesses and tell them they will be expected to give the same testimony at the hearing.

One alternative is to ask the witness to give you a written, signed statement of what they saw, heard, and know. It may also help to have someone with you when you interview the witness, so that he or she can testify to the original statements if the witness changes his or her story at the hearing. The important message here is to be as sure as possible what your witnesses will say before you put them on the witness stand.

Expert Witnesses

Sometimes, especially in custody and alimony cases, it is necessary to have an *expert witness* testify. An expert witness testifies because of his or her special education, training, or experience. Such a person could include a doctor, psychologist, or accountant. An expert witness will testify to something that requires special training to be able to evaluate the material or when a professional opinion is needed.

At the hearing, it is first necessary to have the judge determine that the witness is qualified as an expert. This is usually done by asking the witness to tell his or her profession, and to describe his or her training and job experience. Once this is done, you say to the judge, "I would like this witness to be qualified as an expert."

Notifying Witnesses

The best way to notify witnesses of your hearing date is by having the sheriff serve them with a subpoena. It is a good idea to call your witnesses to let them know of the hearing date and that they will be receiving a subpoena. It is not absolutely necessary to serve a subpoena on a witness who is willing to come voluntarily and help you. Even if your witness is a friend who wants to appear to testify for you, it is a good idea to have him or her served with a subpoena. The subpoena will enable your friend to get off work to come to the hearing. It will also enable you to have the hearing continued to a later date if your friend has car trouble, becomes ill, or cannot make it to the hearing. The judge will probably not continue the hearing so they can testify at a later date—unless they were served with a subpoena.

In order to force someone to appear at the hearing and testify, you will need to have the person served by the sheriff with a subpoena. For doctors, psychologists, school teachers, police officers, etc., it is absolutely necessary that you serve them with subpoenas. This should be done at least five days before the hearing, but no earlier than about two weeks before.

If you just need the person to testify, use a subpoena form commonly used in your state and county. Try asking the court clerk for a form (the subpoena must be issued, or signed, by the clerk, so they may have a form for you to use), look at someone else's court file, or check at your law library for such a form. An example of a typical subpoena is included in Appendix B.

If you want the person to bring documents or other items to be introduced as evidence, you will need to prepare a *subpoena duces tecum*. This will include a directive for the person receiving the subpoena to bring certain items to the hearing. This might include such things as "Your police report relating to...[give the date and names of the persons the report relates to]," "Medical records relating to...[give the person's name]," or "Payroll records relating to...[give the person's name and Social Security number]."

Questioning Witnesses   In questioning witnesses at the hearing, you want to show three basic things:

1. who the witness is;

2. what the witness knows; and,

3. how the witness knows it. (If you are using an expert witness, you will need to ask the witness about his or her education, training, and employment history, then ask the judge to qualify the person as an expert in whatever area you need his or her testimony.)

For each witness you should make a list of the questions you will ask, what the answer will prove, and the expected answer to each question. Keep in mind that most judges try to finish hearings as quickly as possible, so you do not want your witnesses to get off the track of what they need to say to prove your case.

COURTROOM MANNERS

There are certain rules of procedure that are used in a court. These are really the rules of good conduct or good manners, and are designed to keep things orderly. Many of the rules are written down, although some are unwritten customs that have just developed over many years. They are not difficult, and most of them make sense. Following these suggestions will make the judge respect you for your maturity and professional manner. It will also increase the likelihood that you will get the things you request.

Show Respect for the Judge

Show respect for the judge. Do not do anything to make the judge angry at you, such as arguing with him or her. Be polite and call the judge "Your Honor" when you speak to him or her, such as "Yes, Your Honor," or "Your Honor, I brought proof of my income." Although many lawyers address judges as "Judge," this is not proper.

Many of the following rules also relate to showing respect for the court. This also means wearing appropriate clothing, such as a coat and tie for men and a dress or suit for women. This especially means no T-shirts, blue jeans, shorts, or revealing clothing.

Listen

Even if the judge interrupts you, stop talking immediately and listen.

Only One Person can Talk at a Time

Each person is allotted his or her own time to talk in court. The judge can only listen to one person at a time, so do not interrupt your spouse when it is his or her turn. And as difficult as it may be, stop talking if your spouse interrupts you. (Let the judge tell your spouse to keep quiet and let you have your say.)

Talk to the Judge, Not Your Spouse

Many people get in front of a judge and begin arguing with each other. They actually turn away from the judge, face each other, and begin arguing as if they are in the room alone. This can have several negative results. The judge cannot understand what either one is saying, since they both start talking at once. Both you and your spouse look like fools for losing control. The judge gets angry with both of you. So whenever you speak in a courtroom, look only at the judge and talk to the judge—not your spouse.

Try to pretend that your spouse is not there. Remember, you are there to convince the judge that you should have certain things. You do not need to convince your spouse.

Talk Only When It Is Your Turn

The usual procedure is for you to present your case first. When you are done saying all you came to say, your spouse will have a chance to say whatever he or she came to say. Talk only when it is your turn and let your spouse have his or her say. When he or she is finished, you will get another chance to respond to what has been said.

Stick to the Subject

Many people cannot resist the temptation to get off the track and start telling the judge all the problems with their marriage over the past twenty years. This just wastes time and aggravates the judge. Stick to the subject, and answer the judge's questions simply and to the point.

Keep Calm

Judges like things to go smoothly in their courtrooms. They do not like shouting, name calling, crying, or other displays of emotion. Generally, judges do not like family law cases because they get too emotionally charged. Give your judge a pleasant surprise by keeping calm and focusing on the issues.

Show Respect for Your Spouse

Even if you do not respect your spouse, act as if you do. All you have to do is refer to your spouse as "Mr. Smith" or "Ms. Smith" (using his or her correct name, of course).

YOUR HEARING PRESENTATION

As stated in the introduction, this book cannot make you a lawyer. However, you should be aware of a few basic rules of evidence.

Relevancy

The documents you present to the judge and questions that you ask witnesses should be related (relevent) to the facts you need to prove. For example, if you are trying to have a rental property declared non-marital, the fact that your spouse became angry when you went there to make repairs has no relevancy to the issue. You need to determine what information you need to give the judge for the issue at hand, and stick to that information.

Hearsay

Generally, a witness cannot testify to what someone else told him or her. For example, suppose you are trying to get custody due to physical abuse, and your neighbor saw your spouse beat your child with an electric cord. You need the neighbor in court to testify to what he or she saw. You cannot have your cousin testify that the neighbor told him she saw the beating. This can also apply to documents that contain statements made by someone who is not in court to testify. (There are numerous exceptions to the hearsay rule, and many lawyers and judges do not fully understand this area of law. One important exception is that you can use any statements your spouse made to the person testifying.)

Documents

Generally, documents must be introduced at the hearing by someone's testimony. You need someone (it can even be you) who can identify the paper, and say who prepared the paper and how they know who prepared the paper. For example, to introduce documents you received from your spouse's employer, you can testify as to how you got the documents (although it will be much safer to have the employer there to testify).

Examining Witnesses

Asking questions of your witnesses (*direct examination*), and of your spouse's witnesses (*cross-examination*) is called examining witnesses. One problem most nonlawyers have with this is that they tend to start testifying instead of asking questions. This is not the time for you to explain anything. You need to ask simple questions and wait for the witness to answer. You should be particularly careful in cross-examining your spouse's witnesses. If you are not very sure what their answer will be, do not ask. Do not feel that you must ask questions of each witness. It is often best to let the witness go without further damaging your case.

Preparing for the Hearing

To prepare for the hearing, you need to decide what you are going to say, what documents and witnesses (if any) you will present, and the order in which you will present them. You should make a list of each fact you intend to prove, and next to each fact write down how you will prove it. For example:

1. My income at time of judgment: Original Financial Affidavit

2. Spouse's income at time of judgment: Original Financial Affidavit

3. My current income:	My Financial Affidavit and pay stub
4. Spouse's current income:	Spouse's Financial Affidavit
5. Decreased special needs of child:	Testimony of doctor that child no longer needs costly medication
6. Coin collection as nonmarital property:	Testimony of grandfather that he gave me the collection before I was married.

Presenting Your Case

You will want to have your notes ready to keep you on track at the hearing. It also helps to have your documents arranged in the order you will present them. If you have witnesses, you will want to have your written questions arranged in the order you will have them testify.

The judge will know that you do not have a lawyer, and may help you through the hearing by asking you what he or she needs to know, or even by telling you what you need to do to present your case. When you first meet the judge, smile and say, "Good morning, your Honor," or, "Good afternoon, your Honor." Then just follow his or her lead. If the judge starts guiding you or asking questions, just let that control the hearing. Otherwise, be ready to give a brief opening statement, telling the judge that this is a final hearing on a complaint for divorce (or whatever the complaint is called in your state), whether you and your spouse have reached any agreements, and what issues need to be decided by the judge.

NOTE: *Remember, there are basically four issues: property division, alimony, child support, and child custody.*

The judge may stop you before you have the chance to complete your opening statement and ask you to present your proof. This is usually done to save time. If this happens, just present your proof (which may simply be the financial statements filed by you and your spouse). The judge will probably swear you in, then tell you to proceed. What you do to proceed will depend upon what issues need to be decided.

THE JUDGMENT OR DECREE

Be sure to read your state's listing in Appendix A, because many states have special requirements about what needs to be included in the final judgment or decree. A **FINAL JUDGMENT** (see form 11, p.271) is provided in Appendix D, but it can only serve as a guide and starting point for preparing your judgment or decree. You should complete as much of the **FINAL JUDGMENT** as possible before the hearing. The judgment form is designed so that you can complete it at the hearing according to what the judge decides on each issue. You can complete ahead of time any items that you and your spouse have agreed upon. You should give your spouse a copy of the **FINAL JUDGMENT** before the hearing, so that he or she can tell the judge that he or she is aware of what it says, and agrees with it.

To complete the **FINAL JUDGMENT** you need to do the following.

- ❖ Complete the case style according to the instructions in Chapter 9.

- ❖ Type in the complaint title used in your state (from Appendix A) on the line below the case style.

- ❖ Type in your name and your spouse's name in the appropriate blanks in the first paragraph. You will now check the box before each of the paragraphs numbered 1 through 13 that apply to your situation, according to the following guidelines. If a paragraph or provision does not apply to your situation, simply leave it blank.

- ❖ Paragraph 1: Check the box if you and your spouse signed a settlement agreement.

- ❖ Paragraph 2: Check the box if the wife will have her former name restored, and type her restored name in the blank.

- ❖ Paragraph 3: Type in each child's name, date of birth, and either the word "Husband" or "Wife," depending upon which one will take custody of that child.

◈   Paragraph 4: Check the box for "Husband" or "Wife," whichever one will be paying child support. Type in the amount of the support payment, how often it will be paid (weekly, monthly, etc.), and the date the first payment is due.

◈   Paragraph 5: Check either "Husband" or "Wife," whichever will be responsible for health insurance for the children.

◈   Paragraph 6: Check the box for "Husband" or "Wife," whichever one will be paying alimony. Type in the amount of the alimony payment, how often it will be paid (weekly, monthly, etc.), the date the first payment is due, and check the appropriate boxes to indicate when alimony will end. The first box has a blank in which to type the date the alimony payments will end, in the event temporary alimony is awarded.

The second box designates permanent alimony. The law in many states requires the judgment to give the reasons why alimony is or is not awarded.

The third box is for when you and your spouse have agreed on the question of alimony, so just check the appropriate box.

The fourth box is for when the judge decides this question. You will need to type or write in the judge's reasons

◈   Paragraph 7: This paragraph is for the amount of attorney's fees (if any are to be paid by either party), the name of the attorney to be paid, the amount of court costs awarded, and the number of days in which these amounts must be paid.

◈   Paragraphs 8, 9, 10, and 11: these cover the division of your property and debts. If these are the same items covered in your settlement agreement, you can leave these paragraphs blank, because they are already covered in Paragraph 1 of this form. These paragraphs will be used when you do not have a settlement agreement, and the judge has decided who will get what assets and who will pay what debts.

◈   Paragraph 12: Again, if you filed a settlement agreement, you do not need to complete this paragraph. If there is a dispute as to what nonmarital assets and debts belong to you and your spouse, you will need to complete this paragraph after the judge has decided this question.

◈   Paragraph 13: This is a space to write in any other agreements or orders of the judge.

◈   The last (unnumbered) paragraph is for the judge to fill in the date of the judgment.

Be sure to check the box in front of each paragraph that applies to your situation. If a certain paragraph does not apply, simply leave it blank.

If you and your spouse have agreed to everything, you can prepare the **FINAL JUDGMENT** before the hearing and give it to the judge to sign at the end of the hearing. If the judge tells you to change something major in the **FINAL JUDGMENT**, or if you had a contested hearing, it may not be possible to prepare it at the hearing. You will need to make a note of exactly what changes the judge requires or what he or she ordered, then go home and prepare the **FINAL JUDGMENT** the way the judge instructed. You will then need to take the revised form back to the judge for his or her signature.

If you need to prepare the **FINAL JUDGMENT** after the hearing, you will also complete a **CERTIFICATE OF SERVICE** (see form 1, p.245), attach it to the **FINAL JUDGMENT**, and deliver it to the judge's secretary. Give him or her two extra copies, along with a stamped envelope addressed to yourself and a stamped envelope addressed to your spouse. Ask the secretary whether you should sign and date the **CERTIFICATE OF SERVICE**. Sometimes the secretary will handle mailing the judgment after the judge signs it, in which case he or she may sign the **CERTIFICATE OF SERVICE**.

The Future

Once the judge signs your divorce judgment, it is an enforceable order of the court. If you have a settlement agreement, this includes all of the terms of the settlement agreement. You or your spouse are legally required to follow it and are subject to penalties for contempt of court if the terms are not followed. If your spouse does not follow some provision of the judgment, that does not mean that you can retaliate by not following another provision.

Example:

If the noncustodial parent is not paying child support, this does not give the custodial parent the right to withhold visitation. And is the custodial parent denies visitation, that does not give the noncustodial parent the right to stop paying child support.

In any such situation, the proper course of action is to go back to court to complain of your ex-spouse's noncompliance.

Although it is extremely difficult, if not impossible to change your property division, other parts of your divorce judgment are not necessarily forever carved in stone. If circumstances change, it may be possible to change alimony, child support, child custody, or visitation. These matters can be changed if you and your ex-spouse agree to the change. They may also be changed without the agreement of the parties if the circumstances justify a change.

If alimony was not awarded in the divorce judgment, it is very unlikely that you will be able to ask for it later. But if alimony was awarded, it can be increased, decreased, or eliminated if the circumstances warrant.

Child support may be modified (up or down) if the needs of the children change, if the amount of time they spend with each parent changes, or if the income of you or your spouse change. Child custody can be changed (this is more difficult than changing support), but usually this requires proof that the current custodial parent is somehow unfit to have continued custody.

A visitation schedule that becomes unworkable may be changed, although it is more difficult to limit or end a parent's visitation without showing that the children are likely to suffer harm.

Once your divorce is final you are legally free to get married again. If you ever find yourself thinking about marriage, be careful before getting married again, now that you know and appreciate how difficult it can be to get out of a marriage. If you decide to get married, you would be wise to consider a *premarital agreement*. This is an agreement made before marriage, in which both parties disclose all of their property and debts, and agree how things will be handled in the event they separate, or in the event one of them dies. A premarital agreement can avoid a long and costly divorce. You can either see a lawyer for a premarital agreement, or prepare your own with the help of books.

Glossary

A

action. A lawsuit, including a divorce.

affiant. The legal term for the person who signs an affidavit.

affidavit. A written statement, signed before a notary public under oath.

alimony. Money paid by one party to the other, to assist in the other party's financial support. Some states refer to it as *maintenance* or *spousal support*.

annulment. A legal procedure by which a marriage is declared invalid.

answer. The title of a legal pleading that responds to a petition, usually by either admitting or denying the allegations in the petition.

antenuptial agreement. A written, legal contract signed by the parties before their marriage, which spells out what property is owned by each and how property will be divided in the event of divorce.

C

community property. A legal concept of property ownership between a husband and wife, which separates what is jointly owned as part of the marital estate and what is owned separately by each party.

complaint. Title used by some states that begins a divorce case. *See petition*; *verified complaint*.

counterpetition. A response to a petition, which seeks some relief from the court rather than merely admitting or denying the allegations in the petition.

creditor. A person or institution to whom money is owed.

D

debtor. A person or institution who owes money.

deposition. The posing of verbal questions to one party, who is required to answer verbally under oath, usually before a court reporter.

disposition (of an action). The final action taken in a proceeding. This will usually either be a final judgment or a dismissal.

dissolution of marriage. Legal term for divorce used in some states.

domicile. The state of a person's main and permanent residence. This is more than mere residency. A person can have several residences, but only one domicile. Good proof of domicile in a particular state would be that you are registered to vote there, have a driver's license and car registration issued there, are employed or have your principal place of business there, and list that address on your income tax returns.

E

equitable distribution. A legal concept for how marital property is to be divided in a divorce that seeks to divide property in a fair manner, after considering whatever factors are legally required to be considered in a particular state.

F

final judgment. The order of the court at the end of a trial or pursuant to a settlement agreement.

H

homestead. Real estate that is a person's primary place of residence.

I

instrument. A legal term for a document.

interrogatories. Written questions sent by one party to the other, which must be answered in writing under oath.

irretrievably broken. A legal way of saying that a marriage is broken and cannot be repaired.

M

maintenance. Another term, used in some states, for alimony.

marital assets. Assets that are considered the property of both parties to a marriage.

marital property. Property that is considered by state law to be owned by both parties, and is, therefore, subject to being divided between the parties.

motion. A formal written request for the judge to take certain action.

N

nonmarital assets. Assets that are considered the separate property of only one party to a marriage. Generally, these are assets that were acquired before the marriage, or acquired by one party as a separate gift or inheritance.

nonmarital property. Property designated by state law as being the separate property of one of the parties. Nonmarital property is generally not subject to any claims by the spouse.

notary public. A person who is legally authorized by the state to acknowledge signatures on legal documents.

P

party. A person who files a divorce action, or the person one is filed against. The husband and wife are the parties in a divorce action.

payee. The person who is entitled to receive a payment of alimony or child support.

payor. The person who is obligated to pay alimony or child support.

personal property. All property other than land and things permanently attached to the land (such as buildings).

personal service. When legal papers are personally delivered to a person by a sheriff or other authorized process server.

petition. Title of document used by some states that begins a divorce case. *See complaint; verified complaint.*

pleading. A legal document, such as a complaint or an answer filed in a lawsuit that gives a party's position.

premarital agreement. Another term used for antenuptial agreement.

process. The manner in which a person is compelled to appear in court or respond to a lawsuit. Generally, this is done by a summons or a subpoena.

S

separate maintenance. Another term for alimony used in some states.

separate property. Another term for nonmarital property used in some states.

served. 1. To be given official, legal notice of lawsuit papers. 2. Delivered by a sheriff's deputy or other person legally authorized to make official delivery of legal papers. *See service.*

service. To give official, legal notice of legal papers to a person. *See personal service; service by publication.*

service by publication. When a person is given official, legal notice of legal papers by publishing a notice in a newspaper. This is only done when the person cannot be found and given personal service.

service of process. To be served with a summons or a subpoena. *See process; service.*

spousal support. Another term for alimony used in some states.

subpoena. A legal document notifying a witness that he or she must appear at a particular place and time to give testimony. This can either require appearance at court for a trial or hearing, or at some office for a deposition.

subpoena duces tecum. A particular kind of subpoena that also requires the person to bring documents or other items when they appear to testify.

T

title. A document that proves ownership of property.

V

verified complaint. A complaint that has been signed by a party under oath (such as before a notary public or the court clerk).

State Law Information

This appendix contains an alphabetical listing of the laws for every state and the District of Columbia. The following information will help you use the listing for your state.

The Law: This tells you where to find the basic divorce law for your state. It gives the title of the volume of books containing your state's law, and the title, chapter, and article or section number for the portion of the law relating to divorce. In parentheses is an example of how the law is abbreviated. This abbreviation will be used in the following sections to tell you where information is found in your state's laws. There may be additional information to help you find the law for your state.

Case Style/Parties: Explains how the beginning of your legal papers should be prepared. It gives the name of the court, and how you and your spouse should be designated.

Complaint Title: This tells you how to title the paper that will begin your divorce case.

Residency: Most states have some residency requirement that must be met before you can file for divorce. This will tell you what that requirement is for your state.

Which Court: Once the residency requirement is met, there may also be some requirements as to which county you must file your case in. This section will give you that information.

Grounds: The language in quotations will tell you how to phrase the no-fault grounds for divorce in your complaint or petition. Some minimal information may also be given as to other grounds for divorce and legal separations, although this book is designed for no-fault situations.

Property: This gives a summary of your state's law relating to the division of your property.

Alimony: Provides a summary of your state's law relating to alimony.

Child Support: Gives a summary of your state's law relating to child support.

Child Custody: This gives a summary of your state's law relating to child custody.

Misc: This is where you will find any miscellaneous information concerning the divorce laws of your state. This section is not included for all states.

Final Order: The proper title for your divorce judgment or decree is given in all capital letters. This is also where you will find any other information relating to the entry of the final judgment or decree in your state.

Other references may be given for the *Uniform Child Custody Jurisdiction Act* (UCCJA), as well as laws relating to income deduction orders (IDO); temporary alimony, child custody and support, and protection of property (Temporary Relief); protecting yourself and children from an abusive spouse (Domestic Violence); and, Annulment.

WEBSITES

You may find most state statutes on the Internet, although they can vary dramatically in user-friendliness. Some of these sites are maintained by the state government, while others are maintained by private companies or law firms. For a few states, the laws are only available by paying for a subscription service. A single site, **www.findlaw.com**, provides access to all of the state websites. The sites listed below for individual states are the same sites that FindLaw will take you to, but they are provided here because you may wish to skip a few of the steps in getting to them through FindLaw. Occasionally, a state will change its website address, so if you have any problems with the Web addresses listed, try getting to that state's site through **www.findlaw.com**.

States:

Alabama www.legislature.state.al.us/CodeofAlabama/1975/coatoc.htm

Alaska http://old-www.legis.state.ak.us/cgi-bin/folioisa.dll/stattx00?

Arizona www.azleg.state.az.us/ars/ars.htm#Listing

Arkansas www.arkleg.state.ar.us/

Click on folder named "arcode."

California You can try to get information through the FindLaw site, but there does not seem to be a simple way to access the Codes by section numbers.

Colorado http://198.187.128.12/colorado/lpext.dll?f=templates&fn=fs-main.htm&2.0

Use the "Search" for "Dissolution of Marriage," then keep hitting the button for "Next Doc with Hit" until you get to Title 14, then scroll down to the section number you want to see.

Connecticut www.cga.ct.gov/2005/pub/titles.htm

Delaware www.delcode.state.de.us

District of Columbia http://dccode.westgroup.com

Click on "DIVISION II. JUDICIARY AND JUDICIAL PROCEDURE," then click on "TITLE 16. PARTICULAR ACTIONS, PROCEEDINGS AND MATTERS," then click on "CHAPTER 9. DIVORCE, ANNULMENT, SEPARATION, SUPPORT, ETC.," then scroll down to the section number you want to see.

Florida www.leg.state.fl.us/statutes/index.cfm?Mode=ViewStatutes&Submenu=1

Georgia www.legis.state.ga.us/cgi-bin/gl_codes_detail.pl?code=1-1-1

Hawaii www.capitol.hawaii.gov/hrscurrent/?press1=docs

Idaho www3.state.id.us/idstat/TOC/idstTOC.html

Illinois www.ilga.gov

Indiana www.ai.org/legislative/ic/code

Iowa www2.legis.state.ia.us/IACODE/2001

Kansas www.accesskansas.org/legislative/statutes/index.cgi

Kentucky www.lrc.state.ky.us/statrev/frontpg.htm

Louisiana www.legis.state.la.us

Maine	http://janus.state.me.us/legis/statutes
Maryland	http://mlis.state.md.us/cgi-win/web_statutes.exe
Massachusetts	www.state.ma.us/legis/laws/mgl/index.htm
Michigan	www.legislature.mi.gov/mileg.asp?page=chapterindex
Minnesota	www.leg.state.mn.us/leg/statutes.htm
Mississippi	www.sos.state.ms.us
Missouri	www.moga.state.mo.us/STATUTES/STATUTES.HTM
Montana	http://leg.state.mt.us/css/mtcode_const/laws.asp
Nebraska	http://statutes.unicam.state.ne.us
Nevada	www.leg.state.nv.us/NRS/index.cfm
New Hampshire	www.gencourt.state.nh.us/rsa/html/indexes/default.asp
New Jersey	www.njleg.state.nj.us
New Mexico	http://legis.state.nm.us/lcs/default.asp
New York	FindLaw site: http://caselaw.lp.findlaw.com/nycodes/index.html
	NY State Assembly site: http://assembly.state.ny.us/leg/?cl-0
	For either site, click on the subject you want, then try to figure out which "article" or "part" number you need. As most statutes have "section" numbers, this can be difficult to figure out.
North Carolina	www.ncga.state.nc.us
North Dakota	www.nd.gov
Ohio	http://onlinedocs.andersonpublishing.com/revisedcode
Oklahoma	http://oklegal.onenet.net/statutes.basic.html
Oregon	www.leg.state.or.us/ors
Pennsylvania	www.pacode.com
	It does not include the titles on divorce, but this information may be added at some time.
Rhode Island	www.rilin.state.ri.us/Statutes/Statutes.html

South Carolina	www.scstatehouse.net/code/statmast.htm
South Dakota	http://legis.state.sd.us/statutes/index.cfm
Tennessee	www.legislature.state.tn.us
Texas	www.capitol.state.tx.us/statutes/statutes.html
Utah	www.le.state.ut.us/~code/code.htm
Vermont	www.leg.state.vt.us/statutes/statutes2.htm
Virginia	http://leg1.state.va.us/cgi-bin/legp504.exe?000+cod+TOC
Washington	www.leg.wa.gov/wsladm/rcw.htm
West Virginia	www.legis.state.wv.us
Wisconsin	www.legis.state.wi.us/rsb/stats.html
Wyoming	http://legisweb.state.wy.us

ALABAMA

The Law:	Code of Alabama, Title 30, Chapter 2 (C.A. Sec. 30-2-1).
Case Style/Parties:	IN THE CIRCUIT COURT FOR _____ COUNTY, ALABAMA
	In re the marriage of_____, Plaintiff, and _____, Defendant.
Complaint Title:	COMPLAINT FOR DIVORCE
Residency:	No time period if both parties are residents of Alabama, six months if only one is a resident. C.A. Sec. 30-2-5.
Which Court:	Circuit Court of the county where (1) the defendant resides, (2) both parties lived at the time of separation, or (3) where the plaintiff resides if the defendant is not an Alabama resident. C.A. Sec. 30-2-4.
Grounds:	NO-FAULT: (1) "There has been an irretrievable breakdown of the marriage and further attempts at reconciliation are impractical or futile and not in the best interests of the parties or the family." C.A. Sec. 30-2-1(a)(9). (2) "There exists such a complete incompatibility of temperament that the parties can no longer live together." C.A. Sec. 30-2-1(a)(7). TRADITIONAL: (1) physical or mental incapacity at time of marriage; (2) adultery; (3) voluntary abandonment for 1 year; (4) imprisonment in a penitentiary for 2 years, if sentenced to at least 7 years; (5) commission of a "crime against nature"; (6) habitual drunkenness or drug use after marriage; (7) confinement to a mental hospital for 5 years for hopeless and incurable insanity; (8) wife is pregnant by another at time of marriage, without husband's knowledge; (9) violence, or reasonable apprehension of violence, with danger to life or health; (10) wife living separate and apart for 2 years without support; and (11) 2 years after final judgment of divorce from bed and board. C.A. Sec. 30-2-2. LEGAL SEPARATION: Same as traditional divorce, plus cruelty. C.A. Sec. 30-2-30.
Property:	Equitable distribution under case law. Fault may be considered. No statutory factors. Courts recognize separate property as property acquired (1) before marriage; or (2) by gift or inheritance (unless used for the benefit of both parties). See C.A. Sec. 30-4-1 on husband and wife property.
Alimony:	Alimony may be awarded if the party seeking alimony has insufficient property or income for support. Factors: (1) value of each party's estate; and (2) financial condition of recipient spouse's family. C.A. Sec. 30-2-50. However, property acquired before marriage is not considered unless it was regularly used for the common benefit during the marriage. C.A. Sec. 30-2-51. Fault may limit or bar alimony altogether. C.A. Sec. 30-2-52. Alimony must terminate upon remarriage or cohabitation with a member of the opposite sex. C.A. Sec. 30-2-55.
Child Support:	Combined Income Method. Either party may be ordered to pay, "as may seem right and proper, having regard to the moral character and prudence of the parents and age and sex of the children." Where wife abandons family, husband shall have custody if children are at least age 7. C.A. Sec. 30-3-1.
Child Custody:	Factors: (1) moral character of parents; and (2) age and sex of child. Joint custody possible. Where the wife abandons the family, the husband shall have custody if the children are at least 7 years old and if he is suitable. C.A. Sec. 30-3-1.
Misc:	Wife may use former name after divorce. Husband can prevent wife from using his first name or initials after divorce. C.A. Sec. 30-2-11.
Final Order:	JUDGMENT OF DIVORCE FROM BONDS OF MATRIMONY No remarriage is permitted for 60 days after the judgment, or during an appeal. C.A. Sec. 30-2-10.
UCCJA:	C.A. Sec. 30-3-20.
IDO:	C.A. Sec. 30-3-60.
Temporary Relief:	C.A. Secs. 30-3-1 (custody) and 30-2-50 (alimony).
Domestic Violence:	C.A. Sec. 30-5-1.
Annulment:	C.A. Sec. 30-1-1.

ALASKA

The Law:	Alaska Statutes, Title 25, Section 25.24.010 (A.S. Sec. 25.24.010). Supplement in front of volume.
Case Style/Parties:	SUPERIOR COURT FOR THE STATE OF ALASKA #_____ JUDICIAL DISTRICT _____, Petitioner, vs. _____, Respondent. (Standard procedure) In the Matter of the Dissolution of the Marriage of _____, Petitioner, and _____, Respondent. (Simplified procedure)
Complaint Title:	PETITION FOR DIVORCE (Standard procedure) PETITION FOR DISSOLUTION OF MARRIAGE (Simplified procedure, A.S. Sec. 25.24.210)
Residency:	Petitioner must be resident; no time limits. A.S. Sec. 25.24.090.
Grounds:	NO-FAULT: "The parties have an incompatibility of temperament which has caused the irremediable breakdown of the marriage." A.S. Sec. 25.24.050(5)(c). This should be used in either the standard or the simplified procedures. TRADITIONAL: (1) failure to consummate marriage; (2) adultery; (3) conviction of a felony; (4) wilful desertion for 1 year; (5) cruel and inhuman treatment calculated to impair health or endanger the life; (6) personal indignities rendering the other party's life burdensome; (7) habitual gross drunkenness beginning after marriage and continuing for 1 year before filing; (8) incurable mental illness when spouse is confined to institution for 18 months before filing; and (9) drug addiction. A.S. Sec. 25.24.050. LEGAL SEPARATION: None.
Property:	Equitable distribution. Fault is not a factor. All property acquired during marriage is marital property. Factors for dividing marital property: (1) length of marriage and parties' station in life during marriage; (2) age and health of parties; (3) each party's earning capacity, including educational background, training, employment skills, work experience, length of absence from job market, and child custodial responsibilities during the marriage; (4) each party's financial condition, including availability and cost of health insurance; (5) conduct of the parties, including whether there has been unreasonable depletion of marital assets; (6) desirability of the child custodian remaining in the marital home; (7) circumstances and necessities of the parties; (8) time and manner of acquisition of the assets; and (9) the income producing capacity of the property and the value of the property. A.S. Secs. 25.24.160(a)(4) and 25.24.230.
Alimony:	Called "maintenance." Fault not considered. Factors: (1) length of marriage and parties' station in life during marriage; (2) age and health of parties; (3) each party's earning capacity, including educational background, training, employment skills, work experience, length of absence from job market, and child custodial responsibilities during the marriage; (4) each party's financial condition, including availability and cost of health insurance; (5) conduct of the parties, including whether there has been unreasonable depletion of marital assets; (6) property division; and (7) any other relevant factor. A.S. Sec. 25.24.160(a)(2).
Child Support:	Percentage of Income Method. Factors: (1) child's needs; (2) ability of both parties to meet those needs; (3) extent of support by the parent during the marriage; and (4) economic ability of each party to support child after divorce. A.S. Sec. 25.27.060.
Child Custody:	Best interest of the child considering: (1) physical, emotional, mental, religious, and social needs of the child; (2) capability and desire of each party to meet those needs; (3) child's preference, if of suitable age and ability; (4) love and affection existing between child and each party; (5) length of time the child has been in a stable, satisfactory environment, and the desirability of maintaining continuity; (6) desire and ability of each party to allow an open and loving frequent relationship between the child and other party; (7) any evidence of domestic violence, child abuse or neglect in the proposed custodial home, or history of violence between the parties; (8) any evidence that substance abuse by either party or other household member directly affects the child's emotional or physical well-being; (9) any other relevant factor. A.S. Sec. 25.24.150. [Also A.S. Sec. 25.20.060 - 25.20.130.]
Misc:	Either party may change name. A.S. Secs. 25.24.165 & 25.24.210(d).
Dissolution:	This simplified procedure, using the no-fault ground, may be used if: (1) the parties file a joint petition and agree as to custody, visitation, child support, and property and debt division; or (2) the respondent cannot be located after reasonable efforts to find him or her, notice by publication is used, and the respondent cannot be served in or outside of Alaska. A.S. Sec. 25.24.200. The petition must be verified and must include: (1) statement of the grounds and that the above conditions for dissolution are met; (2) that the petitioner, or petitioner and respondent, consent to the court's jurisdiction; (3) a request that the marriage be dissolved; (4) a request for a name change, if desired; (5) the parties' agreement, if a joint petition is filed; (6) each party's occupation; (7) income, assets, and liabilities at time of filing; (8) date and place of marriage; (9) each child's name, date of birth and current custodial status; (10) whether the wife is pregnant; (11) whether either party requires medical care or treatment; (12) whether any domestic violence complaint has been filed during the marriage by a household member; (13) whether petitioner received advice of legal counsel regarding divorce or dissolution; (14) any other facts or circumstances either party wants considered; (15) that the petition constitutes the entire agreement between the parties, if filed jointly; and (16) any other relief sought. A.S. Sec. 25.24.210. Both parties must attend the hearing if a joint petition is filed. A.S. 25.24.220. Forms and instructions are available from the court clerk, or the Department of Health and Social Services. A.S. Sec. 25.24.250.
Final Order:	DECREE OF DIVORCE (Standard procedure) DECREE OF DISSOLUTION OF MARRIAGE (Simplified procedure)

UCCJA: A.S. Sec. 25.30.010.	Temporary Relief: A.S. Sec. 25.24.140.	Annulment: A.S. Sec. 25.24.020.
IDO: A.S. Sec. 25.27.062.	Domestic Violence: A.S. Sec. 25.35.010.	

ARIZONA

The Law:	Arizona Revised Statutes, Section 25-301 (A.R.S. Sec. 25-301).
Case Style/Parties:	IN THE SUPERIOR COURT OF THE STATE OF ARIZONA IN AND FOR THE COUNTY OF _____ In re the marriage of _____, Petitioner, and _____, Respondent.
Complaint Title:	PETITION FOR DISSOLUTION OF MARRIAGE Petition must include: (1) grounds for divorce; (2) each party's birthdate, occupation, address and length of time domiciled in Arizona; (3) date and place of marriage; (4) each child's name, birthdate, and address, and a statement of whether the wife is pregnant; (5) details of any agreements on support, custody, visitation, and alimony; and (6) relief sought.
Residency:	One party must be domiciled in Arizona for at least 90 days before filing. A.R.S. Sec. 25-312.
Which Court:	County where Petitioner resides.
Grounds:	NO-FAULT: "The marriage of the parties is irretrievably broken." A.R.S. Sec. 25-312. TRADITIONAL: None. LEGAL SEPARATION: (1) marriage is irretrievably broken; or (2) one or both parties desire to live separate and apart. One party must be domiciled in the state (no time limit in statute). If respondent objects, then must proceed for dissolution. A.R.S. Sec. 25-313. Also see A.S. Sec. 25-316. COVENANT MARRIAGE: If you have a "covenant marriage," under A.S. Sec. 25-901 through Sec. 25-906, the possible grounds for divorce are: (1) adultery, (2) conviction of a felony and a sentence of death or imprisonment, (3) abandonment for at least 1 year, (4) physical or sexual abuse by your spouse of you, a child, or a relative permanently living in the marital home; or domestic violence or emotional abuse, (5) living separate and apart continuously without reconciliation for at least 2 years, (6) living separate and apart continuously without reconciliation for at least 1 year from the date of a decree of legal separation, (7) habitual abuse of drugs or alcohol, or (8) the husband and wife both agree to divorce.
Property:	Community property. Fault not considered. Each party retains their "sole and separate property." In dividing property the court may consider "excessive or abnormal expenditures, destruction, concealment or fraudulent disposition of community, joint tenancy and other property held in common." No other statutory factors. A.R.S. Sec. 25-318.
Alimony:	Called "maintenance." Alimony may be awarded if the party: (1) lacks sufficient property to provide for his or her reasonable needs; or (2) is unable to support self through employment, or is custodian of young child so is not required to seek employment, or lacks earning ability; or (3) contributed to spouse's education; or (4) is of an age which may preclude adequate employment and the marriage was of long duration. Amount and duration factors: (1) standard of living established during the marriage; (2) duration of marriage; (3) age, employment history, earning ability and physical and emotional condition of the party seeking alimony; (4) ability of the other party to meet his or her own needs while paying alimony; (5) comparative financial resources and earning abilities; (6) contribution of the party seeking alimony to the other's earning ability; (7) extent to which the party seeking alimony has reduced income or career opportunity for the other's benefit; (8) ability of both to contribute to the child's future educational costs; (9) financial resources of the party seeking alimony, and the ability to meet own needs; (10) time needed to acquire education and training to find appropriate employment; and (11) "excessive or abnormal expenditures, destruction, concealment or fraudulent disposition of community, joint tenancy and other property held in common." A.R.S. Sec. 25-319. Parties may agree that alimony may not be modified.
Child Support:	Combined Income Method. Arizona Supreme Court guidelines available from Superior Court Clerk. A.R.S. Sec. 25-320.
Child Custody:	Best interest of the child considering: (1) parties' wishes; (2) child's wishes; (3) interaction and interrelationship between the child and each parent, siblings and other significant persons; (4) child's adjustment to home, school, and community; (5) mental and physical health of all persons involved; and (6) which parent is more likely to allow frequent and continuing contact with the other parent; (7) whether any parent provided primary care; (8) whether there was any coercion or duress by one parent is obtaining a custody agreement; and (9) whether there was any domestic violence. Joint custody may be granted under certain circumstances. A.R.S. Sec. 25-403.
Misc:	Former name may be restored. A.R.S. Sec. 25-325. You may also petition for conciliation to get court assistance in attempting a reconciliation. See A.R.S. Sec. 25-381.10 or get forms and information from court clerk. A person holding a professional license may be subject to license suspension for non-payment of child support. A.R.S. Sec. 25-320. Driver's licenses may also be suspended. A.R.S. Sec. 25-320.01.
Final Order:	DECREE OF DISSOLUTION OF MARRIAGE No hearing may be held until at least 60 days after service of the petition. A.R.S. Sec. 25-329. Must provide for medical insurance for children, and for income withholding. A.R.S. Sec. 25-320.

UCCJA:	A.R.S. Sec. 25-431.	Domestic Violence:	A.R.S. Sec. 13-3601.
IDO:	A.R.S. Sec. 25-323 (Forms are available from court clerk. A.R.S. Sec. 25-323.03).	Annulment:	A.R.S. Sec. 25-301.
Temporary Relief:	A.R.S. Secs. 25-315 (general); 25-324 (attorneys fees); and 25-404 (custody).		

ARKANSAS

The Law:	Arkansas Code of 1987 Annotated, Title 9, Chapter 12, Section 9-12-301 (A.C.A. Sec. 9-12-301).
Case Style/Parties:	IN THE CHANCERY COURT OF _____ ARKANSAS
	_____, Plaintiff, vs. _____, Defendant.
Complaint Title:	COMPLAINT FOR DIVORCE
Residency:	One party must be a resident at least 60 days before filing, and at least 3 months before the final judgment. A.C.A. Sec. 9-12-307.
Which Court:	County where plaintiff resides. If plaintiff is not Arkansas resident, then the county where the defendant resides. A.C.A. Sec. 9-12-303.
Grounds:	NO-FAULT: "The parties have been voluntarily living separate without cohabitation for 18 continuous months." This only means that it is voluntary as to one party. A.C.A. Sec. 9-12-301.
	TRADITIONAL: (1) impotence at time of marriage and continuing; (2) conviction of a felony or infamous crime; (3) habitual drunkenness for 1 year; (4) cruel and barbarous treatment so as to endanger the other's life; (5) one party offering "such indignities to the person of the other as shall render his or her condition intolerable;" (6) adultery; (7) living separate and apart for 3 years without cohabitation by reason of the incurable insanity of one party; and (8) one spouse who is legally obligated to support the other, and has the ability to provide common necessaries of life, wilfully fails to do so. A.C.A. Sec. 9-12-301.
	LEGAL SEPARATION: Called "divorce from bed and board." Same as traditional grounds. A.C.A. Sec. 9-12-301.
Property:	Equitable distribution. Non-marital property is property: (1) acquired prior to marriage; (2) acquired by gift or inheritance; (3) acquired in exchange for non-marital property; (4) designated non-marital by a valid agreement; (5) from an increase in value of, or income from, non-marital property; and (6) claims for workers' compensation, personal injuries, or social security that is for permanent disability or future medical expenses. Marital property is divided equally, unless judge includes his reasons for an unequal distribution considering: (1) length of marriage; (2) age, health and station in life of the parties; (3) occupation; (4) amount and sources or income; (5) vocational skills; (6) employability; (7) each party's estate, liabilities, and needs, and opportunity for further acquisition of capital assets and income; (8) each party's contribution to the acquisition, preservation or appreciation of marital property; and (9) federal income tax consequences. A.C.A. Sec. 9-12-315. Fault may also be considered. A.C.A. Sec. 9-12-301(6).
Alimony:	No statutory factors, other than that it is to be awarded as "reasonable from the circumstances of the parties and the nature of the case." Fault may be considered. A.C.A. Sec. 9-12-312.
Child Support:	Percentage of Income Method. Arkansas Family Support guidelines chart is available from the Chancery Court Clerk. A.C.A. Sec. 9-12-312.
Child Custody:	Only statutory provision is that custody is to be determined "without regard to the sex of the parent but solely in accordance with the welfare and best interests of the children." A.C.A. Sec. 9-12-101.
Misc:	Wife's name before marriage may be restored. A.C.A. Sec. 9-12-318.
	In an uncontested case, a third party affidavit may be used to prove residency, separation, and no cohabitation; and no third party is necessary to prove the grounds for divorce. A.C.A. Sec. 9-12-306. See A.C.A. Sec. 9-12-307 for details of what must be proven.
Final Order:	DECREE OF DIVORCE
	Must include provision for income withholding. A.C.A. Sec. 9-14-218.
	If a property settlement is referred to in the decree, a copy of the property settlement must also be filed. A.C.A. Sec. 9-12-316.
UCCJA:	A.C.A. Sec. 9-13-201.
IDO:	A.C.A. Sec. 9-14-102; 9-14-218; and 9-14-502.
Temporary Relief:	A.C.A. Sec. 9-12-309.
Domestic Violence:	A.C.A. Sec. 9-15-101.
Annulment:	A.C.A. Sec. 9-12-201.

CALIFORNIA

The Law: West's Annotated California Codes, Family, Section 2300. (A.C.C.F., Sec. 2300). Ignore the "Title" numbers. California has several Annotated California Codes, so be sure you have the set marked "Family."

Case Style/Parties: SUPERIOR COURT OF CALIFORNIA, COUNTY OF _____

In re the marriage of _____ , Petitioner, and _____ , Respondent.

Complaint Title: PETITION FOR DISSOLUTION OF MARRIAGE

Residency: The party filing for divorce must be a resident of California for at least 6 months, and of the county for 3 months. A.C.C.F. Sec. 2320.

Which Court: County where person filing resides.

Grounds: NO-FAULT: "The parties have irreconcilable differences which have caused the irremediable breakdown of the marriage." A.C.C.F. Sec. 2310(a).
TRADITIONAL: Incurable insanity. A.C.C.F. Sec. 2310(b).
LEGAL SEPARATION: Same as no-fault and traditional. A.C.C.F. Sec. 2310.

Property: Community property. The court may order arbitration if the parties cannot agree on property division. No statutory factors. The court may order arbitration if the parties cannot agree on property division. A.C.C.F. Sec. 2550-2660.

Alimony: Marital misconduct is not considered. Factors: (1) the extent of each party's earning capacity to maintain the standard of living, considering marketable skills, the job market, the time and expense required for the party requesting alimony to acquire education and training, the need for retraining to acquire other more marketable skills, and the extent earning capacity was impaired by periods of unemployment during the marriage due to domestic responsibilities; (2) the extent the party seeking alimony contributed to the education, training and employment of the other; (3) the spouse's ability to pay; (4) the needs of each party, based on the standard of living; (5) the assets and debts of each party; (6) the duration of the marriage; (7) the ability of the custodial parent to earn without interfering with the best interest of the children; (8) the age and health of the parties; (9) the tax consequences; and (10) any other relevant factor. A.C.C.F. Sec. 4300-4360.

Child Support: Combined Income Method, adjusted by percentage of time each parent has child. Minimum payment amounts established by mandatory forms available from County Clerk. A.C.C.F. beginning with Sec. 4100.

Child Custody: Marital misconduct may be considered. Factors: (1) child's health, safety and welfare; (2) any history of abuse; (3) nature and amount of contact with each parent; and (4) any other factor the court finds relevant. A.C.C.F. Sec. 3011. Joint custody is favored, and the judge may require an investigation. A.C.C.F. beginning with Sec. 3000.

Misc: Official mandatory and optional forms are available from the County Clerk, and may also be found in West's California Judicial Council Forms Pamphlet. A summary dissolution procedure (A.C.C.F. Sec. 2400) may be used if the following conditions are met:
(1) The residency requirement is met.
(2) The divorce is based on the no-fault ground of irreconcilable differences.
(3) There are no children involved.
(4) The parties have not been married for more than 5 years when the petition is filed.
(5) There is no real estate involved, except for a lease expiring within 1 year of the petition being filed.
(6) There are no debts in excess of $4,000, except for auto loans (the amount is adjusted every 2 years).
(7) The parties' community property is less than $25,000; and each party has separate property of no more than $25,000 (not including autos and not allowing for money owed for the property).
(8) The parties have a written agreement as to the property division.
(9) The parties waive their right to alimony.
(10) The parties waive the right to appeal and to file a motion for a new trial.
(11) The parties read and understand a brochure regarding the summary procedure.
(12) The parties both desire a dissolution of the marriage.

Final Order: JUDGMENT OF DISSOLUTION OF MARRIAGE
The judgment is not final until 6 months after service of the petition on or the appearance of the respondent, whichever occurs first. Judgment must state the date it becomes final. A.C.C.F. Sec. 2339.

UCCJA: A.C.C.F. Sec. 3400.
IDO: A.C.C.F. Sec. 5200.
Temporary Relief: A.C.C.F. Secs. 3060 (custody) and 3600 (child support & alimony).
Domestic Violence: A.C.C.F. Sec. 6200.
Annulment: A.C.C.F. Sec. 2200.

COLORADO

The Law:	West's Colorado Revised Statutes Annotated, Title 14, Article 10, Section 14-10-106 (C.R.S.A. Sec. 14-10-106).
Case Style/Parties:	IN THE DISTRICT COURT IN AND FOR THE COUNTY OF _____ AND STATE OF COLORADO In re the Marriage of _____, Petitioner, vs. _____, Respondent.
Complaint Title:	PETITION FOR DISSOLUTION OF MARRIAGE Petition must include: (1) grounds for divorce; (2) each party's residence and length of residence in Colorado; (3) date and place of marriage; (4) date of separation; (5) each child's name, age and address, and a statement as to whether the wife is pregnant; (6) any arrangements of the parties as to custody, child support and alimony; and (7) relief sought. C.R.S.A. Sec. 14-10-107.
Residency:	One of the parties must be a Colorado resident for at least 90 days before filing the petition. C.R.S.A. Sec. 14-10-106.
Which Court:	The county where the respondent resides. If the respondent is not a Colorado resident, or has been served in the county where the petitioner resides, the case may be filed in the county where the petitioner resides.
Grounds:	NO-FAULT: "The marriage of the parties is irretrievably broken." C.R.S.A. Sec. 14-10-106. TRADITIONAL: None. LEGAL SEPARATION: Same as for divorce. C.R.S.A. Sec. 14-10-106.
Property:	Equitable distribution. Fault is not considered. Separate property includes property: (1) acquired before marriage; (2) acquired by gift or inheritance; (3) acquired in exchange for non-marital property; (4) acquired after a legal separation decree; or (5) designated separate by an written agreement of the parties. Factors in dividing marital property: (1) each party's contribution to acquisition of marital property; (2) value of separate property; (3) economic circumstances of the parties, including whether custodial party should remain in marital home; and (4) any increase or decrease in value of separate property during the marriage, and any depletion of separate property for marital purposes. C.R.S.A. Sec. 14-10-113.
Alimony:	Called "maintenance." Fault is not considered. A party may be awarded alimony if he or she: (1) lacks sufficient property to meet own needs; and (2) is unable to support self by employment, or has child custody responsibilities such that employment outside the home is inappropriate. Factors in determining amount and duration of alimony: (1) financial resources and ability of spouse seeking alimony to meet his or her own needs; (2) time needed to obtain education or training to find appropriate employment, and future earning capacity; (3) standard of living established during the marriage; (4) duration of the marriage; (5) age, physical and emotional condition of the party seeking alimony; and (6) ability of other party to meet own needs while paying alimony. C.R.S.A. Sec. 14-10-114.
Child Support:	Combined Income Method. Statutory child support guidelines and tables are in C.R.S.A. Sec. 14-10-115.
Child Custody:	Best interest of the child, considering: (1) parties' wishes; (2) child's wishes, (3) interaction and interrelationship between the child and the parties, siblings and other significant persons; (4) child's adjustment to home, school and community; (5) mental and physical health of all persons involved; (6) custodian's ability to encourage sharing, love, affection and contact with the other party; (7) evidence of the parties' ability to cooperate and make joint decisions; (8) evidence of each party's ability to encourage sharing, love, affection and contact with the other party; (9) whether the past pattern of involvement of the parties with the child reflects a system of values, time commitment, and mutual support which would indicate an ability as joint custodians to provide a positive and nourishing relationship with the child; (10) physical proximity of the parties as relates to practical considerations of awarding joint custody; (11) whether joint custody will promote more frequent or continuing contacts; (12) any history of child abuse or neglect; and (13) any history of spouse abuse. C.R.S.A. Secs. 14-10-124. Joint custody is permitted if the parties file a joint custody plan. C.R.S.A. Sec. 14-10-123.5.
Misc:	Name change not provided for in divorce statute; need to use general name change statute, C.R.S.A. Sec. 3-15-101. Respondent's answer is called a "Response." C.R.S.A. Sec. 14-10-105. For details regarding service by publication, see C.R.S.A. Sec. 14-10-107(4)(a).
Final Order:	DECREE OF DISSOLUTION OF MARRIAGE 90 day waiting period after service. C.R.S.A. Sec. 14-10-106. Must include provision for income withholding in the event of default. C.R.S.A. Sec. 14-10-120.
UCCJA:	C.R.S.A. Sec. 14-13-101.
IDO:	C.R.S.A. Sec. 14-14-105.
Temporary Relief:	C.R.S.A. Sec. 14-10-107(4)(b); 14-10-108; and 14-10-125.
Domestic Violence:	C.R.S.A. Sec. 14-4-101.
Annulment:	C.R.S.A. Sec. 14-10-111.

CONNECTICUT

The Law:	Connecticut General Statutes Annotated, Title 46b, Section 46B-40 (C.G.S.A. Sec. 46b-40). Ignore "Chapter" numbers.
Case Style/Parties:	IN THE SUPERIOR COURT OF THE STATE OF CONNECTICUT
	_____, Plaintiff, vs. _____, Defendant.
Complaint Title:	COMPLAINT FOR DISSOLUTION OF MARRIAGE
Residency:	May be filed at any time if either spouse is a resident. C.G.S.A. Sec. 46b-44. But final judgment can't be entered unless one party has been a resident for at least 12 months, or if one party was a resident at the time of the marriage and returned to become a permanent resident, or if the grounds for the divorce arose in Connecticut. C.G.S.A. Sec. 46b-44.
Which Court:	If support is sought, the county where the Plaintiff resides. Otherwise, in any county most convenient to the parties.
Grounds:	NO-FAULT: (1) "The marriage of the parties has broken down irretrievably." C.G.S.A. Sec. 46b-40. (2) "The parties have lived apart by reason of incompatibility for a continuous period of at least 18 months and there is no reasonable prospect of reconciliation." C.G.S.A. Sec. 46b-40. TRADITIONAL: (1) adultery; (2) fraudulent contract; (3) willful desertion and total neglect of duty for 1 year; (4) absence for 7 years; (5) habitual intemperance (intoxication); (6) intolerable cruelty; (7) commission or conviction of an infamous crime involving a violation of conjugal duty and imprisonment for at least 1 year; and (8) confinement for psychiatric disabilities for 5 years. LEGAL SEPARATION: Same as for divorce. C.G.S.A. Sec. 46b-40.
Property:	Equitable distribution. Factors: (1) length of the marriage; (2) causes of the divorce; (3) age and health of the parties, occupation, vocational skills, and employability of the parties, amount and sources of each party's income, each spouse's needs, estate, liabilities, and prospects for further acquisition of assets and income; (4) contribution of each spouse to the acquisition, preservation or appreciation of assets. C.G.S.A. Sec. 46b-81.
Alimony:	Factors: (1) length of marriage; (2) cause of divorce; (3) age, health, station, occupation, amount and sources of income, vocational skills, employability, estate, and needs of each party; and (4) property division; and (5) desirability of child custodian remaining in marital home. C.G.S.A. Sec. 46b-82.
Child Support:	Combined Income Method. Factors: (1) age, health, station, occupation, earning capacity, amount and sources of income, estate, vocational skills and employability of the parties; and (2) child's age, health, station, occupation, educational status and expectation, amount and sources of income, vocational skills, employability, estate and needs. C.G.S.A. Sec. 46b-84.
Child Custody:	Best interest of the child considering: (1) wishes of the child, if of sufficient age, and (2) causes of divorce as relevant to the child's best interest. C.G.S.A. Sec. 46b-56. Law favors joint custody if both parents agree. C.G.S.A. Sec. 46b-56a.
Misc:	Either party's birth or former name may be restored. C.G.S.A. Sec. 46b-63. The grounds can be proven by both parties signing a statement that the marriage is irretrievably broken, or by both parties so stating in court and submitting a settlement agreement on all matters. C.G.S.A. Sec. 46b-51. Either party can request conciliation order, which will require 2 mandatory consultations. C.G.S.A. Sec. 46b-53.
Final Order:	DECREE OF DISSOLUTION OF MARRIAGE 90 day waiting period from date defendant is to respond. C.G.S.A. Sec. 46b-67.
UCCJA:	C.G.S.A. Sec. 46b-90.
IDO:	C.G.S.A. Sec. 46b-69a.
Temporary Relief:	C.G.S.A. Secs. 46b-44; 46b-56; 46b-80; and 46b-83.
Domestic Violence:	C.G.S.A. Sec. 46b-38a.
Annulment:	C.G.S.A. Sec. 46b-40.

DELAWARE

The Law:	Delaware Code Annotated, Title 13, Section 1502 (D.C.A. 13 Sec. 1502).
Case Style/Parties:	IN THE FAMILY COURT OF THE STATE OF DELAWARE, IN AND FOR _____ COUNTY
	In re the Marriage of _____, Petitioner, and _____, Respondent.
Complaint Title:	PETITION FOR DIVORCE

Complaint Title: PETITION FOR DIVORCE
The petition must contain: (1) age, occupation & residence (including county) of each party, and their length of residence in the state; (2) address where respondent will likely receive mail or that "no address can be ascertained with reasonable diligence;" (3) that it is unlikely jurisdiction can be acquired other than by mail or publication, if appropriate; (4) if respondent is a foreign national or has resided in a foreign country within 2 years, the address of a representative of such country in the U.S.; (5) date of marriage and place registered; (6) date of separation; (7) names, ages and addresses of all children, and whether the wife is pregnant; (8) whether there are any prior marital proceedings, and if so, the date and name and place of the court, and the disposition; (9) an allegation of the no-fault grounds for the divorce; (10) any other relevant facts; and (11) a request for the relief desired. D.C.A. 13 Sec. 1507.
If any children, must also file an affidavit that the children have been advised of certain rights. D.C.A. 13 Sec. 1507 (g).

Residency: One party must be a resident for at least 6 months. D.C.A. 13 Sec. 1504.

Which Court: In the county where either party resides.

Grounds: NO-FAULT: "There has been an irretrievable breakdown of the marriage and reconciliation is improbable." This requires one of the following: (a) voluntary separation; (b) separation due to other party's misconduct or mental illness; (c) separation due to incompatibility. The separation may consist of living in the same house, but not occupying the same bedroom and without having sexual relations within 30 days before the court hears the petition. D.C.A. 13 Sec. 1505. TRADITIONAL: Separation due to mental illness. LEGAL SEPARATION: Not available in Delaware.

Property: Equitable distribution. Nonmarital property includes property: (1) acquired before marriage; (2) acquired after marriage if acquired by inheritance, or in exchange for other nonmarital property; and (3) by written agreement. Fault not considered. Factors: (1) length of the marriage; (2) any prior marriages; (3) each party's age, health, station, amount and sources of income, vocational skills, employability, estate, liabilities and needs; and (4) whether property award is in lieu of, or in addition to, alimony; (5) each party's opportunity for future acquisition of assets and income; (6) contribution or dissipation of assets, including as homemaker or husband; (7) value of separate property; (8) economic circumstances of each party, including whether the custodial parent should remain in the marital home; (9) whether property was acquired as a gift; (10) each party's debts; and (11) tax consequences. D.C.A. 13 Sec. 1513.

Alimony: Marriage for less than 20 years: alimony limited to a time period of 50% of the length of marriage. Marriage of 20 years or more: no limit. Fault is not a factor. Spouse seeking alimony must be (1) dependent upon spouse; (2) lack sufficient property for his or her needs; and (3) unable to support self through employment, or is not required to seek employment because he or she has child custody which makes employment inappropriate. The amount is determined by the following factors: (1) financial resources and ability to meet needs of the party seeking alimony; (2) time and expense required to acquire education and training for employment; (3) standard of living established during the marriage; (4) duration of the marriage; (5) age, physical and emotional condition of each party; (6) contribution of the party seeking alimony to the other's career; (7) ability of the other party to pay and meet his or her own needs; (8) tax consequences; (9) whether either party has foregone or postponed education and career opportunities during the marriage; and (10) any other relevant factor. D.C.A. 13 Sec. 1512.

Child Support: Combined Income Method. Factors: (1) health, relative economic condition, financial circumstances and income of the parties and child; (2) standard of living established during the marriage; and (3) general equities inherent in the situation. D.C.A. 13 Sec. 514. For formula and forms, see *Family Court Civil Rules*, Rule 52(c) and Forms 509 & 509p.

Child Custody: Determined by the best interest of the child, considering: (1) wishes of the parents and the child, (2) interaction and interrelationship of child with parents, siblings, and other significant persons; (3) child's adjustment to home, school and community; (4) mental and physical health of all persons involved. D.C.A. 13 Sec. 721. Must submit affidavit that Petitioner has been advised of the following children's rights: "(1) the right to a continuing relationship with both parents; (2) the right to be treated as an important human being, with unique feelings, ideas, and desires; (3) the right to continuing care and guidance from both parents; (4) the right to know and appreciate what is good in each parent without one parent degrading the other; (5) the right to express love, affection, and respect for each parent without having to stifle that love because of disapproval by the other parent; (6) the right to know that the parents' decision to divorce was not the responsibility of the child; (7) the right not to be a source of argument between the parents; (8) the right to honest answers to questions about the changing family relationships; (9) the right to be able to experience regular and consistent contact with both parents and the right to know the reason for any cancellation of time or change of plans; and (10) the right to have a relaxed, secure relationship with both parents without being placed in a position to manipulate one parent against the other." See D.C.A. 13 Sec. 701.

Misc: Wife may have maiden name or name of former husband restored. D.C.A. 13 Sec. 1514. Parties may be required to attend, and pay for, a "Parenting Education Course." D.C.A. 13 Sec. 1507 (h).

Final Order: DECREE OF DIVORCE

UCCJA:	D.C.A. 13 Sec. 1901.	Domestic Violence:	D.C.A. 13 Sec. 701A.
IDO:	D.C.A. 13 Sec. 516.	Annulment:	D.C.A. 13 Sec. 1506.
Temporary Relief:	D.C.A. 13 Sec. 1509.		

DISTRICT OF COLUMBIA

The Law:	District of Columbia Code, Title 16, Section 901 (D.C.C. Sec. 16-901). Ignore "Chapter" numbers.
Case Style/Parties:	IN THE SUPERIOR COURT OF THE DISTRICT OF COLUMBIA - FAMILY DIVISION _____, Plaintiff vs. _____, Defendant.
Complaint Title:	COMPLAINT FOR DIVORCE
Residency:	One party must be a resident at least 6 months before filing. D.C.C. Sec. 16-902.
Grounds:	NO-FAULT: (1) "The parties have mutually and voluntarily lived separate and apart without cohabitation for a period of at least 6 months." (2) "The parties have lived separate and apart without cohabitation for at least 1 year." TRADITIONAL: None. LEGAL SEPARATION: Called "legal separation from bed and board." (1) mutually and voluntarily living separate and apart without cohabitation; (2) living separate and apart without cohabitation for 1 year; (3) adultery; and (4) cruelty. During the separation period the parties may reside in the same home. D.C.C. Sec. 16-904.
Property:	Equitable distribution. Fault is not a factor. "Sole property" is property (1) acquired before marriage; (2) acquired by gift or inheritance; (3) acquired in exchange for such property; and (4) increased value of sole property. Marital property divided according to following factors: (1) duration of the marriage; (2) any prior marriages; (3) each party's age, health, occupation, amount and sources of income, vocational skills, and employability; (4) each party's assets, debts and needs; (5) child custody provisions; (6) whether property division is in lieu of or in addition to alimony; (7) each party's opportunity for future acquisition of assets and income; (8) each party's contribution to the acquisition, preservation, appreciation, dissipation, or depreciation of marital assets; (9) each party's contribution as a homemaker or to the family unit; and (10) any other relevant factor. D.C.C. Sec. 16-910.
Alimony:	Fault may be considered. Statute merely states that alimony may be awarded "if it seems just and proper." D.C.C. Secs. 16-912 and 16-913. No other statutory factors or guidelines.
Child Support:	Percentage of Income Method. Child support guidelines may be found in D.C.C. Sec. 16-916.1.
Child Custody:	Best interest of the child considering: (1) wishes of the child; (2) wishes of the parties; (3) the interaction and interrelationship between the child and parents, siblings and other significant persons; (4) child's adjustment to home, school and community; (5) mental and physical health of all person involved; (6) any evidence of an "intrafamily offense" under D.C.C. Sec. 16-1001(5); (7) the parents' capacity to communicate and reach shared decisions affecting the child's welfare; (8) the willingness of the parents to share custody; (9) prior involvement of each parent in the child's life; (10) potential disruption of the child's social and school life; (11) geographic proximity of the parents' homes; (12) demands of parental employment; (13) age and number of children; (14) the sincerity of each parent's request; (15) each parent's ability to financially support a joint custody arrangement; (16) any impact on Territory Assistance for Needy Families, Program on Work, Employment, and Responsibilities, and medical assistance; and (17) the benefits to the parents. D.C.C. Secs. 16-911 & 16-914.
Misc:	If a party assumed a new name upon marriage, his or her birth or previous name may be restored. D.C.C. Sec. 16-915.
Final Order:	FINAL DECREE OF DIVORCE
UCCJA:	D.C.C. Sec. 16-4501.
IDO:	D.C.C. Sec. 30-508.
Temporary Relief:	D.C.C. Sec. 16-911.
Domestic Violence:	D.C.C. Sec. 16-1001.
Annulment:	D.C.C. Sec. 16-904(d).

FLORIDA

The Law:	Florida Statutes, Chapter 61, Section 61.001 (F.S. Sec. 61.001). Look for the book *How to File for Divorce in Florida*, from Sourcebooks, Inc. A new set of statute books is published every odd-numbered year. For most current law, look for either the hard-cover Supplement volume published in even-numbered years, or the soft-cover "West's Florida Session Law Service" which is published after each year's legislative session. You may also find a set of "Florida Statutes Annotated," with pocket party supplements. Official forms may be found in the Sphinx book mentioned above, or in the Florida Rules of Court or at the Court Clerk's office.
Case Style/Parties:	IN THE CIRCUIT COURT OF THE _____ JUDICIAL [Each circuit has a number] CIRCUIT, IN AND FOR _____ COUNTY, FLORIDA In re the marriage of _____, Husband, and _____, Wife. [The person who files is referred to as the Petitioner, and the other party as the Respondent. However, the husband is always listed first in the case style.]
Complaint Title:	PETITION FOR SIMPLIFIED DISSOLUTION OF MARRIAGE (Simplified procedure) PETITION FOR DISSOLUTION OF MARRIAGE (Standard procedure)
Residency:	One party must be a resident for at least 6 months before filing. F.S. Sec. 61.021.
Which Court:	The county in which the respondent resides. If the respondent is a non-resident, in the county where the petitioner resides.
Grounds:	(1) "The marriage between the parties is irretrievably broken." or (2) "The Respondent is mentally incompetent." F.S. Sec. 61.052(1). TRADITIONAL: None. LEGAL SEPARATION: None.
Property:	Equitable distribution. Fault is not considered. A "special equity" claim for nonmarital property must be included in the petition. Nonmarital property is property: (1) acquired before marriage; (2) acquired by gift or inheritance; (3) designated nonmarital in an agreement between the parties; (4) acquired in exchange for property in (1), (2), or (3) above; and (5) income from nonmarital property, unless the parties treated or used it as marital income. F.S. Sec. 61.075(5). Marital property includes all retirement, profit-sharing, and deferred compensation plans. F.S.Sec. 61.076. Marital property divided considering: (1) each party's contribution to the marriage; (2) each party's economic circumstances; (3) duration of the marriage; (4) either party's interruption of personal career or educational opportunities; (5) either party's contribution to the personal career or educational opportunities of the other; (6) desirability of retaining any asset intact and free of any claim of or interference from the other; (7) each party's contribution to the acquisition, enhancement, and production of income or the improvement of both marital and nonmarital property; (8) desirability for the custodial parent to remain in the marital home; and (9) any other relevant factor. F.S. Sec. 61.075.
Alimony:	Factors: (1) adultery; (2) standard of living established during marriage; (3) duration of marriage; (4) each party's age, physical and emotional condition; (5) each party's financial resources, and the marital and nonmarital property distribution; (6) time needed to acquire sufficient education and training to find appropriate employment; (7) each party's contribution to the marriage; (8) all sources of income available; and (9) any other relevant factor. F.S. Sec. 61.08.
Child Support:	Combined Income Method. Factors and guidelines are found in F.S. Sec. 61.30.
Child Custody:	Joint custody (referred to as "joint parental responsibility") is preferred, and must be ordered unless judge finds it would be detrimental to the child. F.S. Sec. 61.13(2). Generally this refers to joint responsibility for making decisions for the child's welfare, with one party's home being designated as the "primary residence." Responsibility and primary residence determined by the best interest of the child considering: (1) which party is more likely to allow frequent and continuing contact with the other party; (2) love, affection and other emotional ties existing between the child and each party; (3) each party's capacity and disposition to provide food, clothing, medical care or other material needs for the child; (4) length of time the child has been in a stable, satisfactory environment, and the desirability of maintaining continuity; (5) the permanence, as a family unit, of the existing or proposed custodial home; (6) moral fitness of the parties; (7) mental and physical health of the parties; (8) child's home, school and community record; (9) preference of the child, if of sufficient intelligence, understanding and experience; and (10) any other relevant factor. F.S. Sec. 61.13(3).
Misc:	Approved forms are available through the Circuit Court Clerk. Various forms are required depending upon the circumstances. Simplified procedure is available where there are no children, the wife is not pregnant, the parties agree on the property division, and both parties will attend the final hearing. Name change available if requested in the petition.
Final Order:	FINAL JUDGMENT DISSOLVING MARRIAGE UNDER SIMPLIFIED PROCEDURE (Simplified procedure) FINAL JUDGMENT DISSOLVING MARRIAGE (Standard procedure) Income withholding and health insurance provisions are required. F.S. Secs. 61.13(1)(b).
UCCJA:	F.S. Sec. 61.1304.
IDO:	F.S. Secs. 61.12 and 61.1301. Called "income withholding."
Temporary Relief:	F.S. Secs. 61.071 and 61.11.
Domestic Violence:	F.S. Sec. 741.01.
Annulment:	Available in Florida, but no provisions in statute. Case law only.

GEORGIA

The Law:	Official Code of Georgia Annotated, Title 19, Chapter 5, Section 1 (C.G.A. Sec. 19-5-1). (This is not the same as the Georgia Code, which is a separate and out-dated set of books.)
Case Style/Parties:	IN THE SUPERIOR COURT OF _____, GEORGIA _____, Petitioner, vs. _____, Respondent.
Complaint Title:	PETITION FOR DIVORCE The petition must contain the following: (1) respondent's residence or last known address; (2) a statement showing that the residency requirement has been met; (3) date of marriage and date of separation; (4) name and age of minor children, or a statement that there are no minor children; (5) the no-fault ground for divorce; (6) the property and earnings, if known, if alimony, support or property division is involved. C.G.A. Sec. 19-5-5.
Residency:	One party must be a resident for at least 6 months. C.G.A. Sec. 19-5-2.
Which Court:	Petitioner is a resident: County in which Petitioner resides. Petitioner is not a resident: County in which Respondent resides. C.G.A. Sec. 19-5-2.
Grounds:	NO-FAULT: "The marriage of the parties is irretrievably broken." C.G.A. Sec. 19-5-3(13). TRADITIONAL: (1) marriage within prohibited blood relationships; (2) mental incapacity at time of marriage; (3) impotency at time of marriage; (4) force, menace, duress, or fraud in obtaining the marriage; (5) wife pregnant by another man at time of marriage without husband's knowledge; (6) adultery; (7) willful and continued desertion for 1 year; (8) conviction of an offense involving moral turpitude and sentence of at least 2 years; (9) habitual intoxication; (10) cruel physical or mental treatment so as to justify apprehension of danger to life, limb or health; (11) incurable mental illness; and (12) habitual drug addiction. C.G.A. Sec. 19-5-3. LEGAL SEPARATION: None.
Property:	Equitable distribution. No factors in statute.
Alimony:	To qualify for alimony, proof of the cause of the divorce must be presented. Desertion or adultery is a bar to alimony. See C.G.A. Sec. 19-6-1. The amount is based upon the need of the party seeking alimony and the other party's ability to pay, considering: (1) standard of living established during the marriage; (2) duration of the marriage; (3) age, physical and emotional condition of the parties; (4) financial resources of each party; (5) time needed to acquire education and training to obtain employment; (6) contribution of each party to the marriage; (7) condition of the parties, including the separate estate, earning capacity and fixed liabilities; and (8) any other relevant factor. C.G.A. Sec. 19-6-5.
Child Support:	Percentage of Income Method. Guidelines are found in G.C.A. Sec. 19-6-15. Basically figured as a percent of the payor's gross income, as follows: 17% to 23% for 1 child; 23% to 28% for 2 children; 25% to 32% for 3 children; 29% to 35% for 4 children; and 31% to 37% for 5 or more children. This can be varied by special circumstances also set forth in C.G.A. Sec. 19-6-15.
Child Custody:	No specific factors or provision for joint custody in statute. Child may select parent to live with if at least 14 years of age. G.C.A. Sec. 19-9-1.
Misc:	Maiden or prior name may be restored if asked for in petition. C.G.A. Sec. 19-5-16.
Final Order:	FINAL JUDGMENT AND DECREE OF DIVORCE A form for the judgment may be found in C.G.A. Sec. 19-5-12. Judgment may not be entered until at least 30 days after the respondent is served. C.G.A. Sec. 19-5-3(13).
UCCJA:	C.G.A. Sec. 19-9-20.
IDO:	C.G.A. Sec. 19-6-31.
Temporary Relief:	C.G.A. Secs. 19-6-2 (attorneys fees); 19-6-3 (alimony); and 19-6-14 (child support and custody).
Domestic Violence:	C.G.A. Sec. 19-13-1.
Annulment:	C.G.A. Sec. 19-4-1.

HAWAII

The Law:	Hawaii Revised Statutes, Title 580, Section 580-41 (H.R.S. Sec. 580-41).
Case Style/Parties:	IN THE FAMILY COURT OF THE _____ JUDICIAL CIRCUIT _____, Plaintiff vs. _____, Defendant.
Complaint Title:	COMPLAINT FOR DIVORCE
Residency:	Plaintiff must be a resident for at least 3 months before filing. H.R.S. Sec. 580-1. One party must be resident for at least 6 months before judgment can be entered.
Which Court:	Judicial district where Plaintiff resides, or where parties last lived together.
Grounds:	NO-FAULT: (1) "The marriage of the parties is irretrievably broken." (2) "The parties have lived separate and apart under a decree of separation from bed and board, the term of separation has expired, and no reconciliation has been effected." (3) "The parties have lived separate and apart for a period of 2 years or more under a decree of separate maintenance, and no reconciliation has been effected." (4) "The parties have lived separate and apart for a continuous period of 2 years or more, there is no reasonable likelihood that cohabitation will be resumed, and it will not be harsh or oppressive to the defendant or contrary to the public interest to divorce on this ground." H.R.S. Sec. 580-41. TRADITIONAL: None. LEGAL SEPARATION: "The marriage of the parties is temporarily disrupted." A decree of separation from bed and board may be granted for a period of up to 2 years. H.R.S. Sec. 580-71.
Property:	Equitable distribution. Factors: (1) respective merits of the parties; (2) relative abilities of the parties; (3) condition each party will be in after divorce; (4) burdens imposed on either spouse for the benefit of the children; and (5) any other relevant circumstances. H.R.S. Sec. 580-47.
Alimony:	Called "spousal support and maintenance." Marital misconduct is not considered. Factors: (1) each party's financial resources; (2) ability of party seeking alimony to meet own needs; (3) duration of marriage; (4) standard of living established during marriage; (5) ages of parties; (6) each party's physical and emotional condition; (7) each party's usual occupation during the marriage; (8) vocational skills and employability of party seeking alimony; (9) needs of the parties; (10) either party's child custodial and support responsibilities; (11) ability of party to pay alimony and meet own needs; (12) condition each party will be in after divorce; (13) probable duration of the need for alimony; and (14) any other relevant factor. H.R.S. Sec. 580-47.
Child Support:	Percentage of Income Method for low income families; Combined Income Method for others. Guidelines may be found in H.R.S. Sec. 576D-7.
Child Custody:	Best interest of the child considering: (1) child's wishes, if of sufficient age and capacity to reason; and (2) any evidence of family violence. H.R.S. Sec. 571-46.
Misc:	If the divorce is uncontested, the judge may waive a hearing and enter a decree based on the affidavits of the parties. H.R.S. Sec. 580-42 [NEW].
Final Order:	DECREE OF DIVORCE See H.R.S. Sec. 576E-11 for requirements relating to child support.
UCCJA:	H.R.S. Sec. 583-1.
IDO:	H.R.S. Sec. 576E-16.
Temporary Relief:	H.R.S. Sec. 580-9 (protection and suit money); 580-10 (restraining orders); and 580-11 (custody and child support).
Domestic Violence:	H.R.S. Secs. 586-1.
Annulment:	H.R.S. Sec. 580-21.

IDAHO

The Law:	Idaho Code, Title 32, Chapter 6, Section 32-601 (I.C. Sec. 32-601).
Case Style/Parties:	IN THE DISTRICT COURT OF THE _____JUDICIAL DISTRICT FOR THE STATE OF IDAHO, IN AND FOR THE COUNTY OF_____
	_____, Plaintiff vs. _____, Defendant.
Complaint Title:	COMPLAINT FOR DIVORCE
Residency:	Plaintiff must be a resident for at least 6 weeks before filing. I.C. Sec. 32-701.
Which Court:	The county where the Defendant resides. If defendant is not a resident, in the county where the Plaintiff resides.
Grounds:	NO-FAULT: (1) "The parties have irreconcilable differences." I.C. Secs. 32-603 & 616. (2) "The parties have been living separate and apart without cohabitation for a period of 5 years." I.C. Sec. 32-610. TRADITIONAL: (1) adultery; (2) extreme cruelty; (3) wilful desertion; (4) wilful neglect; (5) habitual intemperance (drunkenness); (6) conviction of a felony; and (7) permanent insanity. I.C. Secs. 32-603. These are further defined in I.C. Secs. 32-604 through 32-608. Complaint based on adultery must be filed within 2 years of becoming aware of the adultery. Complaints based on grounds (3), (4) and (5) must be filed within one year. I.C. Sec. 32-609. Complaint based on conviction of felony must be filed within 1 year of a pardon or end of the sentence. I.C. Sec. 32-615. LEGAL SEPARATION: None.
Property:	Community property. Separate property is property acquired: (1) before marriage; (2) by gift or inheritance; and (3) as proceeds of separate property and acquired with proceeds of separate property. I.C. Sec. 32-903. Marital property is to be divided equally, unless judge gives reasons based upon: (1) duration of marriage; (2) any premarital agreement; (3) each party's age, health, occupation, amount and sources of income, vocational skills, employability, and liabilities; (4) each party's needs; (5) whether property division is in lieu of or in addition to alimony; (6) each party's present and potential earning capacity; and (7) each party's retirement benefits, including social security, civil service, military and railroad pensions. I.C. Secs. 32-712.
Alimony:	Called "maintenance." Either party may be awarded alimony if he or she: (1) lacks sufficient property to be self-supporting; and (2) is unable to be self-supporting through employment. Factors for determining amount and duration: (1) financial resources of the party seeking alimony, including property awarded and ability to meet own needs; (2) time needed to acquire education and training to become employed; (3) duration of marriage; (4) age, physical and emotional condition of party seeking alimony; (5) ability of party paying alimony to meet own needs while paying; (6) tax consequences; (7) fault of either party; and (8) any other relevant factor. I.C. Sec. 32-705.
Child Support:	Combined Income Method. Guidelines are provided by the Idaho Supreme Court. I.C. Sec. 32-706. Check with court clerk or law library.
Child Custody:	Best interest of the child considering: (1) wishes of parties; (2) wishes of child; (3) interaction and interrelationship between the child and parties, siblings or other significant persons; (4) adjustment to home, school and community; (5) mental and physical health of all persons involved; (6) need to promote continuity and stability in the child's life; and (7) any history of domestic violence. I.C. Sec. 32-717. Joint custody is presumed best, unless either party can show otherwise. I.C. Sec. 32-717B.
Misc:	No provision for name change in divorce.
Final Order:	DECREE OF DIVORCE Decree may be granted by default on the uncorroborated testimony of the plaintiff. I.C. Sec. 32-703.

UCCJA:	I.C. Sec. 32-1101.	Domestic Violence:	I.C. Sec. 39-6301.
IDO:	I.C. Sec. 32-1201.	Annulment:	I.C. Sec. 32-501.
Temporary Relief:	I.C. Sec. 32-704.		

ILLINOIS

The Law:	West's Smith-Hurd Illinois Compiled Statutes Annotated, Chapter 750, Act 5, Section 5/101 (750 ILCS 5/101).
Case Style/Parties:	IN THE CIRCUIT COURT OF THE _____JUDICIAL DISTRICT, _____ COUNTY, ILLINOIS In re the Marriage of _____, Petitioner, and _____, Respondent.
Complaint Title:	PETITION FOR DISSOLUTION OF MARRIAGE The petition must be verified, and must contain: (1) age, occupation and residence of each party, and their length of residence in the state; (2) date of marriage and place registered; (3) the no-fault grounds for the divorce; (4) name, age and address of all children, and a statement as to whether the wife is pregnant; (5) any arrangements as to support, custody, visitation and alimony; and (6) the relief sought. 750 ILCS 5/403.
Residency:	One party must be resident for at least 90 days before filing. 750 ILCS 5/401.
Which Court:	The county where either party resides. 750 ILCS 5/104.
Grounds:	NO-FAULT: "Irreconcilable differences have caused the irretrievable breakdown of the marriage, and reconciliation has failed or further attempts at reconciliation are impractical, and the parties have been living separate and apart without cohabitation for more than 2 years." However, if both parties agree, the time period may be reduced to 6 months. TRADITIONAL: (1) impotence; (2) bigamy; (3) adultery; (4) desertion for 1 year; (5) habitual drunkenness for 2 years; (6) drug addiction for 2 years; (7) attempted poisoning or otherwise endangering spouse's life; (8) cruel and inhuman physical or mental treatment; (9) conviction of a felony; and (10) infection of spouse with a communicable disease. 750 ILCS 5/401. LEGAL SEPARATION: Living separate and apart, without fault. 750 ILCS 5/402.
Property:	Equitable distribution. Fault is not considered. Nonmarital property is property: (1) acquired before marriage; (2) acquired after marriage by gift, inheritance, in exchange for other nonmarital property, or after a legal separation; (3) designated nonmarital by written agreement of the parties; (4) designated nonmarital by a judgment from the spouse; or (5) increased value or income from property in (1) through (4). Division of marital property based on following factors: (1) contribution or dissipation of each party; (2) value of separate property; (3) duration of the marriage; (4) economic circumstances of the parties, including whether custodial parent should remain in marital home; (5) prior marriage obligations; (6) any pre-marital agreements; (7) age, health, station, occupation, income, skills, employability, estate, liabilities, and needs of each party; (8) child custody provisions; (9) whether property is in lieu of, or in addition to, alimony; (10) each party's opportunity for future acquisition of assets and income; and (11) tax consequences. 750 ILCS 5/503.
Alimony:	Called "maintenance." Fault is not considered. Factors: (1) income and property of each party; (2) needs of each party; (3) each party's present and future earning capacity; (4) any impairment of earning capacity due to foregoing education and employment opportunities to devote time to domestic duties; (5) time needed for the party seeking alimony for education, training and employment, and whether that party is able to support himself or herself or has custody of a child making it inappropriate to seek employment; (6) standard of living established during the marriage; (7) duration of the marriage; (8) age, physical and emotional condition of each party; (9) tax consequences of the property division; (10) either party's contribution and services to the other's education, training, career or license; (11) any valid agreement of the parties; and (12) any other relevant factor. 750 ILCS 5/504.
Child Support:	Percentage of Income Method. Support guidelines may be found in 750 ILCS 5/505. Basically a percentage of the payor's net income, as follows: 20% for 1 child; 25% for 2 children; 32% for 3 children; 40% for 4 children; 45% for 5 children; and 50% for 6 or more children. Other factors for special needs are listed which may justify more or less.
Child Custody:	Best interest of the child, considering: (1) wishes of parents and child; (2) interaction and interrelationship between the child and the parents, siblings and other significant persons; (3) child's adjustment to home, school and community; (4) mental and physical health of parties and child; (5) any physical threat to the child; (6) each party's willingness to encourage and facilitate continued contact between the other parent and the child. 750 ILCS 5/602. Joint custody factors may be found at 750 ILCS 5/602.1.
Misc:	JOINT SIMPLIFIED PROCEDURE: Parties can file joint petition for simplified dissolution if: (1) no spousal support will be paid; (2) one party has met residency requirements; (3) no-fault grounds are used; (4) there are no children and the wife is not pregnant; (5) the parties have not been married more than 8 years; (6) neither party has any interest in real property; (7) total equity in marital property is less than $10,000; (8) the parties' combined annual gross income is less than $35,00; (9) neither party has an annual gross income of more than $20,000: (10) the parties have disclosed all assets and tax returns for all the years of the marriage; and (11) the parties have a written agreement dividing all the property in excess of $100 in value, and allocating responsibility for all debts and liabilities. 750 ILCS 5/451. Forms, and a brochure describing the procedure, may be obtained from court clerk. Judge may order parties to attend educational program on the effects of divorce on children. 750 ILCS 5/404.1.
Final Order:	JUDGMENT OF DISSOLUTION OF MARRIAGE

UCCJA:	750 ILCS 35/1.	Domestic Violence:	750 ILCS 60/1.
IDO:	750 ILCS 5/706.1.	Annulment:	750 ILCS 5/301.
Temporary Relief:	750 ILCS 5/501, and 5/603.		

INDIANA

The Law: West's Annotated Indiana Code, Title 31, Article 15, Chapter 1, Section 1. (A.I.C. Sec. 31-15-1-1).

Case Style/Parties: _____ COURT OF _____ COUNTY, INDIANA. [The first blank will either be "SUPERIOR," "CIRCUIT," or "DOMESTIC RELATIONS," depending upon the particular county you file in.]

In Re the marriage of _____, Petitioner, and_____, Respondent.

Complaint Title: PETITION FOR DISSOLUTION OF MARRIAGE
Petition must be verified and contain: (1) residence address of each party and length of residence in the state and county; (2) date of marriage; (3) date of separation; (4) name, age and address of living children under age 21, or incapacitated children of any age, and a statement as to whether the wife is pregnant; (5) no-fault grounds for divorce; (6) relief sought. A.I.C. Sec. 31-15-2-5.

Residency: One party must be a resident of Indiana for 6 months, and of the county for 3 months. A.I.C. Sec. 31-15-2-6.

Which Court: County in which either party meets residency requirements. A.I.C. Sec. 31-15-2-6.

Grounds: NO-FAULT: "There has been an irretrievable breakdown of the marriage." A.I.C. Sec. 31-15-2-3.
TRADITIONAL: (1) conviction of a felony subsequent to the marriage; (2) impotence at the time of marriage; and (3) incurable insanity for 2 years. A.I.C. Sec. 31-15-2-3.
LEGAL SEPARATION: "Conditions in the parties' marriage render it currently intolerable for the parties to live together and the marriage should be maintained." See A.I.C. Sec. 31-15-2-3.

Property: Equitable distribution. Fault is not a factor. Property acquired before marriage is a part of the marital estate, although time of acquisition is a factor to be considered in dividing the property. Equal division is presumed. Factors considered in unequal distribution claim are: (1) contribution of each party to acquisition; (2) extent of property acquired prior to marriage, or by gift or inheritance; (3) economic circumstances at the time of distribution, including whether custodial parent should remain in marital home; (4) conduct of the parties as related to disposition or dissipation of assets; (5) the earnings, or earning capacity, of each party; and (6) tax consequences. If insufficient marital property, court may award money to party for contribution to the other's education. See A.I.C. beginning with Sec. 31-15-7-4.

Alimony: Fault is not a factor. Alimony (called "maintenance") may be awarded for a necessary period of time if (1) the party seeking alimony is physically or mentally incapacitated; or (2) lacks financial ability and is custodian of a physically or mentally incapacitated child which requires that party to forego employment. Rehabilitative alimony for up to 3 years may be awarded after considering: (1) each party's educational level at the time of the marriage and at the time the petition was filed; (2) whether the party seeking alimony had his or her education, training or employment interrupted due to homemaking or child care responsibilities; (3) earning capacity of each party; and (4) time and expense required to acquire education and training to obtain employment. A.I.C. Sec. 31-15-7-2.

Child Support: Combined Income Method. Factors considered are: (1) financial resources of custodial parent; (2) standard of living the child could have expected absent the divorce; (3) physical and mental condition of the child and the child's educational needs; (4) financial resources and needs of the non-custodial parent; and (5) any special educational or medical needs of the child. A.I.C. Sec. 31-16-6-1.

Child Custody: Best interest of the child, considering: (1) age and sex of the child; (2) wishes of the parents and child; (3) interaction and interrelationship between the child and the parents, siblings and other significant persons; (4) child's adjustment to home, school and community; and (5) mental and physical health of all persons involved; and (6) any domestic violence. A.I.C. Sec. 31-17-2-8. Joint legal custody may be awarded. A.I.C. beginning with Sec. 31-12-2-13.

Misc: Judgment without a hearing may be entered where: (1) it has been 60 days since petition was filed; (2) petition was verified and signed by both parties; (3) petition contains a waiver of hearing; (4) petition contains either (a) statement that there are no contested issues, or (b) parties have made a written settlement agreement. A.I.C. Sec. 31-15-2-13. If reconciliation seems possible, the judge may continue the hearing and order the parties to counselling. After 45 days either party may move for dissolution; if not, case is dismissed after 90 days. A.I.C. Sec. 31-15-2-15.
Women may have maiden or previous name restored. see A.I.C. Sec. 31-15-2-18.

Final Order: FINAL DISSOLUTION OF MARRIAGE DECREE
No hearing may be held until 60 days after filing the petition. A.I.C. Sec. 31-15-2-10. Parties can waive final hearing if no matters are in dispute. A.I.C. Sec. 31-15-2-13.

UCCJA: A.I.C. Sec. 31-17-3-1.
IDO: A.I.C. Sec. 31-16-15-1.
Temporary Relief: A.I.C. beginning with Sec. 31-15-41. Requires affidavit with factual basis.
Domestic Violence: A.I.C. Sec. 34-4-5.1-1.
Annulment: A.I.C. Sec. 31-7-7-1.

IOWA

The Law:	Iowa Code Annotated, Section 598.1 (I.C.A. Sec. 598.1).
Case Style/Parties:	IN THE DISTRICT COURT OF THE STATE OF IOWA IN AND FOR _____ COUNTY

In Re the Marriage of _____ and _____.

Upon the Petition of)
_____)   Petition for Dissolution
(Petitioner))   of Marriage
and Concerning)   Equity No._____
_____)
(Respondent))

Complaint Title:	PETITION FOR DISSOLUTION OF MARRIAGE Petition must be verified and must include: (1) name, birth date, address and county of residence of petitioner; (2) place and date of marriage; (3) name, birth date, address and county of residence of respondent, if known; (4) name and date of birth of each child; (5) statement of whether a separate action was commenced by respondent, and whether an action is pending in any state; (6) allegation that petitioner has filed this action in good faith and for the purposes set forth in the petition; (7) allegation of the grounds for dissolution; (8) any request for temporary child support or alimony, without stating an amount; (9) any request for permanent alimony or child support, custody, property disposition, attorney's fees and suit money, without stating any amounts; (10) statement of whether the appointment of a conciliator pursuant to section 598.16 may preserve the marriage; and, if the respondent is not a resident or was not personally served, (11) the residency of the petitioner for the past year, specifying the county and length of residence, deducting for any absences, and that the maintenance of the residence has been in good faith and not for purpose of obtaining a marriage dissolution only. I.C.A. Sec. 598.5, Sec. 598.6, and Sec. 598.7. Each party must also file an affidavit of net worth (form available from the court clerk), unless both parties and the judge agree it is not necessary. I.C.A. Sec. 598.13.
Residency:	No time period if defendant is a resident of Iowa and was personally served. Otherwise, 1 year residency of the petitioner. I.C.A. Sec. 598.2.
Which Court:	In the county where either party resides. I.C.A. Sec. 598.2.
Grounds:	NO-FAULT: "There has been a breakdown of the marriage relationship to the extent that the legitimate objects of matrimony have been destroyed and there remains no reasonable likelihood that the marriage can be preserved." I.C.A. Sec. 598.17. TRADITIONAL: None. LEGAL SEPARATION: Called "separate maintenance." Same as no-fault. I.C.A. Sec. 598.28.
Property:	Equitable distribution. Fault is not considered. Separate property is property acquired: (1) by inheritance or gift; or (2) before marriage. Marital property divided considering: (1) length of marriage; (2) property brought into the marriage; (3) each party's contribution to the marriage; (4) each party's age, physical and emotional health; (5) either party's contribution to the other's education, training, and increased earning power; and (6) each party's earning capacity, including educational background, training, employment skills, work experience, length of absence from job market, child custodial responsibilities, and time and expense needed to acquire education and training to become self-supporting at the standard of living established during the marriage; (7) desirability of custodial party remaining in marital home; (8) amount and duration of alimony, and whether property division should be in lieu of or in addition to alimony; (9) each party's other economic circumstances, including pension benefits; (10) tax consequences; (11) any written agreements of the parties; and (11) any other relevant factor. I.C.A. Sec. 598.21.
Alimony:	Factors: (1) length of marriage; (2) age and physical and emotional health of the parties; (3) property distribution; (4) educational level of each party at time of marriage and at time petition is filed; (5) earning capacity of party seeking alimony, including educational background, training, employment skills, work experience, length of absence from job market, child custodial responsibilities, and time and expense needed to acquire education and training to find appropriate employment; (6) the feasibility of the party seeking alimony becoming self-supporting at a standard of living reasonably comparable to that during marriage, and length of time needed to do so; (7) tax consequences; (8) any agreements between the parties; and (9) any other relevant factors. I.C.A. Secs. 598.21.
Child Support:	Percentage of Income Method. Child Support Guidelines published by Department of Human Services.
Child Custody:	Best interest of the child "which will assure the child the opportunity for the maximum continuing physical and emotional contact with both parents." Either party may request joint legal custody. If judge refuses, findings must be in decree, considering various factors in the statute. I.C.A. Sec. 598.41.
Misc:	Either spouse may request change to name on birth certificate or name immediately prior to marriage. Either party may obtain mandatory conciliation efforts. I.C.A. Sec. 598.37.
Final Order:	DECREE OF DISSOLUTION OF MARRIAGE 90 day waiting period from date respondent is served. I.C.A. Sec. 598.19. See I.C.A. Sec. 598.22B for required contents of decree.

UCCJA:	I.C.A. Sec. 598A.1.	Domestic Violence:	I.C.A. Sec. 236.1.
IDO:	I.C.A. Sec. 252D.8.	Annulment:	I.C.A. Sec. 598.29.
Temporary Relief:	I.C.A. Sec. 598.11.		

KANSAS

The Law:	Kansas Statutes Annotated, Section 60-1601 (K.S.A. Sec. 60-1601). You may find these volumes as either "Vernon's Kansas Statutes Annotated, Code of Civil Procedure" or "Kansas Statutes Annotated, Official." The most recent law will probably be found in the supplements, which is a pocket part in "Vernon's" and a separate soft-cover volume in the "Official." Both sets have very poor indexing systems.
Case Style/Parties:	IN THE DISTRICT COURT IN AND FOR THE COUNTY OF_____, KANSAS
	In the matter of the marriage of _____, and _____. [The petitioner's name goes in the first blank, but the designations of "petitioner" and "respondent" are not to be used. K.S.A. Sec. 60-1604.]
Complaint Title:	PETITION FOR DIVORCE
	Petition must include: (1) statutory ground, without any factual details; and (2) each child's name and date of birth; and (3) be accompanied by a Uniform Child Custody Jurisdiction Act Affidavit pursuant to K.S.A. Sec. 38-1309. K.S.A. Sec. 60-1604(c).
Residency:	One party must be a resident for at least 60 days. K.S.A. Sec. 60-1603.
Which Court:	The county where either spouse resides.
Grounds:	NO-FAULT: "The parties are incompatible." K.S.A. Sec. 60-1601.
	TRADITIONAL: (1) failure to perform a material marital duty or obligation; (2) incompatibility due to mental illness or mental incapacity." K.S.A. Sec. 60-1601.
	LEGAL SEPARATION: Called "separate maintenance." Same grounds as no-fault and traditional. K.S.A. Sec. 60-1601.
Property:	Equitable distribution. All property is marital property. Factors for division: (1) age of parties; (2) duration of marriage; (3) property owned by the parties; (4) each party's present and future earning capacity; (5) time, source and manner of acquisition of the property; (6) family ties and obligations; (7) any award of alimony or lack thereof; (8) any dissipation of assets; and (9) any other relevant factor. K.S.A. Sec. 60-1610(b)(1).
Alimony:	Called "maintenance." Limited to 121 months, with one application for 121 month extension. Fault not considered. No statutory factors other than "in an amount the court finds to be fair, just and equitable under all of the circumstances." Payment must be through court clerk or court trustee. K.S.A. Sec. 60-1610(b)(2).
Child Support:	Combined Income Method. Supreme Court Child Support Guidelines are required by K.S.A. Sec. 20-165. Ask court clerk or law librarian.
Child Custody:	Best interest of the child considering: (1) any agreement of the parties; (2) length of time child has been under actual care and control of any person other than a parent and the circumstances involved; (3) desires of the parties; (4) desires of child; (5) interaction and interrelationship between child and parties, siblings and other significant persons; (6) child's adjustment to home, school and community; (7) each party's willingness and ability to respect and appreciate the bond between the child and the other party; (8) any evidence of spousal abuse; and (9) any other relevant factor. K.S.A. Sec. 60-16-1610(a)(3). Four types of custody are recognized, in the following order of preference: (1) joint; (2) sole; (3) divided (if 2 or more children); and (4) non-parental. K.S.A. Sec. 60-1610(a)(4).
Misc:	Former or maiden name may be restored. K.S.A. Sec. 60-1610(c)(1).
	Court may order counseling at the request of either party or on its own. K.S.A. Sec. 60-1608(c).
	No hearing may be held until at least 60 days after filing. K.S.A. Sec. 60-1608(a).
	You may find forms in a set of books called Vernon's Kansas Forms Annotated, Code of Civil Procedure, Sec. 16.1, etc.
Final Order:	DECREE OF DIVORCE
	Must include income withholding provision. K.S.A. Sec. 23-4,107.
UCCJA:	K.S.A. Sec. 38-1301.
IDO:	K.S.A. Secs. 60-1613 and 23-4,107.
Temporary Relief:	K.S.A. Sec. 60-1607.
Domestic Violence:	K.S.A. Sec. 60-3101.
Annulment:	K.S.A. Sec. 60-1602.

KENTUCKY

The Law:	Kentucky Revised Statutes, Chapter 403, Section 010 (K.R.S. Sec. 403.010). These are in a binder, with updates found in the beginning of each volume marked "Current Service."
Case Style/Parties:	_____ CIRCUIT COURT, KENTUCKY [County name goes in blank] In re the Marriage of _____, Petitioner, and _____, Respondent.
Complaint Title:	PETITION FOR DISSOLUTION OF MARRIAGE The petition must contain: (1) age, occupation and residence address of each party, and their length of residence in the state; (2) date of marriage and place registered; (3) a statement that the parties are separated and the date of separation; (4) name, age and address of minor children, and whether the wife is pregnant; (5) any arrangements for custody, visitation, support and alimony; and (6) relief sought. If both parties sign the petition, no service is required. K.R.S. Sec. 403.150.
Residency:	Petitioner must be resident for 180 days before filing. K.R.S. Sec. 403.140.
Which Court:	County where either party resides. K.R.S. Sec. 452.470.
Grounds:	NO-FAULT: "The marriage of the parties is irretrievably broken." K.R.S. Sec. 403.140. TRADITIONAL: None. LEGAL SEPARATION: Same as no-fault, also referred to as "divorce from bed and board." See K.R.S. Secs. 403.050 & 403.140.
Property:	Equitable distribution. Non-marital property is property acquired (1) before marriage; (2) by gift, or inheritance; (3) in exchange for such property; (4) after a legal separation; (5) property set forth as non-marital in a written agreement; and (6) the increase in value of pre-marriage property, unless the increase in value is due to the efforts of the other party. Also, if one party's retirement benefits are non-marital, so are the other's. Marital misconduct not considered. Division of marital property is determined by the following factors: (1) contribution of each party to the acquisition; (2) value of separate property; (3) duration of the marriage; and (4) economic circumstances of the parties, including whether the custodial parent should remain in the marital home. K.R.S. Sec. 403.190.
Alimony:	Fault is not considered. Alimony is only permitted if the person seeking alimony (1) lacks sufficient property to provide for his or her needs; and (2) is unable to be self-supporting through employment, or is custodian of a child whose condition or circumstances make it appropriate not to seek outside employment. Once eligible, the amount is determined by considering the following factors: (1) financial resources of the person seeking alimony; (2) time needed to acquire education and training to become employable; (3) standard of living established during the marriage; (4) duration of the marriage; (5) age, physical and emotional condition of the person seeking alimony; and (6) the ability of the payor to meet his or her own needs while paying alimony. K.R.S. Sec. 403.200.
Child Support:	Combined Income Method. See K.R.S. Sec. 403.212 for child support guidelines and table.
Child Custody:	Best interest of the child, considering: (1) wishes of the parents and child; (2) interaction and interrelationship between the child and parents, siblings and other significant persons; (3) child's adjustment to home, school and community; and (4) mental and physical condition of all persons involved. Judge may grant joint legal custody if it is in the child's best interest. K.R.S. Sec. 403.270.
Misc:	Wife's maiden name may be restored if there are no children. K.R.S. Sec. 403.230. Judge may appoint an advisory committee to counsel the parties. K.R.S. Sec. 403.033. If the wife is pregnant, the judge may continue the case until after the birth. K.R.S. Sec. 403.150(7).
Final Order:	DECREE OF DISSOLUTION OF MARRIAGE If the parties have children, no final hearing may be held until at least 60 days after service of the petition on the respondent. K.R.S. Sec. 403.044. Judgment cannot be entered until parties have "lived apart" (which includes residing together but not having sexual relations) for 60 days. K.R.S. Sec. 403-140. Decree must include an income deduction order to take effect immediately, unless good cause is shown. K.R.S.Sec. 403.215.
UCCJA:	K.R.S. Sec. 403.400.
IDO:	K.R.S. Sec. 403.215.
Temporary Relief:	K.R.S. Secs. 403.160 and 403.280.
Domestic Violence:	K.R.S. Sec. 403.710.
Annulment:	K.R.S. Sec. 403.120.

LOUISIANA

The Law: West's LSA Civil Code (LSA is an abbreviation for Louisiana Statutes Annotated), Article 102 (CC Art 102). The set of books containing the laws of Louisiana is one of the most complicated sets of any state. There are actually several sets, somewhat divided into areas of the law. All sets have the name Louisiana Statutes Annotated (or West's LSA, as they are published by West Publishing Company), which is then followed by the area of law it covers, such as Civil Code, Revised Statutes, Civil Procedure, etc. Most of the laws concerning divorce are found in the Civil Code, although some references to divorce are found in the Code of Civil Procedure (CCP).

Case Style/Parties: _____JUDICIAL DISTRICT COURT, PARISH OF_____, LOUISIANA [District number goes in first blank]

_____, Plaintiff, vs. _____, Defendant.

Complaint Title: PETITION FOR DIVORCE

Residency: One party must be domiciled in Louisiana. C.C.P., Art. 10(A)(7).

Which Court: Parish where either party is domiciled, or where parties were last domiciled while together. C.C.P., Art. 3941.

Grounds: NO-FAULT: (1) "The Plaintiff desires to be divorced from the Defendant." To use this ground you and your spouse must live apart continuously from the date the petition is filed until 180 days after your spouse is served or signs a waiver of service. This means you must actually live apart. You may not live in the same home or apartment. Your petition will also need to allege that one party is domiciled in Louisiana, and that one party is domiciled in the parish (or that the last marital residence was in the parish). C.C., Art. 102. (2) "The parties have been living separate and apart continuously for a period of 6 months or more." This may be used if you and your spouse have been separated for 6 months, and does not require any waiting period before a judgment can be entered. C.C., Art. 103. TRADITIONAL: (1) adultery; (2) conviction of a felony and a sentence of death or hard labor. C.C., Art. 103.
LEGAL SEPARATION: See L.C.C.A. Sec. 138 & 142.
COVENANT MARRIAGE: If parties have a "covenant marriage," under LSA Revised Statutes Sec. 9:272, divorce will only be permitted upon the "complete and total breach of the marital covenant commitment."

Property: Community property. No factors in statute. Although not considered a part of the marital property, it is possible to obtain an award for financial contributions to a spouse's education and training that increased the spouse's earning power, "to the extent that the claimant did not benefit during the marriage from the increased earning power." C.C., Art. 121.

Alimony: Permanent alimony may only be awarded to a spouse without fault and without sufficient means of support. Limited to one-third of the payor's income. Amount determined by following factors: (1) each party's income, means and assets; (2) liquidity of assets; (3) financial obligations and earning capacity; (4) effect of child custody on earning capacity; (5) time needed to acquire education, training or employment; (6) health and age of the parties, and any child support obligations; and (7) any other factor the judge decides is relevant. C.C., Art. 160.

Child Support: Combined Income Method. Based upon (1) needs of the child, and (2) actual resources of each parent. C.C., Art. 131. Guidelines and table are found in LSA Revised Statutes, 9:315.

Child Custody: Joint legal custody is preferred and presumed best for the child. Parties must submit a joint custody plan. If one party requests sole custody, he or she must prove it is in the child's best interest considering the following factors: (1) the child's love, affection and emotional ties with each parent; (2) capacity and disposition of the parties to give love, affection, guidance, education, and religious guidance; (3) capacity and disposition of the parties to give the child food, clothing, medical care, etc., (4) length of time the child has been in a stable, satisfactory environment, and the desirability for continuity; (5) permanence as a family unit of the existing or proposed home; (6) moral fitness of the parties; (7) mental and physical health of the parties; (8) home, school and community record of the child; (9) preference of the child, if old enough; (10) willingness of each party to facilitate a relationship between the child and the other spouse; (11) distance between parties residences; and (12) any other factor the judge decides is proper (except race). C.C., Art. 131 & 134.

Misc: Statute does not provide for name change, but court decisions allow wife to resume her maiden name. Otherwise, use general name-change statute (L.C.C.A. Sec. 13-4751).
Each judicial district may have special rules, which may be found in the Louisiana Rules of Court.
A reconciliation extinguishes a divorce action. C.C., Art. 104.

Final Order: JUDGMENT OF DIVORCE

UCCJA: LSA Revised Statutes, 13:1700.
IDO: LSA Revised Statutes, 46:236.3.
Temporary Relief: C.C., Art. 111 & 131.
Domestic Violence: LSA Revised Statutes, 46:2121.1.
Annulment: C.C., Art. 94.

MAINE

The Law:	Maine Revised Statutes Annotated, Title 19-A, Section 901 (19-A M.R.S.A. Sec. 901). Ignore the "chapter" numbers.
Case Style/Parties:	STATE OF MAINE, _____ COURT, _____ COUNTY [First blank is for either "DISTRICT" or "SUPERIOR," see "Which Court" below.] _____, Plaintiff, vs. _____, Defendant.
Complaint Title:	COMPLAINT FOR DIVORCE
Residency:	One of the following must be met: (1) plaintiff is a resident for 6 months; (2) plaintiff is a resident for any period of time and the parties were married in Maine; (3) plaintiff is a resident for any period of time, and both parties were residents at the time the cause for divorce occurred; or (4) defendant is a resident. 19-A M.R.S.A. Sec. 901.
Which Court:	District Court in county where either spouse resides, but defendant may have case moved to Superior Court.
Grounds:	NO-FAULT: "The parties have irreconcilable marital differences."19-A M.R.S.A. Sec. 902. TRADITIONAL: (1) adultery; (2) impotence; (3) extreme cruelty; (4) desertion for 3 years; (5) alcoholism or drug addiction; (6) nonsupport by spouse capable of support; (7) cruel and abusive treatment; (8) confinement for mental illness for 7 consecutive years. 19-A M.R.S.A. Sec. 902. LEGAL SEPARATION: One or both parties live apart, or desire to live apart, for more than 60 continuous days. 19-A M.R.S.A. Sec. 581.
Property:	Equitable distribution. Fault not considered. Separate property is property: (1) acquired before marriage; (2) acquired by gift or inheritance; (3) acquired in exchange for separate property; (4) acquired after a decree of legal separation; (5) designated separate by agreement of the parties; or (6) increased value of separate property. Marital property is divided considering: (1) each party's contribution to acquisition; (2) value of each party's separate property; and (3) the parties' economic circumstances at the time of division, including whether the child custodian should remain in the marital home. 19-A M.R.S.A. Sec. 953.
Alimony:	Court may award real estate to a party for life as alimony. Fault is not considered. Factors: (1) length of marriage; (2) ability of each to pay; (3) each party's age; (4) each party's employment history and employment potential; (5) each party's income and income potential; (6) each party's education and training; (7) provisions for retirement and health insurance benefits; (8) tax consequences of the property division; (9) each party's health and disabilities; (10) tax consequences of alimony; (11) either party's contribution as homemaker; (12) either party's contribution to the other's education or earning potential; (13) either party's economic misconduct resulting in the diminution of marital property or income; (14) standard of living established during marriage; (15) any other relevant factor, and (16) any willful misuse of the protection from abuse process. 19-A M.R.S.A. Sec. 951.
Child Support:	Combined Income Method. Guidelines found at 19-A M.R.S.A. Secs. 1653, 2001-2008.
Child Custody:	Best interest of the child considering: (1) child's age, (2) child's relationship with each party and other significant persons; (3) preference of child, if of suitable age and maturity; (4) duration and adequacy of child's current living arrangement, and desirability of maintaining continuity; (5) stability of proposed living arrangement; (6) motivation of the parties and their capacity to give love, affection and guidance; (7) child's adjustment to home, school and community; (8) each party's capacity to allow and encourage a relationship between the child and the other party; (9) each party's capacity to cooperate in child care; (10) the methods for assisting parental cooperation and resolving disputes, and each party's willingness to use those methods; (11) effect on the child if one party has sole authority regarding upbringing; (12) any history of domestic abuse; and (13) any other relevant factor. 19-A M.R.S.A. Sec. 1653.
Misc:	Either party may have name changed to any name. 19-A M.R.S.A. Sec. 1051. In uncontested divorce, testimony of corroborating witness in not required. 19-A M.R.S.A. Sec. 901.4.
Final Order:	JUDGMENT OF DIVORCE

UCCJA:	19-A M.R.S.A. Sec. 1701.	Domestic Violence:	19-A M.R.S.A. Sec. 4001.
IDO:	19 M.R.S.A. Sec. 954.	Annulment:	19-A M.R.S.A. Sec. 752.
Temporary Relief:	19-A M.R.S.A. Sec. 904.		

MARYLAND

The Law:	Annotated Code of Maryland, Family Law, Section 7-101 (A.C.M., Family Law Sec. 7-101). These volumes are arranged by subject. Be sure you have the volume marked "Family Law."
Case Style/Parties:	IN THE CIRCUIT COURT FOR _____ COUNTY, MARYLAND _____, Plaintiff, vs. _____, Defendant.
Complaint Title:	BILL FOR DIVORCE
Residency:	Residency of one party, but no time limit if grounds for divorce arose in Maryland. Otherwise, one party must be a resident for at least 1 year before filing. A.C.M., Family Law Sec. 7-101. If ground for divorce is insanity, limit is increased to 2 years. You will need a witness to verify the residency requirement.
Which Court:	In county where either party resides.
Grounds:	NO-FAULT: (1) "The parties have voluntarily lived separate and apart for 12 months without interruption or cohabitation and there is no reasonable expectation of reconciliation." (2) "The parties have lived separate and apart without cohabitation or interruption for 2 years." Both of these require actual living apart. A.C.M., Family Law Sec. 7-103-(a) (3) +(5). TRADITIONAL: (1) adultery; (2) deliberate and final desertion for 12 months with no chance for reconciliation; (3) confinement for incurable insanity of at least 3 years; (4) conviction of a felony or misdemeanor with at least a 3 year sentence or an indeterminate sentence, but only after 1 year has been served. (5) insanity if confined to a mental institution for 3 years, and it is determined by 2 physicians that the insanity is incurable and there is no hope of recovery. A.C.M., Family Law Sec. 7-103. LEGAL SEPARATION: Called "limited divorce," which may be temporary or permanent. Must make good faith effort to reconcile. (1) cruelty of treatment of spouse or child; (2) excessively vicious conduct toward spouse or child; (3) desertion; (4) voluntary separation if living apart without cohabitation and no reasonable expectation of reconciliation. A.C.M., Family Law Sec. 7-102.
Property:	Equitable distribution. Marital property does not include property (1) acquired before marriage; (2) acquired by gift or inheritance; (3) excluded by agreement, and (4) directly traceable to these sources marriage. Marital property divided considering following factors: (1) contributions of each party to the well-being of the family; (2) value of all property interests; (3) economic circumstances of each; (4) circumstances contributing to the divorce; (5) duration of the marriage; (6) ages of the parties; (7) physical and mental condition or the parties; (8) how and when property was acquired, and the efforts of each party to acquire the property; (9) the contribution by either party or nonmarital property to acquire real property as tenants by the entireties; (10) any award of alimony or use of marital home; (11) any other factor the judge considers proper. A.C.M., Family Law Secs. 8-201, 8-203 & 8-205.
Alimony:	Factors: (1) ability of the person seeking alimony to be self-supporting; (2) time needed to gain sufficient education and training; (3) standard of living established during the marriage; (4) duration of the marriage; (5) contributions of each to the well-being of the family; (6) circumstances contributing to the divorce; (7) age of the parties; (8) physical and mental condition of the parties; (9) ability of the payor to meet his or her own needs while paying alimony; (10) any agreement of the parties; (11) financial needs of the parties, including income and assets, property award, nature and amount of financial obligations, and rights to retirement benefits. Generally limited to rehabilitative period, but indefinite alimony may be awarded if (1) it is not reasonable to expect progress due to age, illness, infirmity or disability; or (2) after all progress has been made, the standard of living of the parties will be unconscionably disparate. A.C.M., Family Law Sec. 11-106.
Child Support:	Percentage of Income Method. Child support guidelines and table may be found in A.C.M., Family Law Secs. 12-201 and 12-204.
Child Custody:	No statutory factors, except abuse is mentioned in A.C.M., Family Law Sec. 9-101.
Misc:	Either party can have a former name restored. A.C.M., Family Law Sec. 7-105.
Final Order:	DECREE OF ABSOLUTE DIVORCE
UCCJA:	A.C.M., Family Law Sec. 9-201.
IDO:	A.C.M., Family Law Sec. 10-120.
Temporary Relief:	A.C.M., Family Law Secs. 11-102 (alimony) and 12-101 (child support).
Domestic Violence:	A.C.M., Family Law Sec. 4-501.
Annulment:	A.C.M., Family Law Sec. 8-201.

MASSACHUSETTS

The Law:	Annotated Laws of Massachusetts, Chapter 208, Section 1. (A.L.M., C.208 Sec. 1.)
Case Style/Parties:	COMMONWEALTH OF MASSACHUSETTS, PROBATE COURT

_____, Co-Petitioner, and _____, Co-Petitioner. [If no-fault with a settlement agreement]
_____, Petitioner, and _____, Respondent. [If no-fault without a settlement agreement]
_____, Plaintiff, vs. _____, Defendant. [If traditional ground of fault is alleged]

Complaint Title:	PETITION FOR DIVORCE [If no-fault grounds are used] COMPLAINT FOR DIVORCE [If traditional fault-based grounds are used] The petition or complaint must be accompanied by a statistical report form which may be obtained from the registrar of the probate court.
Residency:	One party must be a resident, with no time limit, if grounds for divorce arose in the State. A.L.M., C.208 Sec. 4. Otherwise, the party filing must be a resident for at least 1 year before filing. A.L.M., C.208 Sec. 5.
Which Court:	County in which the parties last lived together. If neither party resides in that county, then any county where either party resides. A.L.M., C. 208 Sec. 6.
Grounds:	NO-FAULT: "There has been an irretrievable breakdown of the marriage." A.L.M., C. 208 Sec. 1. TRADITIONAL: (1) adultery; (2) impotence; (3) desertion without support for 1 year; (4) alcoholism or drug abuse; (5) cruel and abusive treatment; (6) willful nonsupport; (7) imprisonment for over 5 years. A.L.M., C. 208 Secs. 1, 1A, 1B & 2. LEGAL SEPARATION: (1) failure to provide support without cause; (2) desertion; (3) spouse gave filing party cause to live apart. A.L.M., C. 209.
Property:	Equitable distribution. Factors: (1) length of marriage; (2) conduct of parties during the marriage; (3) age, health, station, occupation, amount and sources of income, vocational skills, employability, estate, liabilities and needs of each; (4) opportunity for future acquisition of capital assets and income; (5) present and future needs of dependent children; (6) contribution of each to acquisition, preservation or appreciation of the property. A.L.M. , C. 208 Secs. 1A & 34.
Alimony:	Same factors as for property. A.L.M., C. 208 Secs. 1A & 34.
Child Support:	Percentage of Income Method. No factors in statute. A.L.M. , C. 208 Sec. 28. Guidelines created by "chief justice for administration and management."
Child Custody:	No factors in statute; only general concepts including best interests of the child. A.L.M., C. 208 Sec. 31.
Misc:	Simplified procedure in no-fault cases: File (1) petition signed by both parties, (2) sworn affidavit that an irretrievable breakdown in the marriage exists, and (3) a notarized separation or settlement agreement signed by both parties. Judgment will be entered 6 months after the court hearing and the judge's approval of separation agreement. A.L.M., C. 208 Sec. 1A. If there is no signed separation agreement, the hearing will be held at least 6 months after filing, and the judgment will be entered if the court finds a continuing irretrievable breakdown of the marriage from the time of filing until the hearing. A.L.M., C. 208 Sec. 1B. For traditional fault-based grounds, some sample forms may be found in the Massachusetts Rules of Court, Appendix of Forms. Wife may have her maiden or former name restored. A.L.M., C. 208 Sec. 23.
Final Order:	JUDGMENT OF DIVORCE The judgment does not become final (or "absolute") until 90 days after it is entered, unless the judge orders a different time. This means there can be no remarriage until the judgment is final.
UCCJA:	A.L.M., C.209B Sec. 1.
IDO:	A.L.M., C.119A Sec. 12; and C. 273A Sec. 10.
Temporary Relief:	A.L.M., C.208 Secs. 17, 18, 19, 20, & 28A.
Domestic Violence:	A.L.M., C.209A Sec. 1.
Annulment:	A.L.M., C.207 Sec. 14.

MICHIGAN

The Law: Michigan Compiled Laws Annotated, Section 552.6 (M.C.L.A. Sec. 552.6). Ignore volume and chapter number and look for section numbers. (Note: Be careful not to use an out-dated set of books called Michigan Statut Annotated (abbreviated M.S.A.).)

Case Style/Parties: STATE OF MICHIGAN
_____JUDICIAL CIRCUIT, _____ COUNTY [Circuit number goes in first blank]

_____, Complainant, vs. _____, Defendant.

Complaint Title: COMPLAINT FOR DIVORCE

Residency: One party must be a resident of the state for 180 days, and of the county for 10 days, before filing. The 10 days in t county may be waived if: (1) the defendant was born in, or is a citizen of, a foreign country; and (2) the parties ha minor children; and (3) there is information which will allow the judge to reasonably conclude there is a danger the child being taken out of the United States by the defendant. M.C.L.A. Sec. 552.9. If the marriage breakdo occurred outside Michigan, one party must be a resident for 1 year , or it must be proven that the parties liv together as husband and wife within the state, before a judgment can be entered. M.C.L.A. Sec. 552.9e & f.

Which Court: County where either party has resided for 10 days before filing. M.C.L.A. Sec. 552.9.

Grounds: NO-FAULT: "There has been a breakdown of the marriage relationship to the extent that the objects of mat mony have been destroyed and there remains no reasonable likelihood that the marriage can be preserved." other explanation or details are allowed. M.C.L.A. Sec. 552.6. TRADITIONAL: None. LEGAL SEPARATIO Same as no-fault. Referred to as "separate maintenance." M.C.L.A. Sec. 552.7.

Property: Equitable distribution. Vested pension benefits accumulated during the marriage are marital assets. M.C.L Sec. 552.18 No specific criteria are listed in the statute; only that the property will be divided as the judge "sh deem just and reasonable." M.C.L.A. Secs. 552.19.

Alimony: Alimony may be awarded if "the estate and effects awarded . . . are insufficient for the suitable support and maint nance of either party and any children of the marriage as are committed to the care and custody of either party." T amount will be determined "as the court considers just and reasonable, after considering the ability of either to p and the character and situation of the parties, and all the other circumstances of the case." M.C.L.A. Sec. 552.23.

Child Support: Combined Income Method. Based on formula developed by the State Friend of the Court Bureau, and found in t *Michigan Child Support Formula Manual* (published by both West Publishing Company and Lawyers Cooperati Publishing); copies may be available at your local office of the Friend of the Court.M.C.L.A. Sec. 552.516. Child su port may be continued beyond the age of 18 if the child is regularly attending high school on a full-time basis, wi a reasonable expectation of graduating while residing with the custodial parent; but in no event beyond the age 19 years, 6 months. M.C.L.A. Sec. 552.16a.

Child Custody: Best interest of the child, considering the following factors: (1) love, affection and other emotional ties existi between the parties and the child; (2) the capacity and disposition of each to give love, affection, guidance a continuation of education and raising the child in its religion; (3) the capacity and disposition of each to provi food, clothing and medical care; (4) length of time the child has lived in a stable, satisfactory environment, a the desirability of maintaining continuity; (5) permanence as a family unit of the existing or proposed custodi home; (6) moral fitness of the parties; (7) mental and physical health of the parties and child; (8) home, sch and community record of the child; (9) preference of the child, if of suitable age; (10) willingness and ability the parties to facilitate and encourage a relationship between the child and the other parent; and (11) any oth relevant factor. M.C.L.A. Sec. 722.23. Joint custody may be considered. M.C.L.A. Sec. 722.26a.

Misc: Official mandatory forms may be available from the Circuit Court Clerk. These forms may also be found in t Michigan Supreme Court Administrative Office Forms Book (titled S.C.A.O. Forms), as well as in the previously me tioned book *How to File for Divorce in Michigan*. All cases will involve some interaction with the Friend of the Cou such as determining child support and custody, alimony, and property division questions; and later enforcement the support, custody, and visitation provisions of the judgment. For details of the operation and duties of the Frie of the Court, see M.C.L.A. beginning with Sec. 552.501.

Final Order: JUDGMENT OF DIVORCE
No hearing may be held until at least 60 days after filing; or 6 months if minor children are involved, unle hardship can be shown. M.C.L.A. Sec. 552.9f. The judgment must include the following provisions: (1) that bo parties must keep the Friend of the Court informed of the name and address of their current employer or oth source of income; (2) that both parties must keep the Friend of the court informed of "any health care covera that is available to him or her as a benefit of employment or that is maintained by him or her; the name of t insurance company, health care organization, or health maintenance organization; the policy, certificate, or co tract number; and the names and birth dates of the persons for whose benefit he or she maintains health ca coverage under the policy, certificate, or contract"; (3) a provision that "one or both parents shall obtain or mai tain any health care coverage that is available to them at a reasonable cost, as a benefit of employment, for t benefit of the minor children of the parties"; and (4) that income withholding shall take effect immediately.

UCCJA: M.C.L.A. Sec. 600.651.
IDO: M.C.L.A. Sec. 552.604.
Temporary Relief: M.C.L.A. Secs. 552.13, 552.14 & 552.15.
Domestic Violence: M.C.L.A. Sec. 600.2950.
Annulment: M.C.L.A. Secs. 552.3 and 552.35 to 552.39.

MINNESOTA

The Law:	Minnesota Statutes Annotated, Section 518.002 (M.S.A. Sec. 518.002).
Case Style/Parties:	STATE OF MINNESOTA DISTRICT COURT, COUNTY OF _____, _____ JUDICIAL DISTRICT In re the Marriage of _____, Co-Petitioner, and _____, Co-Petitioner. [Joint, simplified procedure] In re the Marriage of _____, Petitioner, and _____, Respondent. [Standard procedure]
Complaint Title:	PETITION FOR DISSOLUTION OF MARRIAGE Petition must include: (1) name, address, and social security number of petitioner, and any prior or other names used; (2) name, address, and social security number of respondent and any prior or other names used, if known; (3) place and date of marriage; (4) a statement that the 180 residency requirement has been met; (5) each child's name and any prior name, age, date of birth, and social security number and expected delivery date if the wife is pregnant; (6) whether a separate proceeding for dissolution, legal separation or custody is pending in any state; (7) grounds for dissolution; and (8) any request for temporary or permanent alimony, child support, child custody, property division, attorney's fees, or costs, without stating amounts. M.S.A. Sec. 518.10. See M.S.A. Sec. 518.091 for required language regarding automatic restraining order which must be in the summons. Respondent has 30 days to file an answer. M.S.A. Sec. 518.12.
Residency:	One party must be a resident for at least 180 days before filing. M.S.A. Sec. 518.07.
Which Court:	File in county where either party resides. M.S.A. Sec. 518.09.
Grounds:	NO-FAULT: "There has been an irretrievable breakdown in the marriage relationship." One of the following will have to exist: (1) serious marital discord adversely affecting the attitude of one or both of the spouses toward the marriage, or (2) the parties have been living separate and apart for 180 days before filing. M.S.A. Secs. 518.06 and 518.10. TRADITIONAL: None. LEGAL SEPARATION: The parties "need a legal separation." M.S.A. Secs. 518.06 & 518.10.
Property:	Equitable distribution. Fault not considered. Nonmarital property is property: (1) acquired before marriage; (2) acquired by gift or inheritance; (3) acquired in exchange for or increase in value of nonmarital property; (4) acquired after the valuation date (date of the prehearing settlement conference); or (5) designated in prenuptial agreement M.S.A. Sec. 518.54 subd. 5. Factors for dividing marital property: (1) length of marriage; (2) prior marriages; (3) each party's age, health, station, occupation, amount and sources of income, vocational skills, employability, estate, liabilities, and needs; (4) each party's opportunity for future acquisition of capital assets; (5) each party's income; and (6) each party's contribution to acquisition, preservation, depreciation or appreciation of assets. There is a conclusive presumption the that both parties contributed substantially to the acquisition of property and income during the time they lived together as husband and wife. M.S.A. Sec. 518.58.
Alimony:	Called "maintenance." Fault not considered. Either party may be awarded if he or she: (1) lacks sufficient property to meet own needs; or (2) is unable to be self-supporting through employment, or is not required to seek employment due to responsibilities as child custodian. Amount and duration of alimony determined by: (1) financial resources of party seeking alimony; (2) time needed for education and training to find appropriate employment; (3) standard of living established during the marriage; (4) duration of the marriage, and, for a homemaker, the length of absence from employment and the extent education, skills or experience have become outmoded and earning capacity permanently diminished; (5) any loss of earnings, seniority, retirement benefits, or other employment opportunities foregone; (6) age, physical and emotional condition of the party seeking alimony; (7) ability of the other party to meet own needs while paying alimony; and (8) either party's contribution to acquisition, preservation, depreciation, or appreciation of marital property, and in furtherance of the other's employment or business. M.S.A. Sec. 518.552.
Child Support:	Percentage of Income Method. Child support guidelines may be found in M.S.A. Sec. 518.551. Also see M.S.A. Sec. 518.57.
Child Custody:	Factors: (1) wishes of the parties; (2) preference of the child, if of sufficient age; (3) child's primary caretaker; (4) intimacy of the relationship between child and each party; (5) interaction and interrelationship between child and the parties, siblings, and other significant persons; (6) child's adjustment to home, school and community; (7) length of time in a stable, satisfactory environment, and desirability of maintaining continuity; (8) permanence, as a family unit, of the existing or proposed home; (9) mental and physical health of all persons involved; (10) each party's capacity and disposition to give love, affection, and guidance, and to continue educating and raising the child in the child's culture and religion, if any; (11) child's cultural background; (12) effect of any domestic violence on the child; and (13) any other relevant factor. Also includes additional considerations where joint custody is requested. M.S.A. Sec. 518.17. See M.S.A. Sec. 518.179 for list of criminal acts which prohibit custody.
Misc:	A "summary dissolution" procedure is available if: (1) there are no minor children; (2) the wife is not pregnant; (3) the parties have been married less than 8 years; (4) there is no real estate; (5) total debts are less than $8,000, not including auto loans; (6) total marital assets are not more than $25,000; (7) neither party has nonmarital assets totalling more than $25,000: and (8) there is no domestic abuse. Forms are available from the court clerk. M.S.A. Sec. 518.195. No hearing is required if: (1) there are no children, (2) the parties have a written agreement or the respondent fails to answer; or (1) there are children, (2) the parties have a written agreement, and (3) both parties have an attorney. M.S.A. Sec. 518.13, Sub. 5. Either party can change name to any name. M.S.A. Sec. 518.27. A party's occupational license and driver's license may be suspended for non-payment of child support. (M.S.A. Sec. 518.551, Sub. 12 and Sub. 13.)
Final Order:	DECREE OF DISSOLUTION OF MARRIAGE Decree must include provisions for health insurance (M.S.A. Sec. 518.171); the Social Security number, date of birth, and name and address of the employer of the party paying child support (M.S.A. Sec. 518.613, Sub. 2); and certain custody provisions (M.S.A. Sec. 518.17, Sub. 3b).

UCCJA:	M.S.A. Sec. 518A.01.	Domestic Violence:	M.S.A. Sec. 518B.01.
IDO:	M.S.A. Sec. 518.6111.	Annulment:	M.S.A. Sec. 518.03.
Temporary Relief:	M.S.A. Secs. 518.131; 518.185; and 518.62.		

MISSISSIPPI

The Law:	Mississippi Code 1972 Annotated, Section 93-5-1 (M.C. Sec. 93-5-1).

Case Style/Parties: CHANCERY COURT OF _____ COUNTY, STATE OF MISSISSIPPI

_____, Complainant, vs. _____, Defendant.

Complaint Title: BILL OF COMPLAINT FOR DIVORCE
Only allege the statutory grounds; not any detailed facts to show the grounds. M.C. Sec. 93-5-7. If not using the grounds of irreconcilable differences, complaint must be filed along with an affidavit stating that the complaint is not being filed in collusion with defendant for the purpose of obtaining a divorce, but that the cause or causes of divorce are true as stated. M.C. Sec. 93-5-7.

Residency: One party must have been a resident for at least 6 months before filing, and not have moved to Mississippi for reason of obtaining a divorce. M.C. Sec. 93-5-5.

Which Court: NO-FAULT: (1) If both parties are residents, in the county of either party. (2) If defendant is not a resident, in the county where the complainant resides. TRADITIONAL: (1) If the defendant is a resident, in the county where the defendant resides, or where the parties last lived together. (2) If the defendant is not a resident, in the county where the complainant resides. M.C. Sec. 93-5-11.

Grounds: NO-FAULT: "The parties have irreconcilable differences." No divorce will be granted unless the parties have a written agreement on property, custody, support and alimony; or sign a consent to allow the court to determine these matters. Both parties must agree that there are irreconcilable differences, therefore it may be a good idea to allege one of the traditional grounds (if one applies) as well as irreconcilable differences (just in case your spouse won't agree). M.C. Secs. 93-5-2.
TRADITIONAL: (1) impotence; (2) adultery; (3) imprisonment; (4) willful desertion for at least 1 year; (5) alcoholism or drug addiction; (6) habitual cruel and inhuman treatment; (7) insanity of the defendant at the time of marriage, but only if the complainant did not know of the insanity; (8) bigamy; (9) the wife is pregnant by another at the time of the marriage without husband's consent; (10) incest; and (11) confinement for incurable insanity for 3 years. M.C. Secs. 93-5-1 & 93-5-7.
LEGAL SEPARATION: None. M.C. Sec. 93-5-23.

Property: There are no statutory provisions for property division, which leaves the matter up to the judge interpreting prior appellate court decisions. These are mostly based on the concept of "title," in which each party keeps what is titled in his or her name. Jointly titled property will be divided by the judge. This system has a history of favoring the husband. Recently, judges have offset an otherwise unfair result by liberally awarding lump-sum alimony, or by considering the wife's contributions to acquiring the property.

Alimony: There are no statutory factors. Either party may be awarded alimony. Fault not considered.
See M.C. Sec. 93-5-23.

Child Support: Percentage of Income Method. There are no statutory factors. Generally, child support amount is determined by the relative and proportionate incomes and abilities of the parties.
M.C. Secs. 93-5-23, 93-11-64 & 93-11-65.

Child Custody: No statutory factors. Child may choose if at least age 12. There is a presumption in favor of joint custody, both physical and decision making. The judge may require a custody plan from the parties.
M.C. Secs. 93-3-23 & 93-5-24.

Final Order: DECREE OF DIVORCE
Hearing may not be set until at least 60 days after filing.

UCCJA:	M.C. Sec. 93-23-1.
IDO:	M.C. Sec. 93-12-1.
Temporary Relief:	None in statute.
Domestic Violence:	M.C. Sec. 93-21-1.
Annulment:	M.C. Sec. 93-7-1.

MISSOURI

The Law: Vernon's Annotated Missouri Statutes, Chapter 452, Section 452.300 (A.M.S. Sec. 452.300).

Case Style/Parties: IN THE CIRCUIT COURT OF _____ COUNTY, MISSOURI

In re the Marriage of _____, Co-Petitioner, and _____, Co-Petitioner. [If Petition filed jointly]
In re the Marriage of _____, Petitioner, and _____, Respondent. [If no joint Petition]

Complaint Title: PETITION FOR DISSOLUTION OF MARRIAGE
Petition must include: (1) grounds for divorce; (2) residence of each party and length of residence; (3) date of marriage and place registered; (4) date of separation; (5) each child's name, age and address, and who child has primarily lived with for past 60 days; (6) whether the wife is pregnant; (7) any agreements as to custody, child support, or alimony; (8) each party's social security number and employer's name and address, if known; and (8) relief sought. A.M.S. Secs. 452.310 & 452.312. Respondent's answer is due 30 days after service. A.M.S. Sec. 452.310.

Residency: One party must be a resident for at least 90 days before filing. A.M.S. Sec. 452.305.

Which Court: County where either party resides. A.M.S. Sec. 452.300.

Grounds: NO-FAULT: "The marriage of the parties is irretrievably broken, and there remains no reasonable likelihood that the marriage can be preserved." (But see "Misc." section below). A.M.S. Sec. 452.305 and .310.
TRADITIONAL: None.
LEGAL SEPARATION: "The marriage is not irretrievably broken and there remains a likelihood that the marriage can be preserved." A.M.S. Sec. 452.305.

Property: Equitable distribution. Nonmarital property is property: (1) acquired before marriage; (2) acquired by gift or inheritance; (3) acquired in exchange for (1) or (2); (4) acquired after a decree of legal separation; (5) designated by agreement; or (6) increased in value, except due to marital labor or assets. Factors for dividing marital property: (1) economic circumstances of the parties, including whether custodian should remain in marital home; (2) each party's contribution to acquisition of property; (3) value of nonmarital property; (4) each party's conduct during marriage; (5) custody arrangements; and (6) any other relevant factor. A.M.S. Sec. 452.330.

Alimony: Called "maintenance." Either party may be awarded if he or she: (1) lacks sufficient property to meet own needs; and (2) is unable to be self-supporting through appropriate employment. Amount and duration determined by: (1) financial resources of party seeking alimony; (2) time needed for education and training to obtain appropriate employment; (3) parties' comparative earning capacities; (4) standard of living established during marriage; (5) each party's obligations and assets; (6) duration of marriage; (7) age, physical and emotional condition of party seeking alimony; (8) ability of other party to meet own expenses while paying alimony; (9) each party's conduct during the marriage; and (10) any other relevant factor. Decree must state whether alimony may be modified. A.M.S. Sec. 452.335.

Child Support: Combined Income Method. Factors: (1) financial needs and resources of child; (2) financial resources and needs of the parties; (3) standard of living child would have had if no divorce; (4) child's physical and emotional condition, and educational needs; (5) child's physical and legal custody arrangement, including time spent with each parent and reasonable expenses associated with the custody and visitation arrangement; and (6) reasonable work-related child care expenses of each parent. A.M.S. Sec. 452.340. Check with court clerk for published guidelines. Custody prohibited to party convicted of abuse. A.M.S. Sec. 452.340.

Child Custody: Best interest of the child considering: (1) wishes of the parties; (2) wishes of the child; (3) interaction and interrelationship between child and parties, siblings, and other significant persons; (4) child's adjustment to home, school and community; (5) mental and physical health, and any abuse history, of all persons involved; (6) child's needs for continuing relationship with both parties, and the ability and willingness of each to actively perform their duties as mother and father for the needs of the child; (7) any intention of either party to relocate outside the state; (8) which party is more likely to allow frequent and meaningful contact between the child and the other party; and (9) any other relevant factor. A.M.S. Sec. 452.375. Must submit parenting plan within 30 days after respondent is served. A.M.S. Sec. 452.310.

Misc: The court clerk in some counties has forms available. Name change requires publication in newspaper. See A.M.S. Sec. 527.270 & 290. If respondent denies the marriage is irretrievably broken, the petitioner must prove one of the following: (1) adultery; (2) respondent behaved in such a way that the petitioner cannot reasonably be expected to live with the respondent; (3) abandonment for a continuous period of 6 months; (4) the parties have lived separate and apart by mutual consent for a continuous period of 12 months; or (5) the parties have lived separate and apart for a continuous period of 24 months. Judge may also order counselling. A.M.S. Sec. 452.320.

Final Order: DECREE OF DISSOLUTION OF MARRIAGE
Judgment may not be entered for 30 days. A.M.S. Sec. 452.305.
Must include provision for health insurance (A.M.S. Sec. 452.353), and contain parties' social security numbers (A.M.S. Sec. 452.312 and .305).

UCCJA: A.M.S. Sec. 452.440.
IDO: A.M.S. Secs. 452.350.
Temporary Relief: A.M.S. Secs. 452.315 and 452.380.
Domestic Violence: A.M.S. Sec. 455.010.
Annulment: A.M.S. Sec. 451.020.

MONTANA

The Law:	Montana Code Annotated, Title 40, Chapter 4, Section 40-4-101 (M.C.A. Sec. 40-4-101).

Case Style/Parties: DISTRICT COURT FOR THE STATE OF MONTANA AND FOR THE COUNTY OF _____

In re the Marriage of _____, Co-Petitioner, and _____, Co-Petitioner. [If joint Petition]
In re the marriage of _____, Petitioner, and _____, Respondent. [If standard Petition]

Complaint Title: PETITION FOR DISSOLUTION OF MARRIAGE
Petition must include: (1) grounds for divorce; (2) age, occupation, residence, and length of residence of both parties; (3) date of marriage and place registered; (4) that the residency requirements of M.C.A. Sec. 40-4-104 exist, and the grounds for dissolution; (5) each child's name, age and address, and a statement as to whether the wife is pregnant; (6) any agreements as to child support, custody, visitation, and alimony; and (7) relief sought. M.C.A. Sec. 40-4-105(1). Respondent's answer is called a "response," which is due within 20 days after respondent is served. M.C.A. Sec. 40-4-103.

Residency: One party must be domiciled in the state and county for 90 days. M.C.A. Sec. 40-4-104.

Grounds: NO-FAULT: (1) "There has been an irretrievable breakdown of the marriage due to serious marital discord which adversely affects the attitude of both spouses towards the marriage, and there is no reasonable prospect of reconciliation"; or (2) "There has been an irretrievable breakdown of the marriage and the parties have been living separate and apart for 180 days." M.C.A. Secs. 40-1-104 & 40-4-105. TRADITIONAL: None. LEGAL SEPARATION: Same as no-fault. M.C.A. Sec. 40-104.

Property: Equitable distribution. All property is marital property. Factors: (1) duration of the marriage, and any prior marriages; (2) each party's age, health, station, occupation, amount and sources of income, vocational skills, employability, estate, liabilities, and needs; (3) child custody provisions; (4) whether property division is in lieu of or in addition to alimony; (5) each party's opportunity for future acquisition of capital assets and income; and (6) each party's contribution to or dissipation of the value of property. If property was acquired prior to marriage, by gift or inheritance, in exchange for such property, or increased value of such property, or acquired after a decree of legal separation, the following factors are considered: (1) any nonmonitary contributions of a homemaker; (2) the extent such contribution facilitated maintenance of the property; and (3) whether property division is an alternative to alimony. M.C.A. Sec. 40-4-202.

Alimony: Called "maintenance." Fault not considered. Either party may be awarded alimony if he or she: (1) lacks sufficient property to meet own needs; and (2) is unable to be self-supporting through appropriate employment. Amount and duration determined by: (1) financial resources of the party seeking alimony; (2) time needed for education and training to obtain appropriate employment; (3) standard of living established during marriage; (4) duration of the marriage; (5) age, physical and emotional condition of the party seeking alimony; and (6) the other party's ability to meet own expenses while paying alimony. M.C.A. Sec. 40-4-203.

Child Support: Combined Income Method. Factors: (1) financial resources of child; (2) financial resources of custodial parent; (3) standard of living child would have had in absence of divorce; (4) child's physical and emotional condition, and educational and medical needs; (5) financial resources and needs of noncustodial parent; (6) age of the child; (7) cost of day care; (8) custody arrangements; and (9) needs of any other person either party is legally obligated to support. M.C.A. Sec. 40-4-204. Check with court clerk or library for uniform guidelines required by M.S.A. Sec. 40-5-209.

Child Custody: Factors: (1) parties' wishes; (2) child's wishes; (3) interaction and interrelationship between child and parties, siblings, and other significant persons; (4) child's adjustment to home, school and community; (5) mental and physical condition of all persons involved; (6) any physical abuse, or threat of physical abuse, against a party or the child; (7) any chemical dependency or abuse of either party; and (8) any other relevant factor. M.C.A. Secs. 40-4-212. Joint custody may be granted, but parties will be required to submit custody plan. M.C.A. Sec. 40-4-223.

Misc: Wife's former or maiden name may be restored. M.C.A. Sec. 40-4-108(4).

Summary Procedure: A summary procedure is available if the following conditions are met: (1) the residency requirements of M.C.A. Sec. 40-4-104 are met; (2) irreconcilable differences caused the breakdown of the marriage and both parties agree to dissolution; (3) the wife is not pregnant and either there are no children or all custody and child support issues have been resolved; (4) neither party has any interest in real property (this does not include a party's leased residence as long as there is no option to purchase and the lease terminates within 1 year of filing the petition); (5) there are no unpaid, unsecured debts in excess of $8,000; (6) total assets, excluding secured obligations, are less than $25,000; (7) the parties have a written settlement agreement, and have executed all titles or other papers to transfer ownership; (8) both parties waive alimony; (9) both parties waive their right to appeal and to request a new trial; (10) both parties have read and understand a brochure on the summary dissolution procedure which is available from the court clerk; and (11) both parties desire a dissolution. M.C.A. Sec. 40-4-130. Petition must include: (1) signature of both parties under oath; (2) a statement that the requirements of M.C.A. Sec. 40-4-130 have been met; (3) each party's mailing address; and (4) whether the wife's former or maiden name is to be restored. M.C.A. Sec. 40-4-131. Both parties must appear for the final hearing. M.C.A. Sec. 40-4-133. For more details see M.C.A. Secs. 40-4-130 through 40-4-136, or ask court clerk.

Final Order: DECREE OF DISSOLUTION OF MARRIAGE
Decree may not be entered until 20 days after respondent is served. M.C.A. Sec. 40-4-105(3).
For required child support provisions, see M.C.A. Sec. 40-4-204(6) - (8).
See disclosure requirements of M.C.A. Secs. 40-4-251, 40-4-252, and 40-4-253.

UCCJA:	M.C.A. Sec. 40-7-101.	Domestic Violence:	M.C.A. Sec. 46-6-602.
IDO:	M.C.A. Secs. 40-5-301 and 40-5-401.	Annulment:	M.C.A. Sec. 40-1-401.
Temporary Relief:	M.C.A. Secs. 40-4-121; 40-4-204(4)(c); and 40-4-213.		

NEBRASKA

The Law:	Revised Statutes of Nebraska, Chapter 42, Article 3, Section 42-301 (R.S.N. Sec. 42-301). Supplements are in a separate soft-cover volume.
Case Style/Parties:	IN THE DISTRICT COURT FOR _____ COUNTY, NEBRASKA

_____, Co-Petitioner, and _____, Co-Petitioner. [If joint Petition]
_____, Petitioner, vs. _____, Respondent. [If standard Petition]

Complaint Title: PETITION FOR DISSOLUTION OF MARRIAGE
Petition must be in the form required by the state supreme court, and must include: (1) name and address of petitioner; (2) name and address of respondent, if known; (3) date and place of marriage; (4) each child's name and date of birth; (5) if the petitioner is a party in another action for divorce, separation or dissolution, where that action is pending (court, county and case number); (6) grounds for divorce; and (7) relief sought. R.S.N. Sec. 42-353. Respondent has 30 days after service to file an answer. R.S.N. Sec. 42-354.

Residency: Either: (1) One party must be a resident for 1 year; or (2) no time limit if the parties were married in Nebraska, and one party has lived in Nebraska for the entire time the parties were married. R.S.N. Sec. 42-349.

Which Court: County where either party resides.

Grounds: NO-FAULT: "The marriage of the parties is irretrievably broken." R.S.N. Secs. 42-347 & 42-353.
TRADITIONAL: One party lacked the capacity to consent to marriage, including due to alcohol or drugs. R.S.N. Sec. 42-362.
LEGAL SEPARATION: Same as no-fault, except no residency requirement is specified. R.S.N. Sec. 42-350.

Property: Equitable distribution. All property is marital, although fact that property was acquired before marriage, or by gift or inheritance, is considered as part of the circumstances of the parties. Case of Lord v. Lord, 213 Neb. 557, 330 N.W.2d 492 (1983). Factors: (1) circumstances of the parties; (2) duration of the marriage; (3) each party's contributions to the marriage, including the care and education of the children and any interruption of personal careers or educational opportunities; and (4) the ability of the party seeking alimony to engage in gainful employment without interfering with the interests of a child in that party's custody. R.S.N. Sec. 42-365.

Alimony: Fault not considered. Factors: (1) circumstances of the parties; (2) duration of the marriage; (3) each party's contributions to the marriage, including the care and education of the children and any interruption of personal careers or educational opportunities; and (4) the ability of the party seeking alimony to engage in gainful employment without interfering with the interests of a child in that party's custody. R.S.N. Sec. 42-365.

Child Support: Combined Income Method. Supreme Court child support guidelines are available from the court clerk. R.S.N. Sec. 42-364.

Child Custody: Best interest of the child considering: (1) the relationship of the child and each party; (2) reasonable desires of the child; and (3) the general health, welfare, and social behavior of the child. R.S.N. Sec. 42-364. Shared or joint custody is possible if both parties agree and a hearing shows it is in the best interest of the child. R.S.N. Sec. 42-364(3).

Misc: Either spouse may request restoration of former name. Decree must include both names. R.S.N. Sec. 42-380. No hearing may be held until at least 60 days after respondent is served.

Final Order: DECREE OF DISSOLUTION OF MARRIAGE
See R.S.N. Sec. 42-369 for required provisions.
Decree is final after 6 months. R.S.N. Sec. 42-372.

UCCJA:	R.S.N. Sec. 43-1201.
IDO:	R.S.N. Secs. 42-358(2); 42-364.01; 42-367; and 43-1701.
Temporary Relief:	R.S.N. Sec. 42-357.
Domestic Violence:	R.S.N. Sec. 42-901.
Annulment:	R.S.N. Sec. 42-373.

NEVADA

The Law:	Nevada Revised Statutes Annotated, Chapter 125, Section 125.010 (N.R.S.A. Sec. 125.010).
Case Style/Parties:	IN THE DISTRICT COURT FOR _____ COUNTY, NEVADA _____, Plaintiff, vs. _____, Defendant.
Complaint Title:	COMPLAINT FOR DIVORCE Grounds for divorce should be stated only in the statutory language, with no details of facts. N.R.S.A. Sec. 125.030.
Residency:	One party must be a resident for 6 weeks. No time limit if both parties were domiciled in the state when the grounds for divorce occurred. N.R.S.A. Sec. 125.020.
Which Court:	(1) County where either spouse resides; (2) County where the parties last lived together; or (3) County where the grounds for divorce occurred. N.R.S.A. Sec. 125.020.
Grounds:	NO-FAULT: (1) "The parties are incompatible." (2) "The parties have been living separate and apart without cohabitation for 1 year." N.R.S.A. Sec. 125.010. TRADITIONAL: Insanity existing for at least 2 years before filing. N.R.S.A. Sec. 125.010. LEGAL SEPARATION: Same as for no-fault and traditional, plus desertion for over 90 days. Parties may also agree to separation and make arrangement for support. See N.R.S.A. Sec. 125.190.
Property:	Community property. Separate property is property: (1) acquired before marriage; (2) acquired by gift or inheritance; (3) income or profits from (1) and (2); (4) designated separate by written agreement; (5) acquired after a decree of separate maintenance; and (6) acquired as personal injury damages. Community property to be divided equally, unless the judge "finds a compelling reason" for unequal division and sets forth the reasons in writing. N.R.S.A. Sec. 125.150.
Alimony:	Fault not considered. May be granted to either party "...as appears just and equitable." Alimony for training or education may be awarded upon consideration of: (1) whether the party to pay alimony has obtained greater job skills or education during the marriage; and (2) whether the party seeking alimony provided financial support while the other party obtained job skills or education. If ordered, the decree must state the time within which the training or education must begin. N.R.S.A. Sec. 125.150.
Child Support:	Percentage of Income Method. Based upon following percentage of gross income: 18% for 1 child; 25% for 2 children; 29% for 3 children; 31% for 4 children; and an additional 2% for each additional child. Minimum support of $100 per month per child, unless the judge finds the payor is unable to pay that amount; maximum of $500 per child. Any deviation from these percentages, even where the parties agree, must be explained in the decree, by considering: (1) extraordinary needs of the child are not being met; (2) cost of health insurance; (3) cost of child care; (4) special educational needs; (5) age of the child; (6) the parties' other support obligations; (7) value of services contributed by either party; (8) any public assistance paid to support the child; (9) expenses reasonably related to pregnancy and confinement; (10) cost of transportation for visitation if the custodial party moved from the jurisdiction of the court; (11) amount of time child spends with each party; (12) other necessary expenses for the child's benefit; and (13) the parties' relative incomes. N.R.S.A. Secs. 125B.070 and 125B.080.
Child Custody:	Best interest of the child considering: (1) which party is more likely to allow frequent association and a continuing relationship with the other party; (2) wishes of the child, if of sufficient age and intelligence; (3) "any nomination by a parent of a guardian for the child"; and (4) whether either party has engaged in an act of domestic violence against the child, the other party, or other person residing with the child. Preference is for joint custody. If the parties request joint custody, and it is not ordered, the decree must state reasons. N.R.S.A. Sec. 125.480. See N.R.S.A. Sec. 125.510 for required language in decree relating to custody.
Misc:	Wife's former name may be restored. N.R.S.A. Sec. 125.130. No hearing needed if the parties file a stipulation which: (1) is signed by both parties before the court clerk; (2) states that residency requirements are met; (3) states the grounds for divorce; (4) resolves all issues; and (5) is accompanied by the affidavit of a witness verifying the required residency of one of the parties. N.R.S.A. Sec. 125.127. For default cases, see N.R.S.A. Sec. 125.123 for affidavit requirements.
Summary Procedure:	A summary procedure under N.R.S.A. Secs. 125.181 through 125.184, may be used if: (1) residency requirements are met; (2) grounds for divorce exist; (3) there are no minor children and the wife is not pregnant, or the parties have a written agreement as to custody and support; (4) there is no community or jointly owned property, or the parties have a written agreement to divide such property and have executed all deeds, bills of sale or other transfer documents; (5) the parties waive alimony, or have a written agreement as to alimony; and (6) the parties waive their rights to written notice of decree of divorce, appeal, request for findings of fact and conclusions of law, and to move for a new trial. N.R.S.A. Sec. 125.181. The petition must be signed by both parties under oath, and must include: (1) facts showing residency requirement has been met; (2) grounds for divorce; (3) date and place of marriage; (4) mailing address of both parties; (5) a statement as to whether there are minor children and whether the wife is pregnant; and (6) whether the wife wants her former name restored, and the name. Any settlement agreement must be attached to the petition, and you will also need to file an affidavit of a witness verifying residency. N.R.S.A. Sec. 125.182.
Final Order:	DECREE OF DIVORCE

UCCJA:	N.R.S.A. Sec. 125A.010.	Domestic Violence:	N.R.S.A. Sec. 33.018.
IDO:	N.R.S.A. Sec. 31A.010.	Annulment:	N.R.S.A. Sec. 125.290.
Temporary Relief:	N.R.S.A. Secs. 125.040; 125.050; 125.200; 125.470; 125.510.		

NEW HAMPSHIRE

The Law:	New Hampshire Revised Statutes Annotated 1992, Chapter 458, Section 458:4 (N.H.R.S.A. Sec. 459:4). Ignore "Title" numbers.
Case Style/Parties:	THE STATE OF NEW HAMPSHIRE, SUPERIOR COURT IN AND FOR _____ COUNTY
	_____, Petitioner, vs. _____, Respondent.
Complaint Title:	PETITION FOR DIVORCE Just state statutory grounds for divorce, without detailed facts, unless custody is an issue and the facts are relevant to show a detriment to the child. N.H.R.S.A. Sec. 458:7-a.
Residency:	Either: (1) Both parties are domiciled at time of filing; (2) petitioner is domiciled in the state and the respondent is personally served in the state; (3) petitioner is domiciled in the state for 1 year; or (4) the cause of the divorce arose in New Hampshire when the petitioner was domiciled there. N.H.R.S.A. Secs. 458:5 and 458:6.
Which Court:	County where either party resides.
Grounds:	NO-FAULT: "There are irreconcilable differences which have caused the irremediable breakdown of the marriage." N.H.R.S.A. Sec. 458:7-a. TRADITIONAL: (1) Impotency; (2) adultery; (3) extreme cruelty; (4) conviction of a felony and imprisoned for more than 1 year; (5) treatment "as seriously to injure health or endanger person"; (6) absence for 2 years and "has not been heard of"; (7) habitual drunkenness for 2 years; (8) the other party "has joined any religious sect or society which professes to believe the relationship of husband and wife unlawful, and has refused to cohabit" for 6 months; (9) abandonment and refusal to cohabit for 2 years without sufficient cause or consent of the other; (10) husband absent willingly for 2 years without making suitable provisions for the spouse's support; (11) wife of a citizen being willingly absent for 2 years without consent; (12) wife of a citizen has gone to reside outside the state and remained absent and separate for 10 years without consent; (13) wife is a resident for 2 years and husband has left the U.S. with the intention of becoming a foreign citizen and has not come to claim his marital rights and has not made suitable provisions for wife's support. N.H. R.S.A. Secs. 458:7. LEGAL SEPARATION: Same as no-fault and traditional. N.H.R.S.A. Sec. 458:26.
Property:	Equitable distribution. Fault is a factor. Separate property is property acquired (1) before marriage or in exchange for such property; and (2) by gift or inheritance. Equal division of marital property, unless inequal division is justified considering: (1) duration of the marriage; (2) age, health, social or economic status, occupation, vocational skills, employability, separate property, amount and sources of income, needs and liabilities of the parties; (3) each party's opportunity for future acquisition of capital assets and income; (4) ability of custodial parent to engage in gainful employment without substantially interfering with the interests of the child; (5) custodial parent's need to remain in the marital home; (6) action during the marriage which contributed to the growth or diminution in value of any property; (7) any significant disparity between the parties in relation to contribution to the marriage; (8) any contribution to help educate or develop the career or employability of the other, and any interruption in one party's education or career opportunities for the benefit of the other's career, the marriage, or the children; (9) any expectation of pension or retirement rights acquired prior to or during the marriage; (10) tax consequences; (12) either party's fault for the breakdown of the marriage if fault was the cause and either (a) it caused substantial physical or mental pain and suffering, or (b) it resulted in substantial economic loss to the marital estate or to the injured party; (13) value of each parties' separate property; and (14) any other relevant factor. If division is not equal, the reasons must be stated in the decree. N.H.R.S.A. Sec. 458:19. See N.H.R.S.A. Sec. 458:7 for fault.
Alimony:	Either party may be awarded if that party: (1) lacks income or property to maintain a standard of living similar to that during the marriage; and (2) is unable to support self through employment, or has child custody duties making it inadvisable to be employed; and (3) the party to pay has the ability to pay and meet his or her own needs. Amount and duration of alimony to be determined considering: (1) length of marriage; (2) age, health, social or economic status, occupation, amount and sources of income, property awarded, vocational skills, employability, estate, liabilities, and needs of each party; (3) each party's opportunity for future acquisition of capital assets and income; (4) fault; (5) federal tax consequences; (6) each party's contribution to the acquisition, preservation or appreciation in value of assets and to the family unit. The decree must state the reasons for granting or denying alimony. N.H.R.S.A. Sec. 458:193.
Child Support:	Combined Income Method. Child support guidelines may be found in N.H.R.S.A. Sec. 458-C:1-7. Needs based on a percentage of the parties' combined net income as follows: 25% for 1 child; 33% for 2 children; 40% for 3 children; and 45% for 4 or more children. Each party responsible for a pro rata share of these needs according to income. N.H.R.S.A. Sec. 458-C:3. For criteria allowing departure from these figures see N.H.R.S.A. Sec. 458-C:5.
Child Custody:	Joint legal custody is presumed in the child's best interest, unless abuse is shown. Decree must state reasons if joint legal custody is not ordered. Factors: (1) preference of the child; (2) any domestic violence. N.H.R.S.A. Secs. 458:17.
Misc:	Wife's former or maiden name may be restored, even if not requested in petition. N.H.R.S.A. Sec. 458:24. Counselling may be ordered by the court (N.H.R.S.A. Sec. 458:7-b) or upon the request of both parties (N.H.R.S.A. Sec. 458:15-a).
Final Order:	DECREE OF DIVORCE Must include health care provision. N.H.R.S.A. Sec. 458:17, IX. If alimony is ordered, must include provision requiring each party to provide the Division of Human Services with social security number. N.H.R.S.A. Sec. 458:36.

UCCJA:	N.H.R.S.A. Sec. 458-A:1.	Domestic Violence:	N.H.R.S.A. Sec. 173-B:1.
IDO:	N.H.R.S.A. Sec. 458-B:l.	Annulment:	N.H.R.S.A. Sec. 458:1-3.
Temporary Relief:	N.H.R.S.A. Secs. 458:16 and 458:16-b.		

NEW JERSEY

The Law:	NJSA (for New Jersey Statutes Annotated), Title 2A: Chapter 34, Section 2A:34-2 (N.J.S.A. Sec. 2A: 34-2). Ignore the "article" numbers.
Case Style/Parties:	SUPERIOR COURT OF NEW JERSEY, CHANCERY DIVISION, FAMILY PART, _____ COUNTY _____, Plaintiff, vs. _____, Defendant.
Complaint Title:	COMPLAINT FOR DIVORCE
Residency:	(1) One party must be a resident for 1 year. (2) If the cause of the divorce is adultery which occurred in New Jersey, one party must be a resident (without time limit). N.J.S.A. Sec. 2A: 34-10.
Which Court:	Any county in New Jersey. N.J.S.A. Sec. 2A: 34-8.
Grounds:	NO-FAULT: "The parties have been living separate and apart for 18 months, and there is no reasonable prospect of reconciliation." N.J.S.A. Sec. 2A: 34-2. TRADITIONAL: (1) adultery; (2) willful desertion for 12 months; (3) extreme cruelty (must file 3 months after the last act alleged in the complaint); (4) alcoholism or drug addiction; (5) institutionalization for mental illness for 24 months after the marriage and before filing; (6) imprisonment for 18 months, provided there is no cohabitation after release; (7) deviant sexual conduct voluntarily performed by the defendant without the consent of the plaintiff. N.J.S.A. Sec. 2A:34-2. LEGAL SEPARATION: Same as no-fault and traditional. Called "divorce from bed and board." N.J.S.A. Sec. 2A: 34-3.
Property:	Equitable distribution. Each party keeps property acquired before marriage or by gift or inheritance. Factors: (1) duration of marriage; (2) age, physical and emotional condition of parties; (3) property or income prior to marriage; (4) standard of living established during marriage; (5) any written agreement as to property division; (6) economic circumstances of each; (7) income and earning capacity of each; (8) contribution to the other party's education, training or earning power; (9) contribution to acquisition, dissipation, preservation, depreciation or appreciation of marital property; (10) tax consequences; (11) present value of property; (12) need of custodial parent to remain in the marital home; (13) debts and liabilities of each; (14) need for trust fund to secure foreseeable medical or educational costs for a child or spouse; (15) extent to which a party deferred achieving their career goals; and (16) any other relevant factor. N.J.S.A. Sec. 2A: 34-23-1.
Alimony:	Fault not considered. Factors: (1) actual need and ability of parties to pay; (2) duration of the marriage; and age, physical and emotional condition of the parties; (4) standard of living established during the marriage, and the likelihood each can maintain that standard; (5) earning capacity, educational level, vocational skills and employability of the parties; (6) length of absence from the job market and child custodial responsibilities of the party seeking alimony; (7) time and expense needed for education and training; availability of training and employment; and the opportunity for future acquisition of capital assets and income; (8) contribution of each to the marriage; (9) property division; (10) income available from investment of assets; (11) tax consequences of any alimony award; and (12) any other relevant factor. N.J.S.A. Sec. 2A:34-23.
Child Support:	Combined Income Method. New Jersey Supreme Court child support guidelines may be found in the New Jersey Civil Practice Rules, Appendix IX. Factors: (1) needs of child; (2) standard of living and economic circumstances; (3) income and assets of parties; (4) earning ability of parties; (5) child's need and capacity for education, including higher education; (6) age and health of parties and child; (7) income, assets and earning capacity of child; (8) other child support obligations of parties; (9) debts and liabilities of the parties and child; (10) any other relevant factor. N.J.S.A. Sec. 2A:34-23.
Child Custody:	Best interest of the child, considering the following factors: (1) parents' ability to agree, communicate and cooperate in matters relating to the child; (2) parents' willingness to accept custody and facilitate visitation; (3) interaction and interrelationship between the child and parents and siblings; (4) any history of domestic violence; (5) preference of child, if of suitable age; (6) needs of child; (7) stability of home environment offered; (8) quality and continuity of education; (9) fitness of parents; (10) geographical proximity of the parties' homes; (11) extent and quality of time with the child before and after separation; (12) employment responsibilities; and (13) age and number of children. Judge must follow the parties agreement, unless he determines it is not in the child's best interest. Where parties don't agree, judge may require each party to submit a proposed custody plan. N.J.S.A. Sec. 9:2-4.
Misc:	Either party may resume any name used before marriage, or may assume any surname. N.J.S.A. Sec. 2A: 34-21. If any minor children are involved, there is a mandatory "Parent Education Program," with a $25 fee. N.J.S.A. Sec. 2A: 34-3-12.3 and 12.5.
Final Order:	JUDGMENT OF DIVORCE
UCCJA:	N.J.S.A. Sec. 2A: 34-28.
IDO:	N.J.S.A. Sec. 2A:17-56-18.
Temporary Relief:	N.J.S.A. Sec. 2A:34-23.
Domestic Violence:	N.J.S.A. Sec. 2C:25-17.
Annulment:	N.J.S.A. Sec. 2A: 34-1.

NEW MEXICO

The Law:	New Mexico Statutes 1978 Annotated, Chapter 40, Section 40-4-1 (N.M.S.A. Sec. 40-4-1). Supplement at end of each chapter.

Case Style/Parties:

_____ JUDICIAL DISTRICT COURT
    COUNTY OF _____
       STATE OF NEW MEXICO

_____, Petitioner, vs. _____, Respondent.

Complaint Title:
PETITION FOR DISSOLUTION OF MARRIAGE
Petition must be verified by an affidavit. N.M.S.A. Sec. 40-4-6.

Residency:
One party must be resident for 6 months, and be domiciled in New Mexico. N.M.S.A. Sec. 40-4-5.

Which Court:
County where either party resides. N.M.S.A. Sec. 40-4-4.

Grounds:
NO-FAULT: "The parties are incompatible." N.M.S.A. Sec. 40-4-1.
TRADITIONAL: (1) cruel and inhuman treatment; (2) adultery; (3) abandonment. N.M.S.A. Sec. 40-4-1.
LEGAL SEPARATION: The parties are permanently separated and do not live together or cohabit. See N.M.S.A. Sec. 40-4-3.

Property:
Community property. Separate property is property: (1) acquired before marriage; (2) acquired after a decree of legal separation; (3) designated separate by court order or written agreement of the parties; or (4) acquired by gift or inheritance. N.M.S.A. Sec. 40-3-8. Fault not considered. No statutory factors. N.M.S.A. Sec. 40-4-7.

Alimony:
Called "spousal support." Factors: (1) age, health, and means of support of the parties; (2) current and future earnings and earning capacity; (3) good-faith efforts to maintain employment or to become self-supporting; (4) needs of the parties, including the standard of living, maintenance of medical insurance, and need for life insurance on the payor; (5) duration of marriage; (6) property division; (7) type and nature of each party's assets; (8) type and nature of each party's liabilities; (9) income from property; and (10) any agreements of the parties. N.M.S.A. Sec. 40-4-7.

Child Support:
Combined Income Method. Child support guidelines are found in N.M.S.A. Sec. 40-4-11.1.

Child Custody:
Best interest of the child considering: (1) wishes of parties; (2) wishes of child; (3) interaction and interrelationship between child and parties, siblings and other significant persons; (4) child's adjustment to home, school and community; and (5) mental and physical condition of all persons involved. N.M.S.A. Sec. 40-4-9. Joint custody is presumed in the child's best interest, considering: (1) whether child has established a close relationship with each party; (2) whether each party is capable of providing care; (3) whether each party is willing to accept responsibilities of child care; (4) whether child can best maintain and strengthen a relationship with both parties and profit from such involvement; (5) whether each party is able to allow the other to provide care without intrusion; (6) the suitability of the parenting plan; (7) geographical distance between the parties' residences; (8) the parties' willingness and ability to communicate and cooperate regarding the child's needs; and (9) any court determination of domestic abuse against a child by the party seeking custody. N.M.S.A. Sec. 40-4-9.1.

Final Order:
DECREE OF DISSOLUTION OF MARRIAGE

UCCJA:	N.M.S.A. Sec. 40-10-1.
IDO:	N.M.S.A. Sec. 40-4A-1.
Temporary Relief:	N.M.S.A. Sec. 40-4-7.
Domestic Violence:	N.M.S.A. Sec. 40-13-1. (Family Violence Protection).
Annulment:	N.M.S.A. Sec. 40-1-9.

NEW YORK

The Law:	McKinney's Consolidated Laws of New York Annotated, Domestic Relations Law, Section 170 (C.L.N.Y., D.R.L. Sec. 170). The set of books containing the New York laws is divided into subjects, so be sure you find the volumes marked "Domestic Relations."

Case Style/Parties: SUPREME COURT OF THE STATE OF NEW YORK, _____ COUNTY

_____, Plaintiff, vs. _____, Defendant.

Complaint Title: COMPLAINT FOR DIVORCE
Complaint must be verified.

Residency: No residency time limit if both parties are residents at time of filing and the grounds for divorce arose in New York. If one party is non-resident, then other must be resident for 2 years. However, 1 year residency of one party if (1) parties were married in New York; or (2) both parties once resided in New York; or (3) the grounds for divorce arose in New York.

Which Court: County where either party resides.

Grounds: NO-FAULT: (1) "The parties have been living separate and apart for 1 year under the terms of a written separation agreement which is signed and notarized." [This also requires: (a) proof of compliance with the agreement; and (b) either that a copy of the agreement or a memorandum of the agreement be filed with the county clerk. If a memorandum is filed it must contain the following information: (a) name and address of each party; (b) date of the marriage; (c) date of the separation agreement; and (d) date of signing of the memorandum, and an acknowledgment or proof of the separation agreement.] (2) "The parties have been living separate and apart for 1 year under the terms of a judicial separation agreement."
TRADITIONAL: (1) cruel and inhuman treatment; (2) abandonment for 1 year; (3) imprisonment for 3 years; (4) adultery (but not if in connivance with other party, if adultery is forgiven by word or voluntary cohabitation after knowledge, if the divorce is not filed within 5 years after discovery of adultery, or if the plaintiff is also guilty of adultery) . C.L.N.Y., D.R.L. Secs. 170 & 171.
LEGAL SEPARATION: Same as in traditional divorce, plus failure to support wife. C.L.N.Y., D.R.L. Secs. 200, 230 & 231.

Property: Equitable distribution. Separate property is: (1) property acquired before marriage; (2) property acquired by gift or inheritance; (3) compensation for personal injuries; (4) property acquired in exchange for, or increase in value of, (1) or (2), unless due to the efforts of the other party; and (5) property designated as separate in a written agreement of the parties. Marital property is divided according to the following factors: (1) income and property at time of marriage and at the commencement of the divorce; (2) duration of marriage, and age and health of the parties; (3) need of party with child custody to remain in the marital home; (4) loss of inheritance or pension rights; (5) alimony award, if any; (6) contribution of each to the acquisition of the property; (7) liquidity of the marital property; (8) probable future financial circumstances of each party; (9) difficulty in evaluating an asset or business entity; (10) tax consequences; (11) either party's wasteful dissipation of assets; (12) any transfer or encumbrance in contemplation of divorce without fair consideration; and (13) any other relevant factor. C.L.N.Y., D.R.L. Sec. 236-Part B.

Alimony: Fault not considered. Factors: (1) income and property distribution; (2) duration of marriage, and the age and health of the parties; (3) present and future earning capacity of each; (4) ability of the party seeking alimony to become self-supporting, and the training and time needed; (5) the reduced earning capacity due to career building of the other party; (6) child custody arrangement; (7) tax consequences; (8) contribution to the career of the other party; (9) either party's wasteful dissipation of marital property; (10) any transfer or encumbrance in contemplation of divorce without fair consideration; and (11) any other relevant factor. C.L.N.Y., D.R.L. Sec. 236-Part B.

Child Support: Combined Income Method. Based on a pro-rata share of the child's needs, according to the relative income of the parties. Needs are determined as a percentage of the parties' combined income as follows: 17% for 1 child; 25% for 2 children; 29% for 3 children; 31% for 4 children; and 35% or more for 5 or more children. This amount may be increased if certain special circumstances exist as stated in the statute. A child support chart is available from the Commission of Social Services. C.L.N.Y., D.R.L. Sec. 240.1-b.

Child Custody: Best interests of the child. No statutory factors. See C.L.N.Y., D.R.L Sec. 240.

Misc: Wife's former or maiden name may be restored.

Final Order: JUDGMENT OF DIVORCE

UCCJA:	C.L.N.Y., D.R.L. Sec. 75-a.
IDO:	C.L.N.Y., Civil Procedure Law & Rules Sec. 5241.
Temporary Relief:	C.L.N.Y., D.R.L. Secs. 236-Pt. B (alimony); and 240 (child support and custody).
Domestic Violence:	C.L.N.Y., Social Services Sec. 459-a.
Annulment:	C.L.N.Y., D.R.L. Sec. 140.

NORTH CAROLINA

The Law:	General Statutes of North Carolina, Chapter 50, Section 2 (G.S.N.C. §50-2).
Case Style/Parties:	IN THE GENERAL COURT OF JUSTICE, _____DIVISION, [SUPERIOR or DISTRICT] NORTH CAROLINA, _____ COUNTY
	_____, Plaintiff, vs. _____, Defendant.

Complaint Title: COMPLAINT FOR DIVORCE
Complaint must be verified, and must include: (1) residency of one party for 6 months; (2) facts to show grounds for divorce; (3) name and age of any minors, or a statement that there are no minor children. G.S. N.C. Sec. 50-8.

Residency: One party must be resident for 6 months. G.S. N.C. Sec. 50-6.

Which Court: County where either party resides. G.S.N.C. Sec. 50-3.

Grounds: NO-FAULT: "The parties have been living separate and apart without cohabitation for 1 year." Must actually live apart, but isolated sexual relations during the 1 year period does not preclude a divorce. G.S.N.C. Sec. 50-6. TRA-DITIONAL: (1) confinement for incurable insanity for 3 years; (2) incurable mental illness based on examinations for 3 years. See G.S.N.C. Sec. 50-5.1. LEGAL SEPARATION: (1) abandonment; (2) maliciously turning the spouse out of doors; (3) cruel and barbarous treatment endangering the spouse's life; (4) spouse "offers such indignities to the person of the other as to render his or her condition intolerable and life burdensome"; (5) alcoholism or drug addiction; and (6) adultery. Referred to as "divorce from bed and board." G.S.N.C. Secs. 50-7.

Property: Equitable distribution. Fault not considered. Separate property is property: (1) acquired before marriage, or by gift or inheritance; (2) acquired in exchange for such property; (3) any increase in value of, or income from, separate property; (4) non-transferable professional or business licenses; and (5) non-vested retirement benefits. Division of marital property to be equal, unless judge decides this would not be equitable, considering: (1) income, property and liabilities of each party; (2) obligations of support from prior marriage; (3) duration of marriage, and the age, physical and mental health of the parties; (4) need of child custodian to occupy the marital home; (5) any expectation of non-vested retirement benefits; (6) each party's contribution to the acquisition of property; (7) contributions of either party to the other's education or career development; (8) direct contributions to the increase in value of the other's separate property; (9) liquidity of marital assets; (10) difficulty in evaluating assets or business interests, and the economic desirability of retaining an asset or business interest free of the other's intervention; (11) tax consequences; and (12) acts of either party to maintain, preserve, develop, expand, waste, neglect, devalue, or convert marital property after separation; and any other relevant factor. G.S.N.C. Sec. 50-20.

Alimony: Temporary alimony called "postseparations support." Alimony may be awarded if the party seeking it is a "dependent spouse." No alimony allowed if party seeking it is guilty of adultery and other party is not, or if alimony is barred by a separation agreement. If paying party guilty of adultery and seeking party is not, alimony must be awarded. If both or neither are guilty of adultery, decision to grant or deny alimony (and the amount, duration, and manner of payment) is based on following factors: (1) marital misconduct of either spouse; (2) relative earnings and earning capacities of the spouses; (3) ages and physical, mental, and emotional conditions of the spouses; (4) amount and sources of earned income of both spouses; (5) duration of marriage; (6) contribution by one spouse to the education, training, or increased earning power of the other; (7) extent to which the earning power, expenses, or financial obligations of a spouse will be affected by serving as custodian of a minor child; (8) standard of living established during marriage; (9) education of the spouses and time necessary to acquire education or training to enable the spouse seeking alimony to find adequate employment; (10) assets, liabilities, and debt service requirements of the spouses, including legal obligations of support; (11) property brought to the marriage by either spouse; (12) contribution of a spouse as homemaker; (13) relative needs of the spouses; (14) federal, State, and local tax ramifications of the alimony award; and (15) any other factor relating to the economic circumstances of the parties that the court finds to be just and proper. G.S.N.C. Sec. 50-16.3A.

Child Support: Combined Income Method. Guidelines are available in the Annotated Rules of North Carolina; and from the Department of Human Resources, any child support enforcement office, and the clerk of court. G.S.N.C. Sec. 50-13.4. Can continue past the age of majority if the child is mentally or physically incapable of self-support. G.S.N.C. Sec. 50-13.8.

Child Custody: Custody to be determined "as will best promote interest and welfare of the child." Must consider any acts of domestic violence between the parties, the safety of the child, and safety of either party. G.S.N.C. Sec. 50-13.2. If custody is disputed, mediation may be required. G.S.N.C. Sec. 50-13.1.

Misc: Notice of the trial date is not required where the defendant has not made an appearance. G.S.N.C. Sec. 50-10(b). Wife may resume maiden name, surname of prior husband who is deceased, or surname of a living former husband if there are children with that surname. G.S.N.C. Sec. 50-12. Husband can resume pre-marriage name. G.S.N.C. Sec. 50-12 (a1).

Final Order: DECREE OF DIVORCE

UCCJA:	G.S.N.C. Sec. 50A-1.	Domestic Violence:	G.S.N.C. Sec. 50B-1.
IDO:	G.S.N.C. Sec. 50-13.9 (income withholding).	Annulment:	G.S.N.C. Sec. 50-4.
Temporary Relief:	G.S.N.C. Sec. 50-16.2A (as to alimony).		

NORTH DAKOTA

The Law:	North Dakota Century Code Annotated, Title 14, Chapter 14-05, Section 14-05-01 (N.D.C.C. Sec. 14-05-01).
Case Style/Parties:	STATE OF NORTH DAKOTA, COUNTY OF _____, IN THE DISTRICT COURT, _____ JUDICIAL DISTRICT _____, Plaintiff, vs. _____, Defendant.
Complaint Title:	COMPLAINT FOR DIVORCE
Residency:	Plaintiff must be a resident for 6 months before entry of decree. N.D.C.C. Sec. 14-05-17.
Which Court:	County where defendant resides. If defendant is non-resident, then in any county the plaintiff designates.
Grounds:	NO-FAULT: "The parties have irreconcilable differences." N.D.C.C. Sec. 14-05-03. TRADITIONAL: (1) adultery; (2) extreme cruelty; (3) willful desertion; (4) willful neglect; (5) habitual intemperance (intoxication); (6) conviction of a felony; (7) confinement for insanity for 5 years. N.D.C.C. Sec. 14-05-03. For definitions of each ground see N.D.C.C. Secs. 14-05-04 to 14-05-09.1. LEGAL SEPARATION: Same as no-fault and traditional. N.D.C.C. Sec. 14-06-06.
Property:	Equitable distribution. All property, regardless of how or when acquired (although this is a factor to be considered) will be divided as judge feels is just. No statutory factors. N.D.C.C. Sec. 14-05-24.
Alimony:	Fault is a factor. No other statutory factors. N.D.C.C. Sec. 14-05-24.
Child Support:	Percentage of Income Method. Child support guidelines have been prepared by the North Dakota Department of Human Services. N.D.C.C. Secs. 14-05-24 & 14-09-09.7. Check with court clerk about where to obtain a copy.
Child Custody:	Factors: (1) love, affection and emotional ties between child and each party; (2) each party's capacity and disposition to give love, affection and guidance, and to continue the child's education; (3) each party's disposition to provide food, clothing, medical care and other material needs; (4) length of time the child has been in a stable, satisfactory environment, and the desirability of maintaining continuity; (5) the permanence, as a family unit, of the existing or proposed custodial home; (6) moral fitness of the parties; (7) mental and physical health of the parties; (8) child's home, school and community record; (9) the reasonable preference of the child, if of sufficient intelligence, understanding and experience; (10) any existence of domestic violence; (11) the interaction and interrelationship between the child and parties, siblings and other significant persons; (12) any false abuse allegations not made in good faith; and (13) any other relevant factor. N.D.C.C. Secs. 14-09-06.2. Also see N.D.C.C. Secs. 14-05-22; 14-09-06; and 14-09-06.1.
Misc:	Wife's maiden or former name may be restored.
Final Order:	DECREE OF DIVORCE See N.D.C.C. Sec. 14-09-08.10 regarding medical insurance requirements.
UCCJA:	N.D.C.C. Sec. 14-14-01.
IDO:	N.D.C.C. Sec. 14-09-09.10.
Temporary Relief:	N.D.C.C. Sec. 14-05-23.
Domestic Violence:	N.D.C.C. Sec. 14-07.1-01.
Annulment:	N.D.C.C. Sec. 14-04-01.

OHIO

The Law:	Page's Ohio Revised Code Annotated, Section 3105.01 (O.R.C. Sec. 3105.01). Look for "Title 31 Domestic Relations-Children."
Case Style/Parties:	IN THE COURT OF COMMON PLEAS OF _____ COUNTY, OHIO _____, Plaintiff, vs. _____, Defendant. [Divorce procedure] _____, Petitioner, and _____, Co-Petitioner. [Dissolution of marriage procedure]
Complaint Title:	COMPLAINT FOR DIVORCE [Divorce procedure] PETITION FOR DISSOLUTION OF MARRIAGE [Dissolution of marriage procedure] Petition for dissolution procedure must be signed by both parties, and must have a separation agreement attached which settles the matters of property division, alimony, custody, visitation, and child support. The parties may also file a parenting plan.
Residency:	Divorce procedure: Plaintiff must be resident of Ohio for 6 months, and of the county for 90 days. Dissolution procedure: One party must be a resident for 6 months before filing. O.R.C. Sec. 3105.62.
Which Court:	County where Petitioner or Plaintiff has resided for at least 90 days.
Grounds:	NO-FAULT: Divorce procedure: (1) "The parties are incompatible." A divorce using only this ground can be defeated if your spouse denies incompatibility. (2) "The parties have been living separate and apart without cohabitation for 1 year." Dissolution of marriage procedure: "The parties desire a dissolution of marriage, and have attached a separation agreement." Joint petition procedure may also be filed. TRADITIONAL: (1) bigamy; (2) willful absence of the other party for 1 year; (3) adultery; (4) extreme cruelty; (5) fraudulent contract; (6) gross neglect of duty; (7) habitual drunkenness; (8) imprisonment at the time of filing; and (9) when the divorce decree of another state does not release one party from the marital obligations in Ohio. O.R.C. Sec. 3105.01. LEGAL SEPARATION: Only a suit for alimony may be brought, provided the parties have been living separate and apart, and on the same grounds as traditional divorce. O.R.C. Sec. 3105.17.
Property:	Equitable distribution. Separate property is property: (1) acquired prior to marriage; (2) acquired by inheritance; (3) passive income and appreciation of separate property; (4) acquired after a decree of legal separation; (5) excluded by an antenuptial agreement; (6) obtained as personal injury compensation; or (7) clearly acquired as a gift to only one party. Marital property is divided considering: (1) duration of the marriage; (2) assets and liabilities of each party; (3) desirability of child custodian remaining in the marital home; (4) economic desirability of retaining intact assets or business interests; (5) tax consequences; (6) costs of sale, if sale is necessary; (7) any division pursuant to a separation agreement; and (8) any other relevant factor. O.R.C. Secs. 3105.171.
Alimony:	Referred to as "spousal support." Court will determine property division first. Fault not considered. Factors: (1) income; (2) earning ability; (3) age, physical, mental and emotional condition; (4) retirement benefits; (5) duration of the marriage; (6) extent it would be inappropriate for the party with child custody to seek outside employment; (7) standard of living established during the marriage; (8) education; (9) assets and liabilities; (10) one party's contribution to the other's education, training or earning ability; (11) the time and expense to obtain education and training; (12) tax consequences; (13) income loss due to marital responsibilities; and (14) any other relevant factor. O.R.C. Sec. 3105.18.
Child Support:	Combined Income Method. Factors: (1) child's resources and earning ability; (2) parties' resources and assets; (3) standard of living of each party, and child's standard of living absent a divorce; (4) physical and emotional condition, and needs of child; (5) child's need and capacity for education; (6) child's age; (7) parties' other support obligations; (8) value of services contributed by the custodial parent. Judgment must provide for medical insurance, payment through the child support enforcement agency, and one of the income withholding orders or cash bonds in O.R.C. Sec. 3113,21(D) or (H). O.R.C. Sec. 3105.05.
Child Custody:	Best interest of the child, considering: (1) wishes of parties; (2) child's wishes, if interview by judge; (3) interaction and interrelationship between child and parents, siblings and other significant persons; (4) child's adjustment to home, school and community; (5) mental and physical condition of all persons involved; (6) party more likely to honor and facilitate visitation; (7) compliance with any child support orders; (8) any history of abuse or neglect; (9) any history of visitation denial; and (10) whether a party intends to make his or her residence outside of Ohio. O.R.C. Sec. 3109.04.
Misc:	Neither party may cancel health insurance. O.R.C. Sec. 3105.71.
Dissolution:	A hearing will be held between 30 and 90 days after filing the petition, at which both parties must appear and each must state that he or she voluntarily signed the agreement, is satisfied with the agreement, and desires a dissolution of the marriage. Sample complaint may be found in the Ohio Rules of Civil Procedure, Appendix of Forms, Form #20. Also check for local court rules.
Final Order:	DECREE OF DIVORCE [Divorce procedure] DECREE OF DISSOLUTION OF MARRIAGE [Dissolution of marriage procedure]

UCCJA:	O.R.C. Sec. 3109.21.	Domestic Violence:	O.R.C. Sec. 3113.31.
IDO:	O.R.C. Sec. 3113.21.	Annulment:	O.R.C. Sec. 3105.31.
Temporary Relief:	O.R.C. Sec. 3105.18(B) (alimony).		

OKLAHOMA

The Law:	Oklahoma Statutes Annotated, Title 43, Section 101 (43 O.S.A. Sec. 101).
Case Style/Parties:	STATE OF OKLAHOMA, IN THE DISTRICT COURT, _____ COUNTY
	_____, Plaintiff, vs. _____, Defendant.
Complaint Title:	PETITION FOR DIVORCE Just state the statutory grounds, without any detailed facts. 43 O.S.A. Sec. 107. Petition must be verified. 43 O.S.A. Sec. 105.
Residency:	One party must be resident for 6 months. 43 O.S.A. Sec. 102.
Which Court:	County where plaintiff has resided for 30 days, or county where defendant resides. 43 O.S.A. Sec. 103.
Grounds:	NO-FAULT: "The parties are incompatible." 43 O.S.A. Sec. 101. TRADITIONAL: (1) abandonment for 1 year; (2) adultery; (3) impotence; (4) wife is pregnant by another at the time of marriage; (5) extreme cruelty; (6) fraudulent contract; (7) habitual drunkenness; (8) gross neglect of duty; (9) imprisonment for a felony at time of filing; (10) divorce in another state which does not release the party in Oklahoma of the obligations of marriage; and (11) confinement for incurable insanity for 5 years. 43 O.S.A. Sec. 101. LEGAL SEPARATION: Suit for alimony (called separate maintenance) only, based upon same grounds as no-fault and traditional divorce (i.e., no property division). 43 O.S.A. Sec. 129.
Property:	Equitable distribution. Separate property is property acquired (1) before marriage, or (2) after marriage "in his or her own right." Fault not considered. Marital property divided in a just and reasonable manner. 43 O.S.A. Sec. 121.
Alimony:	Fault not considered. No statutory factors. See 43 O.S.A. Sec. 121.
Child Support:	Combined Income Method. Factors: (1) income and means of the parties, and (2) property and assets of the parties. Child support guidelines and tables are found in 43 O.S.A. Sec. 119 and 56 O.S.A. Sec. 235.
Child Custody:	Statutes list which parent is more likely to allow frequent and continuing contact with the child and other parent (43 O.S.A. Sec. 112); any evidence of ongoing domestic abuse (43 O.S.A. Sec. 112.2); and the child's preference (43 O.S.A. Sec. 113).
Misc:	Wife may have former or maiden name restored. 43 O.S.A. Sec. 121.
Final Order:	DECREE OF DIVORCE Must include income deduction provisions. 43 O.S.A. Sec. 115. Decree is not final for 6 months or until appeal is concluded (i.e. no remarriage except to each other for 6 months plus any time for appeals to be concluded). 43 O.S.A. Sec. 123.
UCCJA:	43 O.S.A. Sec. 501.
IDO:	12 O.S.A. Sec. 1170; 43 O.S.A. Sec. 115; and 56 O.S.A. Sec. 240.
Temporary Relief:	43 O.S.A. Secs. 107.1, 109.1 & 110; and 10 O.S.A. Sec. 21.
Domestic Violence:	22 O.S.A. Sec. 60.
Annulment:	43 O.S.A. Sec. 128.

OREGON

The Law:	Oregon Revised Statutes Annotated, Chapter 107, Section 107.015 (O.R.S. Sec. 107.015).
Case Style/Parties:	IN THE CIRCUIT COURT THE STATE OF OREGON THE COUNTY OF _____ In the Matter of the Marriage of _____ , Co-Petitioner, and _____, Co-Petitioner. [For joint petition] In the Matter of the Marriage of _____, Petitioner, and _____, Respondent. [For regular petition]
Complaint Title:	PETITION FOR DISSOLUTION OF MARRIAGE Petition must include: (1) parties' and children's names, address and social security numbers, if known, children's dates of birth, and the expected birth date if the wife is pregnant; (2) names, addresses and social security numbers, if known, and birth dates, of any children born to the parties before marriage; and (3) whether there are any other domestic relations cases pending in any state. Before or at hearing a written statement must be filed which contains: (1) full names and former names of the parties; (2) each party's residence or legal address; (3) each party's age; (4) each party's social security number; (5) date and place of marriage; and (6) names and ages of children. O.R.S. Sec. 107.085. The petition should only allege the statutory grounds for divorce, unless specific facts of misconduct are relevant to the issue of custody. O.R.S. Sec. 107.036. See O.R.S. Sec. 107.089 for documents that must be given to the other party.
Residency:	Residency of one party if they were married in Oregon. If not married in Oregon, one party must be a resident for 6 months. O.R.S. Sec. 107.075.
Which Court:	County where either party resides. O.R.S.Sec. 14.07. After Respondent is served, files an appearance, or joins in joint petition, there is a 90-day waiting period before hearing can be set. O.R.S. Sec. 107.065.
Grounds:	NO-FAULT: "There are irreconcilable differences between the parties which have caused the irremediable breakdown of the marriage." O.R.S. Sec. 107.025. TRADITIONAL: (1) consent to marriage obtained by fraud, duress or force; (2) marriage of minor without lawful consent; and (3) one party lacked mental capacity to consent (including due to alcohol or drugs). O.R.S. Sec. 107.015. LEGAL SEPARATION: Same as for no-fault. O.R.S. Sec. 107.025.
Property:	Equitable distribution. Fault not considered. O.R.S. Sec. 107.036. All property is divided according to the following factors: (1) cost of any sale of assets; (2) taxes and liens on property; (3) each party's contribution to acquisition of the property, including as homemaker; (4) retirement or social security benefits; (5) life insurance; (6) relationship of property award to alimony. Presumption that both parties contributed equally to acquiring property. O.R.S. Sec. 107.105(1)(f).
Alimony:	Called "support." Fault not considered. O.R.S. Sec. 107.036. Party receiving alimony must make reasonable efforts to become self-supporting within 10 years, or alimony may be terminated. O.R.S. Sec. 107.412. Factors: (1) length of marriage; (2) age, physical and mental health of parties; (3) any contribution to the other's education, training, or earning power; (4) each party's earning capacity; (5) need for education, training or retraining for suitable employment; (6) extent to which earning capacity is impaired due to absence from the job market as a homemaker, job opportunity unavailability due to age, and length of time needed to obtain training or update job skills; (7) any custody responsibilities; (8) tax consequences; (9) amount of long-term financial obligations; (10) costs of health care; (11) standard of living established during the marriage; (12) any court-ordered life insurance to secure support; and (13) any other relevant factor. O.R.S. Sec. 107.105(1)(d).
Child Support:	Combined Income Method. Official child support scales and formulas may be available from the court clerk. O.R.S. Secs. 107.105 & 108.
Child Custody:	Joint custody only awarded where both parties agree. O.R.S. Sec. 107.169. Factors: (1) emotional ties between the child and other family members; (2) each party's interest in and attitude toward the child; (3) desirability of continuing existing relationships; and (4) any abuse of one party by the other; (5) preference given to primary caregiver, if deemed fit by court; and (6) each parent's willingness and availability to facilitate and encourage a close and continuing relationship between the child and the other parent. Conduct and life-style are only considered if it is causing or may cause emotional or physical damage to the child (this will require strong proof). O.R.S. Sec. 107.137. Must file parenting plan. O.R.S. Sec. 107.102.
Misc:	Summary procedure is available if: (1) there are no minor children and the wife is not pregnant; (2) marriage was for no more than 10 years; (3) no real estate is owned; (4) there are no more than $15,000 in debts; (5) the total value of personal property is less than $30,000; (6) the petitioner waives rights to alimony and temporary orders (except temporary orders against spouse abuse); (7) there are no other domestic relations suits in Oregon or any other state. O.R.S. Sec. 107.485. Mandatory forms and instructions for the summary procedure are available from the court clerk. O.R.S. Sec. 107.500 (Forms are also found in the statute). If these situations do not apply, the parties can still file a joint petition. Either party may have prior name restored. O.R.S. Sec. 107.105(1)(h).
Final Order:	DECREE OF DISSOLUTION OF MARRIAGE Decree becomes final after 30 days (or conclusion of any appeal). O.R.S. Sec. 107.115(2).

UCCJA:	O.R.S. Sec. 109.700.	**Domestic Violence:**	O.R.S. Sec. 107.700 (Family Abuse Prevention).
IDO:	O.R.S. Sec. 25.310.	**Annulment:**	O.R.S. Sec. 107.005.
Temporary Relief:	O.R.S. Secs. 107.095, 107.097 and 107.108.		

PENNSYLVANIA

The Law:	*Purdon's* Pennsylvania Consolidated Statutes Annotated, Title 23, Section 3101 (23 Pa.C.S.A. §3101).
Case Style/Parties:	COURT OF COMMON PLEAS, _____ COUNTY, PENNSYLVANIA
	_____, Plaintiff, vs. _____, Defendant.
Complaint Title:	COMPLAINT IN DIVORCE
Residency:	One spouse must be a resident for 6 months. Pa. C.S.A. Sec. 3101.
Which Court:	Either: (1) county where defendant resides; (2) if defendant resides outside of the state, the county where plaintiff resides; (3) county where the parties were domiciled while married, if the plaintiff still resides there; (4) if the parties have not been separated for 6 months and the defendant agrees, the county where the plaintiff resides, or where either resides if both have left the county they lived together in; or (5) if the parties have been separated for 6 months or more, the county where either resides. 23 Pa.C.S.A. Sec. 3104.
Grounds:	NO-FAULT: (1) "The marriage of the parties is irretrievably broken and both parties consent to a divorce." This requires both parties to file affidavits consenting to divorce, and the judgment cannot be entered until 90 days after filing. 23 Pa.C.S.A. Sec. 3301(c). (2) "The marriage of the parties is irretrievably broken, and the parties have lived separate and apart for a period of at least two years." The Plaintiff must file an affidavit stating that the marriage is irretrievably broken and that the parties have lived apart for two years, and either the Defendant must not deny the allegations or the judge must find these facts to exist. If the Defendant denies, the judge may continue the hearing for 90 to 120 days and require counselling for the parties. 23 Pa. C.S.A. Sec. 3301(d). For no-fault grounds, a hearing may not be needed if the grounds are established. 23 Pa.C.S.A. Sec. 3301(c). TRADITIONAL: (1) willful and malicious desertion for 1 year; (2) adultery; (3) cruel and barbarous treatment endangering the life or health of the other; (4) knowing bigamy; (5) spouse being sentenced to imprisonment for 2 or more years; (6) spouse offering such indignities to the other as to render the other's condition intolerable and life burdensome (i.e. mental cruelty) [23 Pa.C.S.A. Sec. 3301(a)]; and (7) insanity or serious mental disorder resulting in confinement to a mental institution for at least the past 18 months, with no reasonable prospect of discharge within the next 18 months. Pa.C.S.A. Sec. 3301(b). LEGAL SEPARATION: None, although a separation agreement may be created as preparation for divorce.
Property:	Equitable distribution. Non-marital property includes property: (1) acquired before marriage, by gift or inheritance; (2) acquired after separation, unless in exchange for marital property; (3) designated non-marital in a valid agreement; (4) sold or mortgaged in good faith and for value before separation; (5) acquired in payment of an award or settlement for a claim accrued prior to the marriage or after separation; or (6) certain veterans benefits. 23 Pa.C.S.A. Sec. 3501. Marital property is divided considering: (1) length of marriage; (2) any prior marriages of the parties; (3) age, health, station, amount and sources of income, vocational skills, employability, estate, liabilities and needs of each party; (4) contribution to the education, training or increased earning power of the other; (5) opportunity of each for future acquisition of capital assets or income; (6) each party's sources of income, including medical, retirement and insurance benefits; (7) each party's contribution or dissipation to the acquisition, preservation, depreciation or appreciation of marital property; (8) value of separate property; (9) standard of living established during the marriage; (10) economic circumstances of the parties, including tax consequences; and (11) whether either party will be custodian of any children. 23 Pa.C.S.A. Sec. 3502(a).
Alimony:	Factors: (1) relative earnings and earning capacities of the parties; (2) ages, physical, mental and emotional condition of the parties; (3) sources of income, including medical, retirement and insurance benefits; (4) "expectations and inheritances"; (5) duration of the marriage; (6) contribution to the education, training or increased earning power of the other party; (7) extent to which the earning power, expenses or financial obligations are affected by serving as child custodian; (8) standard of living established during the marriage; (9) the parties' relative education, and time needed to acquire education and training to become adequately employed; (10) relative assets and liabilities; (11) property brought to the marriage; (12) contribution of a spouse as homemaker; (13) the parties' relative needs; (14) any marital misconduct during the marriage, up to separation; (15) tax ramifications; (16) whether the party seeking alimony lacks sufficient property to provide for his or her needs; and (17) whether the party seeking alimony is incapable of self-support through employment. 23 Pa.C.S.A. Sec. 3701. Cohabitation with a non-relative member of the opposite sex terminates alimony. 23 Pa.C.S.A. Sec. 3706.
Child Support:	Combined Income Method. Check with court clerk for official child support guidelines. 23 Pa.C.S.A. Sec. 4322.
Child Custody:	Best interest of the child based upon which parent is more likely to encourage and allow frequent and continuing contact with the other parent. 23 Pa.C.S.A. Sec. 5301. Counseling may be ordered, with consideration given to counselor's recommendation. 23 Pa.C.S.A. Secs. 5303(c) & 5305. If joint custody is desired, court may require written custody plan. 23 Pa.C.S.A. Sec. 5306.
Final Order:	DECREE OF DIVORCE
	If judge divides property or rules on alimony, reasons must be stated in the decree. 23 Pa.C.S.A. Secs. 3506 & 3701(d); and must provide for mandatory attachment of income, unless the judge finds it is not necessary. 23 Pa.C.S.A. Sec. 4348.

UCCJA:	23 Pa.C.S.A. Sec. 5341.	Domestic Violence:	23 Pa.C.S.A. Sec. 6101.
IDO:	23 Pa.C.S.A. Sec. 4348.	Annulment:	23 Pa.C.S.A. Sec. 3303.
Temporary Relief:	23 Pa.C.S.A. Secs. 3503 (property) and 3702 (alimony).		

RHODE ISLAND

The Law:	General Laws of Rhode Island, Section 15-5-1 (G.L.R.I. Sec. 15-5-1). Ignore "Title" and "Chapter" numbers.
Case Style/Parties:	STATE OF RHODE ISLAND, FAMILY COURT, _____ DIVISION [Check with court clerk for division designation] _____, Plaintiff, vs. _____, Defendant.
Complaint Title:	COMPLAINT FOR DIVORCE Allege statutory grounds only, unless specific facts are relevant to the issue of custody. G.L.R.I. Sec. 15-5-3.1.
Residency:	One party must be domiciled for 1 year. G.L.R.I. Sec. 15-5-12. If only defendant meets this requirement, he or she must actually be served.
Which Court:	County where plaintiff resides. If defendant is the only party meeting the residency requirement, then the county where the defendant resides or in Providence County. G.L.R.I. Sec. 15-5-13.
Grounds:	NO-FAULT: (1) "The parties' have irreconcilable differences which have caused the irremediable breakdown of the marriage." G.L.R.I. Sec. 15-5-3.1. (2) "The parties have been living apart for 3 years." G.L.R.I. Sec. 15-5-3. TRADITIONAL: (1) impotence; (2) adultery; (3) extreme cruelty; (4) willful desertion for 5 years (or less at judge's discretion); (5) alcoholism or drug addiction; (6) husband's neglect and refusal to provide for wife for 1 year while able to do so; and (7) "gross misbehavior and wickedness . . . repugnant to and in violation of the marriage covenant." G.L.R.I. Sec. 15-5-2. LEGAL SEPARATION: Called "divorce from bed and board." Same as no-fault and traditional. Court determines proper residency period. G.L.R.I. Sec. 15-5-9.
Property:	Equitable distribution. Separate property is property acquired before marriage or by gift or inheritance. Factors for dividing marital property: (1) length of the marriage; (2) conduct of parties during marriage; and (3) each party's contribution to the acquisition, preservation or appreciation in value of the asset, including as homemaker; (4) health and age; (5) amount and sources of income; (6) occupation and employability; (7) opportunity for future acquisition of capital assets and income; (8) contribution by one party to the education, training; licensure, business, or increased earning power of the other; (9) need of custodial parent to occupy or own marital residence; (10) either party's wasteful dissipation of assets or improper transfer or encumbrance of assets; and (11) any other "just and proper" factor. G.L.R.I. Sec. 15-5-16.1.
Alimony:	Factors: (1) length of marriage; (2) conduct during marriage; (3) each party's health, age, station, occupation, amount and sources of income, vocational skills, and employability; and (4) each party's "state" [probably intended to be "estate"], liabilities and needs; (5) effect that being primary custodian of a child has on the parent's ability to be employed; (6) absence from employment due to homemaking responsibilities, and extent to which education, skills, or experience have become outmoded and earning capacity diminished; (7) time and expense needed to acquire education to find employment and probability of party completing education to become self-supporting; (8) standard of living during marriage; (9) opportunity to acquire capital assets and income; (10) ability of payor to pay; and (11) any other relevant factor. G.L.R.I. Sec. 15-5-16.
Child Support:	Combined Income Method. Family Court child support guidelines are used. Variations from guidelines if certain statutory factors exist. G.L.R.I. Sec. 15-5-16.2.
Child Custody:	Best interest of the child. No statutory factors, except domestic violence. C.L.R.I. Sec. 15-5-16.
Misc:	Wife may have name changed. C.L.R.I. Sec. 15-5-17.
Final Order:	FINAL JUDGMENT OF DIVORCE Waiting period of 60 days between filing and final hearing, unless court orders otherwise. G.L.R.I. Sec. 15-5-14. Judgment not final until after 3 months. G.L.R.I. Sec. 15-5-23. For required income deduction provisions, see G.L.R.I. Sec. 15-5-24.
UCCJA:	G.L.R.I. Sec. 15-14-1.
IDO:	G.L.R.I. Secs. 15-16-1 and 15-5-24.
Temporary Relief:	G.L.R.I. Secs. 15-5-18 and 15-5-19.
Domestic Violence:	G.L.R.I. Sec. 15-15-1.
Annulment:	G.L.R.I. Sec. 15-5-1 (Use divorce grounds and grounds in Sec. 15-1-1 through 15-1-5).

SOUTH CAROLINA

The Law:	Code of Laws of South Carolina, Title 20, Section 20-3-10 (C.L.S.C. Sec. 20-3-10).
Case Style/Parties:	STATE OF SOUTH CAROLINA, THE _____ COURT OF THE _____JUDICIAL CIRCUIT [Either "CIRCUIT" or "FAMILY" will be typed in the first blank; and the circuit number in the second blank] _____, Plaintiff, vs. _____, Defendant.
Complaint Title:	COMPLAINT FOR DIVORCE
Residency:	If both parties are residents, plaintiff must be resident for 3 months. Otherwise, plaintiff or defendant must be a resident for 1 year. C.L.S.C. Sec. 20-3-30.
Which Court:	If both parties are residents, either the county where the Defendant resides, or the county where the parties last lived together. If Defendant is not a resident, then the county where Plaintiff resides. C.L.S.C. Sec. 20-3-60.
Grounds:	NO-FAULT: "The parties have been living separate and apart without cohabitation for 1 year." C.L.S.C. Sec. 20-3-10(5). TRADITIONAL: (1) adultery; (2) alcoholism or drug addiction; (3) physical cruelty; (4) desertion for 1 year. C.L.S.C. Sec. 20-3-10. LEGAL SEPARATION: Called "separate maintenance." See C.L.S.C. Sec. 20-3-140.
Property:	Equitable distribution. Nonmarital property is property (1) acquired before marriage; (2) acquired by gift or inheritance; (3) acquired after an order in a divorce or separate maintenance action; (4) acquired after signing a settlement agreement; (5) acquired after a permanent court order regarding property; (6) acquired in exchange for any of the above property; (7) designated as such in a written agreement of the parties; and (8) any increase in value of any such property, unless due to the other's efforts. The court has no jurisdiction to award one party the other's nonmarital property. C.L. S.C. Sec. 20-7-473. Marital property divided considering: (1) duration of marriage, and the parties' ages at the time of marriage and now; (2) any marital misconduct or fault; (3) value of marital property, and each party's contribution to the acquisition, preservation, depreciation or appreciation of assets; (4) each party's income, earning potential and opportunity for future acquisition of capital assets; (5) each party's physical and emotional health; (6) each party's need for training or education; (7) each party's nonmarital property; (8) existence of any vested retirement benefits; (9) whether alimony was awarded; (10) whether the custodial party should remain in the marital home; (11) tax consequences; (12) any other support obligations; (13) any encumbrances on property, and other debt; (14) any child custody arrangements and obligations; and (15) any other relevant factor. C.L.S.C. Sec. 20-7-472.
Alimony:	Either party may be awarded alimony. Factors: (1) duration of marriage, and the parties' ages at the time of marriage and now; (2) each party's physical and emotional condition; (3) educational background, and need for additional training or education; (4) employment history and earning potential; (5) standard of living established during marriage; (6) current and reasonably anticipated earnings; (7) current and reasonably anticipated expenses and needs; (8) all property; (9) any child custody conditions and circumstances; (10) any marital misconduct or fault; (11) tax consequences; (12) any other support obligations; and (13) any other relevant factor. C.L.S.C. Sec. 20-3-130.
Child Support:	Combined Income Method. Same factors as for custody, and ". . . a fair and reasonable sum according to his or her means, as may be determined by the court." C.L.S.C. Secs. 20-3-160 and 20-7-40.
Child Custody:	Determined "...as from the circumstances of the parties and the nature of the case and the best spiritual as well as other interests of the children as may be fit, equitable and just." C.L.S.C. Secs. 20-3-160.
Misc:	Forms may be available from the court clerk. May have former or maiden name restored. C.L.S.C. Sec. 20-3-180.
Final Order:	DECREE OF DIVORCE 3 month waiting period between filing and final decree, except where the grounds are desertion or separation for 1 year. C.L.S.C. Sec. 20-3-80.
UCCJA:	C.L.S.C. Sec. 20-7-782.
IDO:	C.L.S.C. Sec. 20-7-1315.
Temporary Relief:	C.L.S.C. Secs. 20-3-110; 20-3-120; and 20-3-130.
Domestic Violence:	C.L.S.C. Sec. 20-4-10.
Annulment:	C.L.S.C. Sec. 20-1-530 (called "declaration of invalidity").

SOUTH DAKOTA

The Law:	South Dakota Codified Laws, Title 25, Chapter 25-4, Section 25-4-1 (S.D.C.L. Sec. 25-4-2).
Case Style/Parties:	STATE OF SOUTH DAKOTA, COUNTY OF _____, IN THE CIRCUIT COURT, _____ JUDICIAL DISTRICT _____, Plaintiff, vs. _____, Defendant.
Complaint Title:	COMPLAINT FOR DIVORCE
Residency:	Plaintiff must be a resident at time of filing, and continue to be resident until divorce is final. S.D.C.L. Sec. 25-4-30.
Which Court:	County where either party resides, but Defendant can have case moved to his or her county upon request. S.D.C.L. Sec. 25-4-30.1.
Grounds:	NO-FAULT: "The parties have irreconcilable differences." S.D.C.L. Sec. 25-4-2, and Sec. 25-4-17.1. TRADITIONAL: (1) adultery; (2) extreme cruelty; (3) willful desertion; (4) willful neglect; (5) habitual intemperance (intoxication); (6) confinement for incurable insanity for 5 years; or (7) conviction of felony. S.D.C.L. Secs. 25-4-2 & 25-4-18. See S.D.C.L. Secs. 25-4-3 through 25-4-17.1. for definitions of each ground. LEGAL SEPARATION: Same as no-fault and traditional. S.D.C.L. Secs. 25-4-17.2 & 25-4-40.
Property:	Equitable distribution. No separate property mentioned in the Code. Fault not considered. S.D.C.L. Sec. 25-4-45.1. Only factor in statute is "the equity and circumstances of the parties", which courts have interpreted by using the usual factors, including the value of each party's property. See S.D.C.L. Sec. 25-4-44.
Alimony:	Only factor in statute is the "circumstances of the parties." Fault is considered. S.D.C.L. Sec. 25-4-41.
Child Support:	Combined Income Method. Child support obligation schedule is found in S.D.C.L. Secs. 25-7-6.2 through 25-7-6.10.
Child Custody:	"The best interests of the child in respect to the child's temporal and mental and moral welfare." Court may consider child's preference if child is "of sufficient age to form an intelligent preference." S.D.C.L. Sec. 25-4-45. Joint custody is also possible, determined by factors set forth in S.D.C.L. Sec. 25-5-7.1.
Misc:	Simplified procedure: Where both parties consent to using no-fault grounds, court may grant divorce solely upon the parties' affidavits of residency and grounds, and without either party appearing for hearing. S.D.C.L. Sec. 25-4-17.3. Wife's former or maiden name may be restored. S.D.C.L. Sec. 25-4-47.
Final Order:	DECREE OF DIVORCE Waiting period of 60-days until final decree may be entered, or hearing may be held. S.D.C.L. Sec. 25-4-34.
UCCJA:	S.D.C.L. Sec. 26-5A-1.
IDO:	S.D.C.L. Sec. 25-7A-23.
Temporary Relief:	S.D.C.L. Sec. 25-4-33.1 (upon filing there is an automatic injunction against either party harassing the other, hiding or disposing of assets, or interfering with each other's access to children); and Sec. 25-4-38 (alimony, child support, and suit money).
Domestic Violence:	S.D.C.L.Sec. 25-10-1.
Annulment:	S.D.C.L. Sec. 25-3-1.

TENNESSEE

The Law:	Tennessee Code Annotated, Title 36, Section 36-4-101 (T.C.A. Sec. 36-4-101).
Case Style/Parties:	IN THE _____ COURT OF _____ COUNTY, TENNESSEE [The type of court which handles divorce cases in your county will go in the first space. Usually this will be "CHANCERY" or "CIRCUIT."]

_____, Petitioner, vs. _____, Respondent.

Complaint Title: PETITION FOR DIVORCE
Petition contents: (1) grounds in statutory language; (2) full name of husband; (3) full maiden name of wife; (4) both parties' mailing address, date and place of birth, race, and number of previous marriages; (5) date and place of marriage; (6) number of minor children and whether there is any other custody litigation in any state [T.C.A. Sec. 36-4-106]; and (7) a verified affidavit that "the facts stated in the petition are true to the best of the petitioner's knowledge and belief, that the complaint is not made out of levity or by collusion with the defendant, and that the complaint is made in sincerity and truth for the causes mentioned in the complaint." [T.C.A. Sec. 36-4-107].

Residency: If grounds arose in Tennessee, Petitioner must be a resident when grounds arose. Otherwise, one party must be a resident for 6 months. T.C.A. Sec. 36-4-104.

Which Court: County in which parties lived at time of separation, or county in which Respondent resides. If Respondent is not a resident or is in prison, then county in which Petitioner resides. T.C.A. Sec. 36-4-105.

Grounds: NO-FAULT: (1) "There are irreconcilable differences between the parties." To use this ground, you and your spouse must have a written agreement as to custody, child support, and property division. If you have children, no hearing will be held for at least 90 days after filing; if you have no children, the waiting period is only 60 days. A divorce may not be granted on this ground if your spouse denies there are irreconcilable differences, unless you have both signed a valid separation agreement. T.C.A. Sec. 36-4-101(11) and Sec. 36-4-103 and (2). "The parties have lived in separate residences for a continuous period of 2 or more years, and have not cohabited as man and wife during such period, and there are no minor children of the parties." T.C.A. Sec. 36-4-101(12). TRADITIONAL: (1) Either party was involuntarily impotent and incapable of procreation at the time of the marriage and continuing at the time of filing; (2) knowing bigamy by either party; (3) adultery of either, but see defenses in T.C.A. Sec. 36-4-112; (4) willful and malicious desertion or absence for at least 1 year without reasonable cause; (5) conviction of a crime which renders the party infamous; (6) conviction of a felony resulting in confinement to a penitentiary; (7) attempted murder of spouse; (8) refusal of spouse to move to Tennessee without reasonable cause, and willfully absenting self from the spouse in Tennessee for 2 years; (9) the wife was pregnant by another at the time of the marriage, without her husband's knowledge; (10) habitual drunkenness or abuse of narcotic drugs, beginning after marriage; (11) cruel and inhuman treatment or "inappropriate marital conduct"; (12) the husband offered such indignities to wife as to render her condition intolerable and thereby forcing her to withdraw; (13) husband abandoned wife, or turned her out of doors, and refused or neglected to provide for her; and (14) two years have passed since the entry of a decree of divorce from bed and board, or for separate maintenance, and there has been no reconciliation. T.C.A. Sec. 36-4-101. LEGAL SEPARATION: Referred to as "divorce from bed and board." Same as grounds for divorce (11), (12) & (13). T.C.A. Sec. 36-4-102.

Property: Equitable distribution. Separate property is property acquired (1) before marriage; (2) in exchange for such property; (3) as income or appreciation from such property; and (4) by gift or inheritance. Marital property divided according to following factors: (1) duration of the marriage; (2) each party's age, physical and mental health, vocational skills, employability, earning capacity, estate, financial liabilities and needs; (3) either party's tangible and intangible contribution to the education, training or increased earning power of the other; (4) the parties' relative abilities for future acquisition of capital assets and income; (5) each party's contribution to the acquisition, preservation, appreciation or dissipation of marital or separate property; (6) value of separate property; (7) estate of each at time of marriage; (8) economic circumstances at the time of property division; (9) tax consequences; and (10) any other relevant factor. T.C.A. Sec. 36-4-121.

Alimony: Factors: (1) Relative earning capacity, obligations, needs and financial resources; (2) relative education and training, and opportunity to secure education and training, and necessity to secure education and training, to improve earning capacity; (3) duration of the marriage; (4) age, physical and mental condition of each party; (5) any limitation on a party's earning capacity due to child custody responsibilities; (6) separate assets; (7) property division; (8) standard of living established during the marriage; (9) contribution to the marriage, and to the other's education, training and increased earning power; (10) relative fault of the parties; and (11) any other relevant factor, including tax consequences. T.C.A. Sec. 36-5-101.

Child Support: Percentage of Income Method. Tennessee Supreme Court child support guidelines and forms are available from court clerk. T.C.A. Sec. 36-5-101(e).

Child Custody: Best interests of the child considering the following factors: (1) love, affection and emotional ties between parents and child; (2) disposition of parents to provide food, clothing, medical care, education and other necessary care, and degree to which a parent has become the primary caregiver; (3) importance of continuity in the child's life and length of time child has lived in a stable, satisfactory environment; (4) stability of the family unit; (5) mental and physical health of parents; (6) child's home, school and community record; (7) reasonable preference of child if at least 12 years of age, although court may hear preference of younger child and is to give more weight to preference of older children; (8) any evidence of physical or emotional abuse of child, parent or others; and (9) character and behavior of any person who resides in or frequents the home and that person's interaction with the child. T.C.A. Sec. 36-6-101.

Final Order: FINAL DECREE OF DIVORCE

UCCJA:	T.C.A. Sec. 36-6-201.	Domestic Violence:	T.C.A. Sec. 71-6-101.
IDO:	T.C.A. Sec. 36-5-501 (referred to as "assignment of income").	Annulment:	T.C.A. Sec. 36-4-101.
Temporary Relief:	T.C.A. Secs. 36-5-101 and 36-6-101.		

TEXAS

The Law:	Vernon's Texas Codes Annotated; Family Code, Chapter 3, Section 3.001 (T.C.A.F.C. Sec. 3.001).
Case Style/Parties:	IN THE DISTRICT COURT OF _____ COUNTY, TEXAS, _____ JUDICIAL CIRCUIT
	In the Matter of the Marriage of _____, Petitioner, and _____, Respondent.
Complaint Title:	ORIGINAL PETITION FOR DIVORCE
	Petition must include: (1) statutory grounds only, no detailed facts. T.C.A.F.C. Sec. 6.402; (2) whether there are children under the age of 18 or otherwise entitled to support under Chapter 154. If there are such children, the petition must include numerous other provisions set forth in T.C.A.F.C. Sec. 102.008. Petition must also include a specific paragraph regarding alternative dispute resolution as set forth in T.C.A.F.C. Secs. 6.403 and 102.0085.
Residency:	One party must be domiciled in Texas for 6 months, and in the county for 90 days. T.C.A.F.C. Sec. 6.301.
Which Court:	County where at least one party has resided for 90 days.
Grounds:	NO-FAULT: (1) "The marriage of the parties has become insupportable because of discord or conflict of personalities that has destroyed the legitimate ends of the marriage relationship and prevents any reasonable expectation of reconciliation." T.C.A.F.C. Sec. 6.001.TRADITIONAL: (1) cruel treatment of a nature that renders further living together insupportable; (2) adultery; (3) conviction of a felony and imprisonment for at least 1 year in a state or federal penitentiary without being pardoned; (4) abandonment for 1 year; (5) confinement to a mental hospital at the time of filing for at least 3 years, with no likelihood of adjustment, or that if adjusted a relapse will occur. T.C.A.F.C. Secs. 6.002 through 6.007. LEGAL SEPARATION: None.
Property:	Community property. Separate property is that acquired before marriage, by gift or inheritance, or as personal injury recovery. T.C.A.F.C. Sec. 3.001.
Alimony:	Alimony (called maintenance) may be granted if (1) spouse to pay alimony was convicted of a criminal offense constituting act of family violence within the past 2 years; or (2) the duration of the marriage ws at least 10 years and the spouse seeking alimony is unable to provide for his or her own needs. T.C.A.F.C. Sec. 8.051. If granted, amount and duration determined by (1) financial resources of spouse seeking alimony, (2) education and employment skills of each; (3) duration of marriage; (4) age, employment history, earning ability, and physical and emotional condition of party seeking alimony; (5) ability of paying spouse to meet his or her own needs and pay child support; (6) acts of either spouse resulting in excessive or abnormal expenditures or destruction, concealment, or fraudulent disposition of jointly owned property; (7) the parties' comparative financial resources; (8) any contribution of one spouse to the other's education, training, or increased earning power; (9) property brought into the marriage by either spouse; (10) contribution of a spouse as homemaker; (11) any marital misconduct of spouse seeking alimony; and (12) the efforts of spouse seeking alimony to pursue available employment counseling. T.C.A.F.C. Sec. 8.052. There is a presumption against alimony (Sec. 8.053); duration may not generally exceed 3 years (Sec. 8.054); and alimony is limited to the lesser of $2,500 per month or 20% of payor's gross income (Sec. 8.055).
Child Support:	Percentage of Income Method. Child support guidelines found in T.C.A.F.C. §§154.061 through 154.133. Medical support provision also required by the sections beginning with Sec. 154.181.
Child Custody:	Called managing conservatorship. Petition must include a "suit affecting the parent-child relationship." T.C.A.F.C. beginning with Sec. 153.001. Factors: (1) whether the child's physical, psychological, and emotional needs will benefit from joint managing conservatorship; (2) ability of parents to give priority to child's welfare and reach shared decisions; (3) whether each parent can encourage and accept a positive relationship between the child and the other parent; (4) whether both parents participated in child rearing; (5) the geographic proximity of the parents' residences; (6) the child's preference, if at least 10 years of age; (7) any other factor the judge deems relevant. T.C.A.F.C. Sec. 153.134. The judge must also consider any acts of domestic violence. T.C.A.F.C. Sec. 153.004. A standard possession order in provided in T.C.A.F.C. beginning with Sec. 153.311.
Misc:	No remarriage for 30 days, except to each other, or by court order. T.C.A.F.C. Sec. 6.801. Either party may obtain name change. T.C.A.F.C. Sec. 6.706.
Final Order:	DECREE OF DIVORCE
	Waiting period of 60 days before divorce can be granted. T.C.A.F.C. Sec. 6.702.
	Custody order must contain the parties' and child's social security number and driver's license number, if any. Decree must include the following paragraphs [T.C.A.F.C. Secs. 105.006(d) & (e)]:
	(1) "Failure to obey a court order for child support or for possession of or access to a child may result in further litigation to enforce the order, including contempt of court. A finding of contempt of court may be punished by confinement in jail for up to six months, a fine of up to $500 for each violation, and a money judgment for payment of attorney's fees and court costs."
	(2) "Failure of a party to make a child support payment to the place and in the manner required by a court order may result in the party not receiving credit for making the payment."
	(3) "Failure of a party to pay child support does not justify denying that party court-ordered possession of or access to a child. Refusal by a party to allow possession of or access to a child does not justify failure to pay court-ordered child support to that party."
	(4) "Each person who is a party to this order or decree is ordered to notify the clerk of this court within 10 days after the date of any change in the party's current address, mailing address, home telephone number, name of employer, address of place of employment, or work telephone number. The duty to furnish this information to the clerk of the court continues as long as any person, by virtue of this order or decree, is under an obligation to pay child support or is entitled to possession of or access to a child. Failure to obey the order of this court to provide the clerk with the current mailing address of a party may result in the issuance of a capias for the arrest of the party if that party cannot be personally served with notice of a hearing at an address of record." [If you can show that providing your address is likely to cause harassment, harm or injury, the judge may allow you not to provide the information. T.C.A.F.C. Sec. 154.130(c)].
	See T.C.A.F.C. Sec. 14.057 for child support provisions required to be in final decree.

UCCJA:	T.C.A.F.C. Sec. 152.001	Annulment:	T.C.A.F.C. Sec. 6.101.
IDO:	T.C.A.F.C. Sec. 8.101; 158.001.	Domestic Violence:	T.C.A.F.C. Sec. 71.001.
Temporary Relief:	T.C.A.F.C. Sec. 6.502 (in general); Sec. 105.001 (alimony); Sec. 109.001 (custody).		

UTAH

The Law:	Utah Code Annotated 1953, Title 30, Chapter 3, Section 30-3-1 (U.C. Sec. 30-3-1).
Case Style/Parties:	IN THE DISTRICT COURT OF THE _____ JUDICIAL DISTRICT, IN AND FOR _____ COUNTY, STATE OF UTAH
	_____, Plaintiff, vs. _____, Defendant.
Complaint Title:	COMPLAINT FOR DIVORCE
Residency:	Plaintiff must be resident of state and county for 3 months. U.C. Sec. 30-3-1(2).
Which Court:	County where Plaintiff meets residency requirements.
Grounds:	NO-FAULT: (1) "There are irreconcilable differences in the marriage." U.C. Sec. 30-3-1(3)(h). (2) "The parties have been living separately without cohabitation for 3 years under a judicial decree of separation." U.C. Sec. 30-3-1(3)(j).
	TRADITIONAL: (1) impotence; (2) adultery; (3) willful desertion for more than 1 year; (4) willfully neglecting to provide Plaintiff with common necessaries of life; (5) habitual drunkenness; (6) conviction of a felony; (7) cruel treatment to the extent of "bodily injury or great mental distress"; and (8) incurable insanity. U.C. Sec. 30-3-1(3).
	LEGAL SEPARATION: (1) willful desertion; (2) living separate and apart without cohabitation; (3) gross neglect. For desertion, the Defendant must be a Utah resident, or own the Utah property in which the Plaintiff resides. U.C. Sec. 30-4-1.
Property:	Equitable distribution. All property divided equitably, regardless of how or when acquired. No statutory factors. See U.C. Secs. 30-3-5.
Alimony:	Factors: (1) financial condition and needs of recipient; (2) recipient's earning capacity; (3) ability of payor to pay; (4) length of marriage; (5) whether recipient has custody of a minor child; (6) whether recipient worked in a business owned or operated by the payor; (7) whether recipient directly contributed to payor's skill by paying for payor's education or allowing payor to attend school during marriage; and (8) fault. U.C. Sec. 30-3-5.
Child Support:	Combined Income Method. No statutory factors or guidelines. See U.C. Secs. 30-3-5.
Child Custody:	Best interest of the child considering: (1) past conduct and demonstrated moral standards of the parties; (2) child's wishes; (3) which party is most likely to act in the child's best interest, including allowing contact with the other party; and (4) any other relevant factor. U.C. Sec. 30-3-10. Judge may grant joint custody. U.C. Sec. 30-3-10.2.
Misc:	Need to use general name change statute. See U.C. Sec. 42-1-1.
	Sample complaint for divorce may be found in the Utah Rules of Civil Procedure, Appendix of Forms, Form #18. Parties may be required to attend course for divorcing parents if children are involved. U.C. Sec. 30-3-4(1)(c).
Final Order:	DECREE OF DIVORCE
	Generally, there is a waiting period of 90 days before divorce may be granted. U.C. Sec. 30-3-18.
	Must include provisions for income deduction, U.C. Sec. 30-3-5.1; and medical insurance for children, U.C. Sec. 30-3-5(1).
	See U.C. Sec. 30-3-5 for required provisions in decree.
UCCJA:	U.C. Sec. 78-45a-1.
IDO:	U.C. Secs. 30-3-5.1 and 62A-11-403.
Temporary Relief:	U.C. Sec. 30-3-3 (for alimony, child support and suit money).
Domestic Violence:	U.C. Sec. 30-6-1.
Annulment:	U.C. 30-1-17.4.

VERMONT

The Law:	Vermont Statutes Annotated, Title 15, Section 551 (15 V.S.A. Sec. 551). Ignore "Chapter" numbers.
Case Style/Parties:	STATE OF VERMONT, SUPERIOR COURT, _____ COUNTY
	_____, Plaintiff, vs. _____, Defendant.
Complaint Title:	COMPLAINT FOR DIVORCE Must also file affidavit of income and assets on form available from the court administrator. 15 V.S.A. Sec. 662.
Residency:	One party must be a resident for 6 months before filing, and for 1 year before final decree is entered. 15 V.S.A. Sec. 592.
Which Court:	County where either party resides. 15 V.S.A. Sec. 593.
Grounds:	NO-FAULT: "The parties have been living separate and apart for 6 consecutive months and the resumption of marital relations is not reasonably probable." 15 V.S.A. Sec. 551(7). TRADITIONAL: (1) adultery; (2) imprisonment for 3 years or more; (3) "intolerable severity"; (4) willful desertion for 7 years; (5) persistent refusal or failure to provide spouse with suitable maintenance while able to do so; and (6) incurable insanity; 15 V.S.A. Secs. 551 & 631. LEGAL SEPARATION: Same as for no-fault and traditional divorce. 15 V.S.A. Sec. 555.
Property:	Equitable distribution. All property divided regardless of how or when acquired, but how and by whom acquired is a factor. Concept of "separate property" is recognized, but not defined in the statute. Factors: (1) length of marriage; (2) age and health of parties; (3) each party's occupation, and sources and amount of income; (4) each party's vocational skills and employability; (5) either party's contribution to the education, training and increased earning power of the other; (6) value of property, liabilities, and needs of each; (7) whether property division is in lieu of or in addition to alimony; (8) each party's opportunity for future acquisition of capital assets or income; (9) desirability of the custodial parent remaining in the marital home; (10) the party through whom the property was acquired; (11) each party's contribution to the acquisition, preservation, depreciation and appreciation of the property; and (12) the "respective merits of the parties." 15 V.S.A. Sec. 751.
Alimony:	Fault not considered. May be awarded if (1) party seeking alimony lacks sufficient income or property to provide for his or her reasonable needs; and (2) is unable to support self through appropriate employment at the same standard of living established during the marriage, or is custodian of a child. Factors in determining amount and duration: (1) financial resources of the party seeking alimony, the property apportioned to him or her, ability to meet his or her own needs, and the extent to which child support contains an amount for him or her as custodian; (2) time and expense needed to acquire education and training to find appropriate employment; (3) standard of living established during marriage; (4) duration of marriage; (5) age, and physical and emotional condition of the parties; (6) ability of the person to pay alimony to meet his or her own needs while paying; and (7) "inflation with relation to the cost of living." 15 V.S.A. Sec. 752.
Child Support:	Combined Income Method. Official child support guidelines may be obtained from the Vermont Department of Human Services. 15 V.S.A. Secs. 650 through 663.
Child Custody:	Best interest of the child considering: (1) relationship of the child and each party, and each party's ability and disposition to provide love, affection and guidance; (2) ability and disposition to provide food, clothing, medical care, other material needs, and a safe environment; (3) ability and disposition to meet the child's present and future developmental needs; (4) quality of the child's adjustment to present housing, school and community, and potential effect of a change; (5) ability and disposition to foster a continuing relationship with the other party; (6) quality of the child's relationship with the primary care giver; (7) child's relationship to other significant persons; (8) ability and disposition of the parties to make joint decisions; and (9) any evidence of abuse. 15 V.S.A. Sec. 665.
Misc:	Wife may resume use of former or maiden name. 15 V.S.A. Sec. 558. Check with the court clerk for where to obtain a statistical data sheet which must be filed with the complaint. Children's names may also be changed. 15 V.S.A. Sec. 559.
Final Order:	DECREE OF DIVORCE See 15 V.S.A. Secs. 663 & 781 for required child support provisions which must be in decree. Final after 3 months, unless court fixes an earlier date. 15 V.S.A. Sec. 554.
UCCJA:	15 V.S.A. Sec. 1031.
IDO:	15 V.S.A. Secs. 663 & 780.
Temporary Relief:	15 V.S.A. Sec. 594a.
Domestic Violence:	15 V.S.A. Sec. 1101.
Annulment:	15 V.S.A. Sec. 511.

VIRGINIA

The Law:	Code of Virginia 1950, Title 20, Section 20-91 (C.V. Sec. 20-91). Ignore the "Chapter" numbers, and look for "Title" and "Section" numbers.
Case Style/Parties:	VIRGINIA: IN THE _____ COURT OF _____ [The first blank will either be "CIRCUIT COURT," "DOMESTIC RELATIONS COURT," or "EXPERIMENTAL FAMILY COURT." Call the court clerk to find out which applies in your county.] _____, Plaintiff, vs. _____, Defendant.
Complaint Title:	COMPLAINT FOR DIVORCE
Residency:	One party must be a resident and domiciled in the state for 6 months. C.V. Sec. 20-97.
Which Court:	The county where the Defendant resides, or where the parties last lived together. If the Defendant is a non-resident, then the county where the Plaintiff resides.
Grounds:	NO-FAULT: (1) "The parties have been living separate and apart without cohabitation for 1 year." (2) "The parties have been living separate and apart without cohabitation for 6 months without interruption, there are no minor children, and the parties have entered into a separation agreement." C.V. Sec. 20-91(9). TRADITIONAL: (1) adultery, including homosexual acts, but no divorce if there is cohabitation after knowledge of the act, or if the case is not filed for more than 1 year after; (2) conviction of a felony and imprisonment for 1 year, and no cohabitation after knowledge of the felony; or (3) either party is "guilty of cruelty, caused reasonable apprehension of bodily hurt, or willfully deserted or abandoned the other" (decree may not be entered until one year after the date of act). C.V. Sec. 20-91. LEGAL SEPARATION: Called "divorce from bed and board." Same grounds as (3) for divorce. C.V. Secs. 20-95.
Property:	Equitable distribution. Separate property is property acquired (1) before marriage; (2) by gift or inheritance; (3) by exchange for separate property, provided it was always maintained as separate property; and (4) any income from, or increase in value of, such property, unless the income or increase was from the efforts of the spouse. Factors for dividing marital property: (1) each party's contribution to the well-being of the family; (2) each party's contribution to the acquisition and care and maintenance of marital property; (3) duration of marriage; (4) age, physical and mental condition of the parties; (5) circumstances and factors contributing to the divorce; (6) how and when property was acquired; (7) each party's debts and liabilities, and the basis for, and property securing, such debts and liabilities; (8) liquid or nonliquid character of all marital property; (9) tax consequences; and (10) any other relevant factor. C.V. Sec. 20-107.3.
Alimony:	Factors: (1) obligations, needs and financial resources of the parties; (2) standard of living during marriage; (3) duration of marriage; (4) age and physical and mental condition of the parties and any special circumstances of the family; (5) whether a party should not seek outside employment due to the age, physical, or mental condition or special circumstances of any child; (6) contributions of each party to the well-being of the family; (7) property interests of each party; (8) provisions made for marital property under Sec. 20-107.3; (9) each party's earning capacity, including skills, education, and training and the present employment opportunities; (10) the opportunity for, ability of, and time and costs involved for a party to acquire appropriate education, training and employment to enhance earning capacity; (11) the parties' decisions regarding employment, career, economics, education, and parenting arrangements during marriage and how they affect present and future earning potential; (12) extent to which either party contributed to the education, training, and career position of the other; and (13) any other appropriate factor, such as tax consequences.
Child Support:	Combined Income Method. Child support guidelines and tables are found in C.V. Secs. 20-108.1 & 108.2. See also C.V. Sec. 20-60.1.
Child Custody:	Best interest of the child, considering: (1) age, physical and mental condition of the child and parties; (2) relationship between the child and each party; (3) needs of the child; (4) the role each party played, and will play, in the child's upbringing and care; (5) any history of family abuse; (6) propensity of each parent to support a relationship and contact with the child and the other parent; (7) child's preference if of suitable age, intelligence and understanding; and (8) any other relevant factor. C.V. Sec. 20-124.3.
Misc:	Former name may be restored if it was changed when married. C.V. Sec. 20-121.4. Defendant may waive service by signing a form in front of the court clerk or notary. C.V. Sec. 20-99.1:1. Must have corroborating witness; can't get divorce just on the testimony of the parties. C.V. Sec. 20-99. For information on service by publication, see C.V. Secs. 8-01, and 20-104 to 20-105.
Final Order:	DECREE OF DIVORCE See C.V. Sec. 20-60.3 for what needs to be in the decree regarding child support and income withholding.
UCCJA:	C.V. Sec. 20-125.
IDO:	C.V. Sec. 63-1.
Temporary Relief:	C.V. Sec. 20-103.
Domestic Violence:	C.V. Sec. 16.1-227.
Annulment:	C.V. Sec. 20-89.1.

WASHINGTON

The Law:	West's Revised Code of Washington Annotated, Title 26, Chapter 26.09, Section 26.09.010 (R.C.W.A. Sec. 26.09.030). Must use required forms. R.C.W.A. Sec. 26.09.006.
Case Style/Parties:	IN THE _____ COURT OF THE STATE OF WASHINGTON, ["SUPERIOR" or "FAMILY"] IN AND FOR THE COUNTY OF _____

In re the marriage of _____, Petitioner, and _____, Respondent. |
| Complaint Title: | PETITION FOR DISSOLUTION OF MARRIAGE
Check with the court clerk about where to get required forms before you prepare any papers. Petition must include: (1) each party's last known address; (2) date and place of marriage; (3) date of separation, if any; (4) name, age and address of each dependent child, and a statement of whether the wife is pregnant; (5) any agreement as to custody, child support and alimony; (6) a statement of whether there is community or separate property to be disposed of; and (7) the relief sought. It must also be accompanied by a certificate on a form provided by the Department of Health. R.C.W.A. Sec. 29.09.020. |
| Residency: | Petitioner must be a resident (no time limit). |
| Which Court: | County where petitioner resides. R.C.S.A. Sec. 26.09.010(2). |
| Grounds: | NO-FAULT: "The marriage of the parties is irretrievably broken." R.C.W.A. Sec. 29.09.030.
TRADITIONAL: None.
LEGAL SEPARATION: Same as no-fault. |
Property:	Community property. Separate property is property acquired before marriage, or by gift or inheritance, and any income or increase in value of such property. R.C.W.A. Secs. 26.16.010 and 26.16.020. Factors in dividing marital property: (1) nature and extent of community property; (2) nature and extent of separate property; (3) duration of marriage; (4) each party's economic circumstances, including whether the custodial party should remain in the marital home; and (5) any other relevant factor. Sec. 26.09.080.
Alimony:	Fault not considered. Factors: (1) financial resources of the party seeking alimony; (2) time needed to acquire education and training to find employment suitable to the party's skills, interests, life style, and other circumstances of the party seeking alimony; (3) standard of living established during the marriage; (4) duration of marriage; (5) age, physical and emotional condition, and the financial obligations of the party seeking alimony; and (6) the ability of the other party to meet his or her own needs while paying alimony. R.C.W.A. Sec. 26.09.090.
Child Support:	Combined Income Method. Official child support guidelines and worksheets may be obtained from the administrator for the courts. R.C.W.A. Secs. 26.09.050, 26.09.100, 26.19.001 to 26.19.100.
Child Custody:	Where minor child is involved, the Petition must include a proposed parenting plan which must be filed the earlier of 30 days after filing and service of a notice for trial, or 180 days after filing. R.C.W.A. Sec. 26.09.181 For the contents of the plan see R.C.W.A. Sec. 26.09.184. If the judge decides custody, the following factors are used: (1) each party's relative strength, nature and stability of the relationship with the child, including which party has taken greater responsibility for the child; (2) any agreement of the parties; (3) each party's past and potential for future performance of parenting functions; (4) child's emotional needs and development; (5) the child's relationship with siblings and any other significant adults, and involvement in his or her physical surroundings, school, and other activities; (6) the wishes of the parties and the child; and (7) each party's employment schedule. The greatest weight is given to factor (1) above. R.C.W.A. Sec. 26.09.187.
Misc:	You must use the official mandatory forms approved by the administrator for the courts. Check with the court clerk about where to obtain these forms. R.C.W.A. Sec. 26.09.006.
Either party's name may be restored or changed. R.C.W.A. Sec. 26.09.150.
The parties must file a Washington Department of Health and Human Services Certificate with the Petition. Check for local court rules in the Washington Local Court Rules, Rule 94.04.
The respondent's answer is called a "Response." R.C.W.A. Sec. 26.09.010(4).
Final Order:	DECREE OF DISSOLUTION OF MARRIAGE
Waiting period of 90 days after filing and service on Respondent.

For required provisions see R.C.W.A. Secs. 26.09.105 (medical insurance for children); 26.09.165 (miscellaneous provisions); 26.18.060 (wage assignments); and 26.23.050 (other child support provisions). |
UCCJA:	R.C.W.A. Sec. 26.27.010.
IDO:	R.C.W.A. Sec. 26.18.060 (wage assignment).
Temporary Relief:	R.C.W.A. Sec. 29.09.060.
Domestic Violence:	R.C.W.A. Sec. 26.50.010.
Annulment:	R.C.W.A. Sec. 29.09.040.

WEST VIRGINIA

The Law: West Virginia Code, Chapter 48, Article 2, Section 48-2-1 (W.V.C. Sec. 48-2-1).

Case Style/Parties: CIRCUIT COURT OF _____ COUNTY, WEST VIRGINIA

In Re the marriage of _____, Petitioner and _____, Respondent.

Complaint Title: COMPLAINT FOR DIVORCE

Residency: One party must be a resident. W.V.C. Sec. 48-2-6. No time limit if parties were married in West Virginia; 1 year residency otherwise. W.V.C. Sec. 48-2-7.

Which Court: If Defendant is a resident, the county where Defendant resides, or where parties last lived together. If Defendant is non-resident, then county where Plaintiff resides, or where parties last lived together. W.V.C. Sec. 48-2-8.

Grounds: NO-FAULT: (1) "Irreconcilable differences have arisen between the parties." This can only be used if the defendant files an answer admitting there are irreconcilable differences. An answer form is available in W.V.C. Sec. 48-2-4a and from court clerk. W.V.C. Sec. 48-2-4(a)(10). (2) "The parties have been living separate and apart without cohabitation and without interruption for 1 year."
TRADITIONAL: (1) adultery; (2) conviction of a felony; (3) abandonment for 6 months; (4) cruel and inhuman treatment, including false accusation of adultery or homosexuality; (5) alcoholism or drug addiction; (6) confinement for incurable insanity for 3 years; (7) abuse or neglect of a child or the other party. W.V.C. Sec. 48-2-4.
LEGAL SEPARATION: Same as no-fault and traditional divorce. W.V.C. Secs. 48-2-7 & 48-2-28.

Property: Equitable distribution. Separate property is property: (1) acquired before marriage; (2) acquired in exchange for such property; (3) designated separate by a written agreement; (4) acquired by gift or inheritance; (5) acquired after separation of the parties; and (6) increases in value of separate property not due to the efforts of the parties. Fault is not considered. Marital property to be divided equally, but this may be altered upon consideration of: (1) extent each party contributed to acquisition, preservation and maintenance, or increase in value of marital property; (2) extent each party expended efforts during the marriage which limited or decreased that party's income earning ability, or increased the other party's income earning ability; (3) conduct of either party which dissipated or depreciated value of marital property. W.V.C. Sec. 48-2-32.

Alimony: Fault is a factor. Alimony is barred if party requesting (1) was adulterous, (2) was convicted of a felony during the marriage, or (3) deserted or abandoned spouse for 6 months. Factors: (1) length of marriage; (2) period of time during marriage the parties actually lived together; (3) present income and recurring earnings; (4) income earning abilities of the parties; (5) property division, as it affects earnings, need for alimony or ability to pay alimony; (6) age, physical, mental and emotional condition of each; (7) educational qualifications of each; (8) Likelihood that party seeking alimony can substantially increase his or her income earning abilities within a reasonable time by acquiring additional education or training; (9) anticipated expense of obtaining education and training; (10) cost of educating minor children; (11) cost of providing health care to both parties and children; (12) tax consequences; (13) extent to which it would be inappropriate for custodial party to seek employment outside home; (14) financial needs of both parties; (15) legal obligations of each party to support self or any others; and (16) any other relevant factors. W.V.C. Sec. 48-2-16.

Child Support: Combined Income Method. Same factors as for alimony. W.V.C. Sec. 48-2-16. Child support guidelines may be obtained from the West Virginia Child Advocate Office. See W.V.C. Secs. 48-2-15, 48-2-15a, 48-2-16 & 48A-2-8.

Child Custody: No statutory factors. Presumption in favor of primary caretaker. W.V.C. Sec. 48-2-15.

Misc: Check with court clerk to see if standard financial disclosure forms are needed, and where they are available.
Simplified procedure: If Plaintiff files a verified Complaint, and the Defendant files a verified Answer (form is available from the court clerk), no witnesses will be needed to prove irreconcilable differences. W.V.C. Sec. 48-2-4(a)(10).
Either party may restore name to their name prior to their first marriage, or to the name of a former spouse if there are any living children by that former spouse. W.V.C. Sec. 48-2-23.

Final Order: DECREE OF DIVORCE
For required provisions see W.V.C. Sec. 48-2-15a (health care), and W.V.C. Sec. 48-2-15b (income withholding).

UCCJA: W.V.C. Sec. 48-10-1.
IDO: W.V.C. Secs. 48-2-15b and 48A-5-3.
Temporary Relief: W.V.C. Sec. 48-2-13.
Domestic Violence: W.V.C. Sec. 48-2A-1.
Annulment: W.V.C. Sec. 48-2-2.

WISCONSIN

The Law:	West's Wisconsin Statutes Annotated, Section 767.001 (W.S.A. Sec. 767.001). Ignore "chapter" numbers.
Case Style/Parties:	STATE OF WISCONSIN: CIRCUIT COURT, _____ COUNTY
	In re the marriage of _____, Joint-Petitioner, and _____, Joint-Petitioner. [If joint Petition is filed]
	In re the marriage of _____, Petitioner, and _____, Respondent. [If regular Petition is filed]
Complaint Title:	PETITION FOR DIVORCE
	Petition must include: (1) name, birthdate, social security number, and occupation of each party, and date and place of marriage, and facts relating to residence; (2) each child's name and birthdate, and whether the wife is pregnant; (3) grounds for divorce (statutory only); (4) whether there are any pending or prior divorce actions, whether either party has any previous marriages, and if so, how they were terminated, and the name of any court and time and place of judgment; (5) whether the parties have any written agreements, if so, attach a copy; and (6) the relief requested. W.S.A. Sec. 767.085. If seeking an order affecting a minor child (custody), the petition should also request the "department of health and social services to provide services on behalf of the minor child under Sec. 46.25." For contents of summons see W.S.A. Sec. 767.085(2m). For service of petition see W.S.A. Secs. 767.14 and 801.01. If a joint petition is filed, it must contain: "The parties consent to personal jurisdiction and waive service of a summons." W.S.A. Sec. 767.05(3).
Residency:	One party must be a resident of the state for 6 months, and the county where the Petition is filed for 30 days. W.S.A. Sec. 767.05. Waiting period of 120 days after Respondent is served (or joint petition is filed) before hearing will be set. W.S.A. Sec. 767.083.
Which Court:	County in which residency requirement is met. W.S.A. Sec. 767.05.
Grounds:	NO-FAULT: (1) "The parties jointly request a divorce be granted as there has been an irretrievable breakdown of the marriage." [This requires a joint petition]. W.S.A. Secs. 767.07 and 767.12. (2) "There has been an irretrievable breakdown of the marriage." [This requires the judge to determine that there is no chance of reconciliation, based upon the reasons given by the Petitioner at the hearing]. TRADITIONAL: None. LEGAL SEPARATION: Same as no-fault. W.S.A. Secs. 767.05 & 767.07.
Property:	Community property. Separate property is property acquired: (1) before marriage; (2) by gift or inheritance; or (3) with funds obtained before marriage or by gift or inheritance. (However, these types of property may even be divided to prevent hardship to a party). Fault is not considered. Marital property divided considering: (1) length of marriage; (2) property brought to marriage by each; (3) whether one party has substantial assets not subject to division by the court; (4) contribution of each party to marriage; (5) age, physical and emotional health of each; (6) contribution of one party to the other's education, training or increased earning power; (7) earning capacity of each, custodial responsibilities, and time and expense needed to acquire education or training to become self-supporting at a standard of living reasonably comparable to that during marriage; (8) desirability of custodial party remaining in marital home; (9) amount and duration of alimony or family support, and whether property division is in lieu of such payments; (10) other economic circumstances of the parties; (11) tax consequences; (12) any written agreements; and (13) any other relevant factor. W.S.A. Secs. 766.01 & 767.255.
Alimony:	Called "maintenance." Fault is not considered. Either party may be granted alimony after considering: (1) length of marriage; (2) age, physical and emotional health of the parties; (3) property division; (4) each party's educational level at the time of marriage and now; (5) earning capacity of party seeking alimony, including custodial responsibilities, and time and expense needed to acquire education or training to find appropriate employment; (6) feasibility that party seeking alimony can become self-supporting at a standard of living similar to that during marriage, and length of time needed; (7) tax consequences; (8) any agreement of the parties; (9) either party's contribution to the other's education, training, or increased earning capacity; and (10) any other relevant factor. W.S.A. Secs. 767.26.
Child Support:	Percentage of Income Method. Basically, 17% for one child; 25% for two children; 29% for three; 31% for four; 34% for five or more. May be combined with alimony into a "family support" payment. W.S.A. 767.261. Support guidelines in DWD 40 of Wisconsin Administrative Code. Official support guidelines are available from the court clerk.
Child Custody:	Referred to as "legal custody and physical placement." Best interest of the child considering: (1) wishes of parties; (2) wishes of child; (3) interaction and interrelationship between child and the parties, siblings, and any other significant person; (4) child's adjustment to home, school and community; (5) mental and physical health of all parties involved; (6) availability of public or private child care services; (7) whether one party is likely to unreasonably interfere with the child's continuing relationship with the other party; (8) any evidence of child abuse; (9) any evidence of interspousal battery or domestic abuse; (10) whether either party has had a significant problem with alcohol or drug abuse; and (11) any other relevant factor. W.S.A. Sec. 767.24.
Misc:	Where minor children are involved, a child support form must be obtained from the court clerk and filed with the petition. A guide to court procedures will be provided by the court clerk when the Petition is filed.
Final Order:	DECREE OF DIVORCE

UCCJA:	W.S.A. Sec. 822.01.	Domestic Violence:	W.S.A. Sec. 813.12.
IDO:	W.S.A. Sec. 767.265.	Annulment:	W.S.A. Sec. 767.03.
Temporary Relief:	W.S.A. Sec. 767.23.		

WYOMING

The Law:	Wyoming Statutes Annotated, Title 20, Chapter 2, Section 20-2-104 (W.S.A. Sec. 20-2-104).
Case Style/Parties:	IN THE DISTRICT COURT IN AND FOR _____ COUNTY, WYOMING _____, Plaintiff, vs. _____, Defendant.
Complaint Title:	COMPLAINT FOR DIVORCE
Residency:	Plaintiff must be a resident for 60 days; or, if less than 60 days, have been a resident since the time of the marriage if the parties were married in Wyoming. W.S.A. Sec. 20-2-107. Waiting period of 20 days between filing and divorce decree.
Which Court:	County in which either party resides. W.S.A. Sec. 20-2-104.
Grounds:	NO-FAULT: "The parties have irreconcilable differences." W.S.A. Sec. 20-2-104. TRADITIONAL: Confinement for incurable insanity for 2 years. W.S.A. Sec. 20-2-105. LEGAL SEPARATION: Same as no-fault and traditional divorce. W.S.A. Sec. 20-2-106.
Property:	Equitable distribution. All property is divided, regardless of how and when acquired, although this is a factor. Fault is a factor. Factors: (1) respective merits of the parties; (2) condition each party will be left in after divorce; (3) the party through whom the property was acquired; and (4) the burdens imposed on the property for the benefit of either party or their children. W.S.A. Sec. 20-2-114.
Alimony:	Either party may be awarded ". . . reasonable alimony out of the estate of the other having regard for the other's ability." No other statutory factors. Fault is not considered. W.S.A. Sec. 20-2-114.
Child Support:	Combined Income Method. Child support guidelines at W.S.A. Sec. 20-2-301 through Sec. 20-2-309. See W.S.A. Sec. 20-2-401 regarding medical support for children.
Child Custody:	Best interest of the child considering: (1) quality of relationship with each parent; (2) ability of each parent to provide adequate care (including care by others); (3) relative competency and fitness of each parent; (4) willingness to accept responsibilities of parenting; (5) how parents and child can best maintain and strengthen a relationship with each other; (6) how parents and child interact and communicate with each other; (7) ability and willingness to allow other parent to provide care without intrusion; (8) geographic distance between parents' homes; (9) current physical and mental ability of each parent to care for the child; and (10) any other relevant factor. W.S.A. Sec. 20-2-201.
Misc:	A Complaint for Divorce form may be found in Wyoming Rules of Civil Procedure, Appendix of Forms, Form #15.
Final Order:	DECREE OF DIVORCE
UCCJA:	W.S.A. Sec. 20-5-101.
IDO:	W.S.A. Sec. 20-6-201.
Temporary Relief:	W.S.A. Secs. 20-2-109; 20-2-110; 20-2-111; and 20-2-112.
Domestic Violence:	W.S.A. Sec. 35-21-101.
Annulment:	W.S.A. Sec. 20-2-101.

Sample Case with Completed Forms

This appendix reconstructs the paper trail of a typical uncontested divorce. Many of the filled-in forms in this appendix are also found in Appendix D as blank forms. These forms might provide guidance when filling out the same forms in Appendix D. (Forms that are in this appendix but not in Appendix D are included because of their relevance to the case, but are typically forms that must be obtained by the court or the court clerk's office.)

The following nine forms, relating to a typical uncontested divorce described on page 203, are found in this appendix.

form A: Petition for Dissolution of Marriage (Complaint for Divorce) 206

form B: Uniform Child Custody Jurisdiction Act Affidavit 210

form C: Summons 212

form D: Answer and Waiver 213

form E: Marital Settlement Agreement 214

form F: Notice of Hearing...............................**217**

form G: Certificate of Service.........................**218**

form H: Certificate of Corroborating Witness..........**219**

**form I: Decree of Dissolution of Marriage
(Final Decree of Divorce)**.............................**220**

The next five forms, relating to various situations, are also included.

form J: Motion to Enter Default.......................**223**

form K: Affidavit of Nonmilitary Service.............**224**

form L: Motion for Service by Publication............**225**

form M: Notice of Action..............................**226**

form N: Subpoena Duces Tecum..........................**227**

James and Lisa decide to get a divorce, and James moves into his own apartment. They have reached an agreement on all issues, but James has not done anything to help begin divorce proceedings. Lisa has talked to him several times about getting together to prepare the papers, but James just cannot seem to get around to it. Lisa decides that she will have to get things rolling on her own, and hopes that James will cooperate once she files. Their state does not have any special simplified procedure, and does not provide for a joint petition. The listing for their state in Appendix A gives Lisa the following information:

Case Style/Parties: IN THE CIRCUIT COURT OF THE _____ JUDICIAL CIRCUIT

_____ COUNTY, STATE OF COLUMBIA

In re the Marriage of _____, Petitioner, and _____, Respondent.

Complaint Title: PETITION FOR DISSOLUTION OF MARRIAGE

Residency: One party must be a resident for at least 60 days before filing.

Which Court: Where either party resides.

Grounds: "There has been an irretrievable breakdown of the marriage."

Final Order: DECREE OF DISSOLUTION OF MARRIAGE

First, Lisa prepares the **PETITION FOR DISSOLUTION OF MARRIAGE** (form A), a **FINANCIAL AFFIDAVIT** (this form is not included in this Appendix, although a blank form can be found in Appendix C), a **UNIFORM CHILD CUSTODY JURISDICTION ACT AFFIDAVIT** (form B), and a **SUMMONS** (form C). She files the originals with the court clerk and delivers copies to the sheriff's office for service on James. Lisa also calls James and tells him that she has filed for divorce, and he will be receiving copies from the sheriff's office.

When James receives the papers from the sheriff deputy, he calls Lisa and asks her what he needs to do next. She provides him with an **ANSWER** (form D), which he signs and files within the twenty-day time period stated in the **SUMMONS**.

Next, they get together and write down their agreement regarding property division, alimony, child custody, and child support. This agreement is spelled out in a **MARITAL SETTLEMENT AGREEMENT** (form E), which is then filed with the court clerk.

Lisa then obtains a court date from the judge's secretary and prepares a **NOTICE OF HEARING** (form F). The **NOTICE OF HEARING** is mailed to James and a copy of it is filed with the court clerk. Lisa also files a **CERTIFICATE OF SERVICE** (form G) with the court clerk, to verify that a copy of the **NOTICE OF HEARING** was sent to James.

By going to the courthouse and looking at someone else's divorce file, Lisa learns that she needs a form called a **CERTIFICATE OF CORROBORATING WITNESS** to prove that she meets her state's residency requirement. Lisa goes to the law library and makes a copy of this form from a book containing divorce forms. Sometime before the hearing, Lisa prepares her own **CERTIFICATE OF CORROBORATING WITNESS** (form H) and has her friend, Melissa, sign it to verify that she has known Lisa since at least sixty days before the petition was filed, and that she knows that Lisa has lived in the state for at least sixty days before filing the petition. This form is filed with the court clerk.

Lisa prepares the **DECREE OF DISSOLUTION OF MARRIAGE** (form I), and goes to the court hearing. Since she and James have agreed on everything, and have both signed the **MARITAL SETTLEMENT AGREEMENT**, she can prepare the decree before the hearing. At the hearing, she answers the judge's questions and hands the judge the decree. The judge signs the decree, and Lisa and James are divorced.

If James did not respond to the Petition within twenty days after being served (as required by the **SUMMONS**), Lisa would need to file a **MOTION TO ENTER DEFAULT** (form J). After the clerk signed the bottom portion of this form, Lisa would contact the judge's secretary to schedule a court hearing. In this situation, she would need to present any evidence she obtained to the judge and ask the judge for what she wants. She would then prepare the decree according to what the judge decides.

If the sheriff was not able to find James, or Lisa does not know where James can be found, she would need to pursue **SERVICE BY PUBLICATION** (after researching her state's requirements). First, she would need to be sure that James was not in the military. If she knows for certain that he is not in the military, she would file an **AFFIDAVIT OF NONMILITARY SERVICE** (form K). If she is not sure, she would need to mail a copy of a **REQUEST FOR CERTIFICATE OF MILITARY SERVICE** to each branch of the service and wait for a reply. (This form is not included in this appendix, but a blank form can be found in Appendix C.) She would then take a **MOTION FOR SERVICE BY PUBLICATION** (form L) and a **NOTICE OF ACTION** (form M) to the court clerk. The court clerk will then complete and sign the **NOTICE OF ACTION**. Lisa will then make arrangements with the local legal newspaper to publish a copy of the **NOTICE OF ACTION** for the number of times required in her state.

If James will not sign the agreement, and did not file a **FINANCIAL AFFIDAVIT** or provide any income information, Lisa will need to subpoena James' employer to testify at the hearing. In this case, Lisa will want the employer to bring certain papers to the hearing, so she will prepare a **Subpoena Duces Tecum** (form N). The clerk will issue the subpoena, then Lisa will have the sheriff serve the subpoena on the employer's payroll clerk.

NOTE: *Not all blanks will be filled in. Depending upon your circumstances, different information will be required on the forms. Further, some information is completed by the clerk or some other person. These blanks have not been completed in these sample forms, as it is not something you would complete.*

Form A

IN THE CIRCUIT COURT OF THE FIRST JUDICIAL CIRCUIT

KING COUNTY, STATE OF COLUMBIA

_____ LISA SMITH _____,

CASE NO._____

_____ JAMES SMITH _____,

__PETITION FOR DISSOLUTION OF MARRIAGE__

The _____Petitioner_____ (hereinafter called the _____Wife_____), for his/her _____Petitioner_____ against the _____Respondent_____ (hereinafter called the _____Husband_____), alleges and states:

1. RESIDENCE. The ☐ Husband ☒ Wife   has been a resident of the State of _____Columbia_____ since _____3/18/96_____, and of the County of _____King_____ since _____3/18/96_____, and otherwise meets all residency requirements for filing this action.

2. HUSBAND'S STATISTICAL FACTS:
    A. Name: _James Smith_____
    B. Previous Names, if any: _____
    C. ☒ Current   ☐ Last known Address: __142 Balmoral Street, #201__
        _Jackson, Columbia 22102_____
    D. Length of Residency: _10 years, 11 months_____
    E. Date of Birth: _11/14/58_____
    F. Social Security Number: _999-99-9999_____
    G. Occupation: _Architecture Advisor_____
    H. Employer's Name and Address: _Old Buildings-R-Us, 721 Wright Drive,_
        _Jackson, Columbia 22102_____

3. WIFE'S STATISTICAL FACTS:
    A. Name: _Lisa Smith_____
    B. Previous Names, if any: _Lisa Jackson_____
    C. ☒ Current   ☐ Last known Address: _2476 Highgrove Way_____
        _Jackson, Columbia 22102_____
    D. Length of Residency: _10 years, 11 months_____
    E. Date of Birth: _____7/1/61_____
    F. Social Security Number: _888-88-8888_____
    G. Occupation: _Child Care Worker_____
    H. Employer's Name and Address: _Save the World Foundation, 29 Bleeding_
        _Heart Lane, Jackson, Columbia 22102_____

4. The parties were married on _____7/29/91_____, at _____Washington D.C._____;
and the marriage is registered at _Washington D.C._____.

5. The parties were separated on _11/6/05_____.

6. DECLARATION REGARDING MINOR CHILDREN OF THIS MARRIAGE:
   A. ❏ There are no minor or dependent children of the parties.
   B. ❏ The wife is pregnant, with an expected delivery date of _____.
   C. ❏ The wife is not pregnant.
   D. ☒ The parties have the following minor or dependent children:

Name	Address	Birth Date	Age	Sex	Current Custody
Rebecca Ann	Same as Wife	6/21/95	10	F	Wife
Christine Marie	Same as Wife	9/15/96	8	F	Wife

   E. ☒ A Uniform Child Custody Jurisdiction Act Affidavit is being completed
   and filed along with this _____Petition_____.

7. The ❏ Husband ☒ Wife seeks a _____Dissolution of Marriage_____
on the following grounds:
There has been an irretrievable breakdown of the marriage.

8. ❏ The parties have entered into the settlement agreement attached hereto, resolv-
ing the matters of:
   ❏ Property division
   ❏ Child custody
   ❏ Child support
   ❏ Alimony
   ❏ Other:

9. The parties ❏ DO ☒ DO NOT have marital property to be divided.

   A. ☒ The parties have already divided their property, and each party will keep
   the property in his or her possession.
   B. ❏ The parties have entered into the attached settlement agreement, which
   provides for the division of their property.
   C. ❏ A Financial Affidavit including the parties' assets and debts is being completed and filed along with this _____.
   D. ❏ The following are the Husband's nonmarital assets and obligations:

E.   ❑ The following are the Wife's nonmarital assets and obligations:

10.   ☒ The ❑ Husband   ☒ Wife requests that his/her name be changed/restored
to: ___Lisa Jackson_____.

11.   This action is being filed in good faith, for the purposes and reasons set forth herein.

12.   RELIEF REQUESTED. The   ❑ Husband   ☒ Wife requests the following
relief from this court:

A.   Grant the parties a   ❑ divorce from the bonds of marriage   ☒ dissolution
of the marriage.

B.   ☒ Legal child custody of the child(ren) be awarded to:
        ❑ Husband   ☒ Wife
        ❑ Other:_____

C.   ☒ Physical custody (primary residence) of the child(ren) be awarded to:
        ❑ Husband   ☒ Wife
        ❑ Other:_____

D.   ☒ Child visitation rights be granted to the party without physical custody
as follows:
        ☒ Liberal   ❑ Reasonable   ❑ Scheduled (attach schedule)
        ❑ Restricted or Supervised as follows: _____
        _____

E.   ☒ Child support be awarded to: ❑ Husband   ☒ Wife

F.   ☒ Medical/dental insurance for child(ren) be provided by:
        ☒ Husband   ❑ Wife

G.   ☒ Unusual medical/dental expenses be provided by:
        ☒ Husband   ❑ Wife

H.   ❑ Alimony be awarded to: ❑ Husband   ❑ Wife

I.   ❑ Property rights be determined.

J.   ☒ Wife's former name restored to: Lisa Jackson

K.   Any other injunctive or other orders as may be proper.

L.   ❏ Other specific relief:

DATED: February 15, 2006   *Lisa Smith*
                                      Signature

                                      Name Lisa Smith

                                      Address 2476 Highgrove Way

                                                  Jackson, Columbia 22102

                                      Telephone No. (201) 555-7739

I DECLARE UNDER PENALTY OF PERJURY, that the facts stated herein are true and correct.

                                      Lisa Smith
                                      Signature

     SWORN TO AND subscribed before me on _____,
20_____, by _____, who ❏ is personally known to me ❏ produced _____ as identification.

_____

NOTARY PUBLIC
My Commission Expires:

Form B

IN THE CIRCUIT COURT OF THE FIRST JUDICIAL CIRCUIT

KING COUNTY, STATE OF COLUMBIA

_____LISA SMITH_____,
Petitioner

CASE NO. _____

_____JAMES SMITH_____,
Respondent

UNIFORM CHILD CUSTODY JURISDICTION ACT AFFIDAVIT

1. The name and present address of each child (under 18) in this case is:

    Rebecca Ann Smith and Christine Marie Smith
    2476 Highgrove Way
    Jackson, Columbia 22012

2. The places where the child(ren) has/have lived within the last 5 years are:
    Same as above.

3. The name(s) and present address(es) of custodians with whom the child(ren) has/have lived within the past 5 years are:

    With parents for past 5 years.

4. I do not know of, and have not participated (as a party, witness, or in any other capacity) in, any other court decision, order, or proceeding (including divorce, separate maintenance, child neglect, dependency, or guardianship) concerning the custody or visitation of the child(ren) in this state or any other state, except: [specify case name and number and court's name and address]

    None.

5.   I do not have information of any pending proceeding (including divorce, separate maintenance, child neglect, dependency, or guardianship) concerning the custody or visitation of the child(ren), in this state or any other state except: [specify case name and number and court's name and address]
None.

       That proceeding   ____ is continuing   ____ has been stayed by the court.

    ____ Temporary action by this court is necessary to protect the child(ren) because the child(ren) has/have been subjected to or threatened with mistreatment or abuse or is/are otherwise neglected or dependent.
Attach explanation.

6.   I do not know of any person who is not already a party to this proceeding who has physical custody of, or who claims to have custody or visitation rights with, the child(ren), except: [state name(s) and address(es)]
None.

7.   The child(ren)'s "home state" is _____ Columbia _____. ["Home State" means the state in which the child(ren) immediately preceding the time involved lived with his or her parents, a parent, or a person acting as a parent, for at least 6 consecutive months, and, in the case of a child less than 6 months old, the state in which the child lived from birth with any of the persons mentioned. Periods of temporary absence of the named persons are counted as a part of the 6 month or other period.]

I acknowledge a continuing duty to advise this court of any custody or visitation proceeding (including dissolution of marriage, separate maintenance, child neglect, or dependency) concerning the child(ren) in this state or any other state about which information is obtained during this proceeding.

DATED: _February 15, 2006_   *Lisa Smith* _____
                              Signature of Affiant

                              Name _Lisa Smith_____
                              Address _276 Highgrove Way_____
                                         _Jackson, Columbia 22102_____
                              Telephone No. _(201) 555-7739_____

     SWORN TO AND subscribed before me on _____,
20_____, by _____, who ❑ is personally known to me ❑ produced _____ as identification.

_____
NOTARY PUBLIC
My Commission Expires:

Form C

IN THE CIRCUIT COURT OF THE FIRST JUDICIAL CIRCUIT

KING COUNTY, STATE OF COLUMBIA

In re the Marriage of   CASE NO: _____

_____ LISA SMITH _____,
                    Petitioner

_____ JAMES SMITH _____,
                    Respondent

SUMMONS

TO Each Sheriff of the State of Columbia:

    YOU ARE COMMANDED to serve this summons and a copy of the petition in this action on the Respondent:

    James Smith
    142 Balmoral Street, #201
    Jackson, Columbia 22102

    The Respondent is required to serve written defenses to the petition on the Petitioner.
    Lisa Smith
    2476 Highgrove Way
    Jackson, Columbia 22102

Within 20 calendar days after this Summons is served on the Respondent, exclusive of the day of service, and to file the original of the defenses with the clerk of this court either before service on the Petitioner or immediately thereafter. If the Respondent fails to do so, a default will be entered against the Respondent for the relief demanded in the petition.

    DATED on _____, 20_____.

                                    Clerk of the Court

                       By _____

                           As Deputy Clerk

Form D

IN THE CIRCUIT COURT OF THE FIRST JUDICIAL CIRCUIT
KING COUNTY, STATE OF COLUMBIA

_____LISA SMITH_____,
Petitioner

CASE NO. _____06-2837_____

_____JAMES SMITH_____,
Respondent

ANSWER AND WAIVER

The _____Respondent_____, _____James Smith_____, answers the
_____Petition for Dissolution of Marriage_____ as follows:

1. The _Respondent_ admits all of the allegations contained in the ___Petition___, and agrees to all relief requested therein.

2. The _____Respondent_____ waives appearance at the final hearing.

3. The _____Respondent_____ requests that a copy of the final judgment entered in this case be forwarded to him/her at the address below.

_James Smith_____
Signature

Name _James Smith_____
Address _142 Balmoral Street, #201_____
_____Jackson, Columbia 22102_____
Telephone No. _(201) 555-1066_____

SWORN TO AND subscribed before me on _____, 20_____, by _____, who ❏ is personally known to me ❏ produced _____ as identification.

_____
NOTARY PUBLIC
My Commission Expires:

Form E

IN THE CIRCUIT COURT OF THE FIRST JUDICIAL CIRCUIT

KING COUNTY, STATE OF COLUMBIA

_____LISA SMITH_____,
Petitioner

CASE NO. ____06-2837____

_____JAMES SMITH_____,
Respondent

MARITAL SETTLEMENT AGREEMENT

We, _____Lisa Smith_____, and _____James Smith_____, were married on _____7/29/91_____. We desire to terminate our marriage, and we have made this agreement to settle once and for all the matters set forth below. Each of us states that we have honestly disclosed our property, debts, and income to each other, and each of us states that we believe the other one has been open and honest in preparing this agreement. Each of us agrees to sign and exchange any papers that might be needed to complete this agreement. This agreement is based upon our current circumstances as indicated in the financial affidavits filed in this case.

CHILD CUSTODY

❑   We will share in parenting responsibilities; however, physical custody of the minor child(ren), _____ shall be awarded to the Husband; and the Wife shall have reasonable and liberal visitation rights.

☒   We will share in parenting responsibilities; however, physical custody of the minor child(ren), __Rebecca Ann Amith and Christine Marie Smith__ shall be awarded to the Wife; and the Husband shall have reasonable and liberal visitation rights.

❑   Other:

CHILD SUPPORT

☒   The   ☒ Husband   ❑ Wife agrees to pay the sum of $____600.00____ per ____month____ as support and maintenance for the minor child(ren) in the physical custody of the other parent.

☒   The   ☒ Husband   ❑ Wife agrees to maintain health insurance coverage for the minor child/children as long as such insurance is available at a reasonable group rate.

❑   Other:

DIVISION OF PROPERTY

We shall each keep our own personal clothing and effects, unless otherwise indicated below. We divide our property as follows:

1.   Husband transfers to Wife as her sole and separate property:
A.   All property currently in the Wife's possession
B.
C.
D.
E.
F.
G.
❏   Continued on Additional Sheet.

2.   Wife transfers to Husband as his sole and separate property:
A.   All property currently in the Husband's possession
B.
C.
D.
E.
F.
G.
❏   Continued on Additional Sheet.

DIVISION OF DEBTS

We divide responsibility for payment of our debts as follows:

3.   Husband shall pay the following debts and will not at any time hold Wife responsible for them:
A.   Loan on 2002 BMW auto, Loan No. 20987
B.
C.
D.
E.
F.
G.
❏   Continued on Additional Sheet.

4.   Wife shall pay the following debts and will not at any time hold Husband responsible for them:
A.   Mortgage on Wife's residence
B.
C.
D.
E.
F.
G.
❏   Continued on Additional Sheet.

ALIMONY

☒   No alimony shall be awarded to either party.

❑   The   ❑ Husband   ❑ Wife shall pay alimony to the other party in the sum of
      $_____ per _____, for a period of _____;
      or until the   ❑ Husband   ❑ Wife dies or remarries, whichever occurs first.

❑   Other:

DATED: _____February 21, 2006_____   DATED: _____February 21, 2006_____

*James Smith*_____   *Lisa Smith*_____
Husband's signature   Wife's signature

Name James Smith_____   Name Lisa Smith_____

Address 142 Balmoral Street #201____   Address 2476 Highgrove Way_____

Jackson, Columbia 22102_____   Jackson, Columbia 22102_____

Telephone No. (210) 555-1066_____   Telephone No. (210) 555-7739_____

      SWORN TO AND subscribed before me on _____, 20_____,
by _____, who   ❑   is personally
known to me   ❑ produced _____ as identification.

_____
NOTARY PUBLIC
My Commission Expires:

Form F

IN THE CIRCUIT COURT OF THE FIRST JUDICIAL CIRCUIT
KING COUNTY, STATE OF COLUMBIA

_____LISA SMITH_____,
             Petitioner

                                      CASE NO. _____06-2837_____

_____JAMES SMITH_____,
             Respondent

NOTICE OF HEARING

TO: James Smith
       142 Balmoral Street, #201
       Jackson, Columbia 22102

PLEASE TAKE NOTICE that the _____Petition for Dissolution of Marriage_____ will be called for hearing on _Wednesday_, the _22nd_ day of _____March_____, _2006_, at _9:00_ _A_. M., before the Honorable _____Henry Whitaker_____, Judge of the above-titled court, _in his chambers at the King County Courthouse,_ _Jackson, Columbia_ .

                          *Lisa Smith*_____
                          Signature

                          Name _Lisa Smith_____
                          Address _2476 Highgrove Way_____
                                _Jackson, Columbia 22101_____
                          Telephone No. _(201) 555-7739_____

Form G

IN THE CIRCUIT COURT OF THE FIRST JUDICIAL CIRCUIT

KING COUNTY, STATE OF COLUMBIA

_____ LISA SMITH _____,
Petitioner

CASE NO. _____ 06-2837 _____

_____ JAMES SMITH _____,
Respondent

CERTIFICATE OF SERVICE

I HEREBY CERTIFY that a true and correct copy of the __Notice of Hearing__

_____

WAS: ☒ mailed   ❑ hand delivered to the parties or persons listed below, this __6th__ day of _____ March _____, __2006__ .

Name __James Smith_____

Address __142 Balmoral Street, #201__

__Jackson, Columbia 22102_____

Telephone No. __(210) 555-1066_____

Name _____

Address _____

_____

Telephone No. _____

_Lisa Smith_____
Signature

Name __Lisa Smith_____

Address __2476 Highgrove Way_____

_____Jackson, Columbia 22101_____

Telephone No. __(201) 555-7739_____

Form H

IN THE CIRCUIT COURT OF THE FIRST JUDICIAL CIRCUIT

KING COUNTY, STATE OF COLUMBIA

_____LISA SMITH_____,
Petitioner

CASE NO. _____06-2837_____

_____JAMES SMITH_____,
Respondent

CERTIFICATE OF CORROBORATING WITNESS

UNDER PENALTY OF PERJURY, I CERTIFY that I am a resident of the State of _____Columbia_____; I have known _____Lisa Smith_____ for more than _____60 days_____ before the date of filing the _____Petition_____ in this action, and know of my own personal knowledge that such person has resided in the State of _____Columbia_____ for at least that period of time.

*Melissa White*_____
Witness' Signature

_10 Longpier Place_____
Witness' Residence Address

_Melissa White_____
Witness' Name (Typed or Printed)

_Jackson, Columbia 22102_____
City, State, Zip Code

Sworn to and subscribed before me

on _____, 20_____.

_____

NOTARY PUBLIC

My Commission Expires:

Form I

IN THE CIRCUIT COURT OF THE FIRST JUDICIAL CIRCUIT

KING COUNTY, STATE OF COLUMBIA

_____ LISA SMITH _____,
Petitioner

CASE NO. _____ 06-2837 _____

_____ JAMES SMITH _____,
Respondent

DECREE FOR DISSOLUTION OF MARRIAGE

This action was heard before the Court. On the evidence presented,

IT IS ADJUDGED that the bonds of marriage between the Husband, _____ James Smith _____ and the Wife, _____ Lisa Smith _____, are dissolved.

IT IS FURTHER ADJUDGED that:

☒   1.   The settlement agreement between the parties filed in this action was executed voluntarily after full disclosure and is approved and incorporated in this judgment by reference, and the parties are ordered to comply with it.

☒   2.   The Wife's former name is restored and she shall hereafter be known as: _____ Lisa Jackson _____.

☒   3.   The parties shall share parenting responsibilities; however, physical custody of the minor child(ren) of the parties shall be awarded to the party designated below:

Name of Child	Child's Birthdate	Custody Awarded to:
Rebecca Ann	6/21/95	Wife
Christine Marie	9/15/96	Wife

Each party shall have the right to visit any child not in his or her physical custody at reasonable times and places after reasonable notice to the custodial party.

☒   4.   The ☒ Husband ❏ Wife shall pay child support to the other party in the sum of $ 600.00 per month, beginning April 1, 20 06.

☒   5.   The ☒ Husband ❏ Wife shall provide health insurance coverage for the minor child(ren) whenever such insurance is reasonably available.

Form I

❏   6.   The   ❏ Husband   ❏ Wife shall pay alimony to the other party in the sum
            of $_____ per _____, beginning _____, 20_____,
            to terminate:
            ❏ On _____, 20_____, or on the death or remarriage of said
               other party, whichever occurs first.
            ❏ Upon the death or remarriage of the other party.
            ❏ Alimony is   ❏ Awarded   ❏ Not Awarded   pursuant to the request
               and agreement of the parties.
            ❏ Alimony is   ❏ Awarded   ❏ Not Awarded   based upon the following
               reasons:

❏   7.   The   ❏ Husband   ❏ Wife shall pay the other party's attorney's fees, set
            at $_____ (to be paid to _____), and court
            costs, taxed at $_____, both of which shall be paid within _____ days of
            the date of this judgment.

☒   8.   The Husband shall transfer to the Wife as her sole and separate property:
            All property currently in Wife's possession

☒   9.   The Wife shall transfer to the Husband as his sole and separate property:
            All property currently in Husband's possession

☒   10.   The Husband shall pay the following debts and shall not at any time hold the
            Wife responsible for them:
            Loan on 2002 BMW auto, Loan No. 20987

☒   11.   The Wife shall pay the following debts and shall not at any time hold the Husband responsible for them:

Mortgage on Wife's residence

❏   12.   The parties' nonmarital assets and debts shall be distributed as follows:

❏   13.   Other Provisions:

ORDERED at _____Jackson_____, _____Columbia_____, on this __24th__ day of _____March_____, 20_06_.

_____

Judge

Form J

IN THE CIRCUIT COURT OF THE FIRST JUDICIAL CIRCUIT

KING COUNTY, STATE OF COLUMBIA

_____ LISA SMITH _____,
Petitioner

CASE NO. _____ 06-2837 _____

_____ JAMES SMITH _____,
Respondent

MOTION TO ENTER DEFAULT

The _____ Petitioner _____ hereby moves for the entry of a default against the
_____ Respondent _____ for failure to serve or file a timely response to the
_____ Petition for Dissolution of Marriage _____ as
required by law.

DATED: __ March 15, 2006 __

Lisa Smith _____
Signature

Name __ Lisa Smith _____

Address __ 2476 Highgrove Way _____

__ Jackson, Columbia 22101 __

Telephone No. __ (201) 555-7739 _____

DEFAULT

A default is entered in this action against the _____ Respondent _____ for failure
to serve or file a response as required by law.

DATED: _____

CLERK OF COURT

By: _____

Form K

IN THE CIRCUIT COURT OF THE FIRST JUDICIAL CIRCUIT

KING COUNTY, STATE OF COLUMBIA

_____LISA SMITH_____,
Petitioner

CASE NO. _____06-2837_____

_____JAMES SMITH_____,
Respondent

AFFIDAVIT OF NONMILITARY SERVICE

STATE OF   Columbia   )
COUNTY OF   King   )

_____Lisa Smith_____, being first duly sworn, states under penalty of perjury:

__x__   1.   That I know of my own personal knowledge that the ___Respondent___ is not in the Armed Forces of the United States.

_____   2.   That I have inquired of the Armed Forces of the United States and the U.S. Public Health Service to determine whether the _____ is a member of the armed services and am attaching certificates stating that the _____ is not now in the Armed Forces.

DATED: ___March 23, 2006___   *Lisa Smith* _____
                                    Signature of Affiant

                                    Name _Lisa Smith_____
                                    Address _2476 Highgrove Way_____
                                         _Jackson, Columbia 22101_____
                                    Telephone No. _(201) 555-7739_____

    SWORN TO AND subscribed before me on _____, 20_____,
by _____, who ❏ is personally known to me
❏ produced _____ as identification.

_____
NOTARY PUBLIC
My Commission Expires:

Form L

IN THE CIRCUIT COURT OF THE FIRST JUDICIAL CIRCUIT
KING COUNTY, STATE OF COLUMBIA

In re the Marriage of

_____ LISA SMITH _____,
                              Petitioner

CASE NO: ___06-2837_____

_____ JAMES SMITH _____,
                              Respondent

MOTION FOR SERVICE BY PUBLICATION

The Petitioner moves this court to issue a Notice of Action for service by publication in this action, and states under penalty of perjury that:

1. I have made diligent search and inquiry to discover the name and residence of Respondent: (Specify details of search)

    __x__ I have made inquiry with the postal authorities.

    __x__ I have checked telephone directories.

    __x__ I have inquired of relatives, friends, and/or acquaintances.

    _____ Other (specify) _____.

2. The age of Respondent is ____over ____under the age of 18 years (or ____ is unknown).

3. __x__ The residence of Respondent is unknown to Affiant.

    _____ The residence of Respondent is in some state or county other than the State of Columbia, and Respondent's last known address is: _____
    _____.

    _____ The Respondent, having residence in Columbia, has been absent therefrom for more than 60 days prior to the making of this affidavit, or conceals him(her)self so that process cannot be served personally upon him (her), and that Affiant believes that there is no person in the state upon whom service of process would bind said absent or concealed Respondent.

                                   *Lisa Smith*_____
                                   Signature of Petitioner
                                   Name __Lisa Smith_____
                                   Address __2476 Highgrove Way_____
                                   _____Jackson, Columbia 22101__
                                   Telephone No. _(201) 555-7739_____

Sworn to and signed before me on _____, 20____

_____
NOTARY PUBLIC

My Commission Expires:

Form M

IN THE CIRCUIT COURT OF THE FIRST JUDICIAL CIRCUIT
KING COUNTY, STATE OF COLUMBIA

In re the Marriage of

_____ LISA SMITH _____ ,
                    Petitioner

                                      CASE NO: ___06-2837___

_____ JAMES SMITH _____ ,
                    Respondent

NOTICE OF ACTION - DISSOLUTION OF MARRIAGE

TO: James Smith

    YOU ARE HEREBY NOTIFIED that an action for dissolution of marriage has been filed against you and you are required to serve a copy of your written defenses, if any, to _____ Lisa Smith _____ , Petitioner, whose address is _2476 Highgrove Way,_ _Jackson, Columbia 22102_____ , on or before _____, 20____, and file the original with the clerk of this court before service on Petitioner or immediately thereafter. If you fail to do so, a default will be entered against you for the relief demanded in the petition.

    WITNESS my hand and the seal of this Court on _____.

CLERK OF THE COURT

By _____

Deputy Clerk

Form N

IN THE CIRCUIT COURT OF THE FIRST JUDICIAL CIRCUIT
KING COUNTY, STATE OF COLUMBIA

In re the Marriage of

_____LISA SMITH_____,
Petitioner

CASE NO: ___06-2837_____

_____JAMES SMITH_____,
Respondent

SUBPOENA DUCES TECUM

THE STATE OF COLUMBIA:

TO: Payroll Clerk
Old Buildings-R-Us
721 Wright Drive
Jackson, Columbia 22102

    YOU ARE HEREBY COMMANDED to appear before the Honorable __Henry___ __Whitaker, Circuit Judge__, at the _____King_____ County Courthouse in __Jackson__, __Columbia__, on ___April 6___, 20_06_, at __9:00__ A.M., to testify in this action and to have with you at that time and place the following:

    If you fail to appear, you may be in contempt of court. You are subpoenaed to appear by the following person or attorney and unless excused from this subpoena by said person or attorney or the court, you shall respond to this subpoena as directed.

DATED: _____

CLERK OF THE CIRCUIT COURT

PARTY REQUESTING SUBPOENA:

Name: _Lisa Smith_____   By _____

Address: _2476 Highgrove Way_____   As Deputy Clerk

      _Jackson, Columbia 22101___

Telephone No. _(201) 555-7739_____

Worksheets

This Appendix contains blank worksheets that may be helpful as you prepare your divorce case. All of the worksheets are discussed throughout the text. The worksheets can also be found on the CD-ROM.

Worksheet 1: Personal Information 230

Worksheet 2: Document Checklist 232

Worksheet 3: Property Inventory 233

Worksheet 4: Debt Inventory 234

Worksheet 5: Child Support Worksheet—
Percentage of Income Method 235

Worksheet 6: Child Support Worksheet—
Combined Income Method 237

Worksheet 7: Divorce File Cover Sheet 240

Worksheet 8: Divorce File Document Index 241

Worksheet 1: Personal Information

<u>YOU</u>:

Your Name (as it appears on your marriage certificate): _____

Address: _____

Home Phone: _____

Home Fax: _____

Work Phone: _____

Email Address: _____

Social Security Number: _____

Date of Birth: _____ Age: _____

Date of Marriage: _____

Place of Marriage: _____

Date of Separation: _____

Employer: _____

Employer's Address: _____

Employer's Phone: _____

<u>YOUR SPOUSE</u>:

Spouse's Name (as it appears on your marriage certificate): _____

Address: _____

Home Phone: _____

Home Fax: _____

Work Phone: _____

Email Address: _____

Social Security Number: _____

Date of Birth: _____ Age: _____

Date of Marriage: _____

Place of Marriage: _____

Date of Separation: _____

Employer: _____

Employer's Address: _____

Employer's Phone: _____

<u>YOUR CHILDREN:</u>

Child's Name (as it appears on birth certificate): _____
Current Address: _____
Residence Address(es) for past 5 years: _____

_____
Social Security Number: _____
Date of Birth: _____ Age: _____

Child's Name (as it appears on birth certificate): _____
Current Address: _____
Residence Address(es) for past 5 years: _____

_____
Social Security Number: _____
Date of Birth: _____ Age: _____

Child's Name (as it appears on birth certificate): _____
Current Address: _____
Residence Address(es) for past 5 years: _____

_____
Social Security Number: _____
Date of Birth: _____ Age: _____

Child's Name (as it appears on birth certificate): _____
Current Address: _____
Residence Address(es) for past 5 years: _____

_____
Social Security Number: _____
Date of Birth: _____ Age: _____

Worksheet 2: Document Checklist

❏ Most recent paystubs (you and spouse)

❏ Most recent income tax return

❏ Last year's W-2 forms (you and spouse)

❏ Bank statements

❏ Brokerage account statements

❏ Real estate deeds

❏ Motor vehicle titles and registrations (including boats, RVs, etc.)

❏ Your will

❏ Your spouse's will

❏ Any trust documents

❏ Life insurance policies

❏ Disability insurance policies

❏ Pension or retirement fund statements

❏ Health insurance cards, policies, and statements

❏ Credit card statements

❏ Mortgage documents

❏ Motor vehicle loan documents

❏ Other loan documents

❏ Most recent utility bills (electric, gas, phone)

❏ Other:

Worksheet 3: Property Inventory

(1) N-M	(2) DESCRIPTION	(3) ID#	(4) VALUE	(5) BALANCE OWED	(6) EQUITY	(7) OWNER H-W-J	(8) H	(9) W

Worksheet 4: Debt Inventory

(1) N-M	(2) CREDITOR	(3) ACCOUNT NO.	(4) NOTES	(5) MONTHLY PAYMENT	(6) BALANCE OWED	(7) DATE	(8) OWNER H-W-J	(9) H	(10) W

Worksheet 5: Child Support Worksheet—
Percentage of Income Method

NOTE: *If your state uses the percentage of income method, complete this worksheet. If your state uses the combined income method, complete* **WORKSHEET 6** *instead. See the listing for your state in Appendix A to determine which method you should use.*

CAUTION:

The calculation of child support is often a complicated procedure, and varies greatly from state to state. Therefore, this form is very general in nature. It includes information that is common to many states, however, any given income, deduction, or other item may or may not be used in your state. Be sure to refer to Appendix A—as well as any other source you consult—for information about how your state calculates child support, to determine whether a particular item on this form applies to your state. For example, some states use gross income, while others allow deductions for such things as income taxes and FICA.

USE MONTHLY AMOUNTS.

Noncustodial Parent

Gross Income:

Salary or Wages: _____

Bonuses, Commissions, Overtime, Tips, etc.: _____

Self-employment income: _____

Disability/SSI: _____

Workers' Compensation: _____

Unemployment Compensation: _____

Pension/Retirement Income: _____

Annuity Payments: _____

Social Security Benefits: _____

Interest Income: _____

Dividends: _____

Rental Income: _____

Income from Royalties, Trusts, and Estates: _____

Alimony Actually Received: _____

Other Income: _____

_____   _____

_____   _____

_____   _____

_____   _____

_____   _____

TOTAL GROSS INCOME: _____

Deductions From Income:

Federal Income Tax: _____

State Income Tax: _____

Local Income Tax: _____

FICA: _____

Self-Employment Tax: _____

Medicare Payments: _____

Mandatory Union Dues: _____

Mandatory Retirement Payments: _____

Health Insurance Premiums: _____

Court-Ordered Child Support for Children
    from Another Relationship: _____

Court-Ordered Alimony: _____

Other Allowed Deductions:

_____   _____

_____   _____

_____   _____

_____   _____

_____   _____

TOTAL DEDUCTIONS: _____

TOTAL NET INCOME: _____

Percentage Based Upon
    Number of Children: x _____
BASIC MONTHLY CHILD SUPPORT   _____

Other Adjustments Allowed
    By Your State:

_____   _____

_____   _____

_____   _____

_____   _____

TOTAL CHILD SUPPORT: _____

Worksheet 6: Child Support Worksheet—
Combined Income Method

NOTE: *If your state uses the combined income method, complete this worksheet. If your state uses the percentage of income method, complete* **WORKSHEET 5** *instead. See the listing for your state in Appendix A to determine which method you should use.*

CAUTION:

The calculation of child support is often a complicated procedure, and varies greatly from state to state. Therefore, this form is very general in nature. It includes information that is common to many states, however, any given income, deduction, or other item may or may not be used in your state. Be sure to refer to Appendix A of this book—as well as any other source you consult—for information about how your state calculates child support, to determine whether a particular item on this form applies to your state. For example, some states may only allow deductions for income taxes and FICA, while others allow one or more of the additional deductions listed below.

USE MONTHLY AMOUNTS.

	Noncustodial Parent	Custodial Parent
Gross Income:		
Salary or Wages:	_____	_____
Bonuses, Commissions, Overtime, Tips, etc.:	_____	_____
Self-Employment Income	_____	_____
Disability/SSI:	_____	_____
Workers' Compensation:	_____	_____
Unemployment Compensation:	_____	_____
Pension/Retirement Income:	_____	_____
Annuity Payments:	_____	_____
Social Security Benefits:	_____	_____
Interest Income:	_____	_____
Dividends:	_____	_____
Rental Income:	_____	_____
Income from Royalties, Trusts, and Estates:	_____	_____
Alimony Actually Received:	_____	_____
Other Income:		
_____	_____	_____
_____	_____	_____
_____	_____	_____
_____	_____	_____
TOTAL GROSS INCOME:	_____	_____

	Noncustodial Parent	Custodial Parent
Deductions From Income:		
Federal Income Tax:	_____	_____
State Income Tax:	_____	_____
Local Income Tax:	_____	_____
FICA:	_____	_____
Self-Employment Tax:	_____	_____
Medicare Payments:	_____	_____
Mandatory Union Dues:	_____	_____
Mandatory Retirement Payments:	_____	_____
Health Insurance Premiums:	_____	_____
Court-Ordered Child Support for Children from Another Relationship:	_____	_____
Court-Ordered Alimony:	_____	_____
Other Allowed Deductions:		
_____	_____	_____
_____	_____	_____
_____	_____	_____
_____	_____	_____
_____	_____	_____
TOTAL DEDUCTIONS:	_____	_____

1. TOTAL NET INCOME: a. _____   b. _____

2. COMBINED NET INCOME (a + b):   2. _____

3. BASIC MONTHLY CHILD SUPPORT: 3. _____
   [from state table or chart]

4. PERCENT OF BASIC MONTHLY
   SUPPORT: a. _____   b. _____
        1a divided by line 2   1b divided by line 2

5. SHARE OF BASIC MONTHLY
   SUPPORT: a. _____   b. _____
        3 x 4a   3 x 4b

	<u>Noncustodial Parent</u>	<u>Custodial Parent</u>
6. Other Adjustments Allowed By Your State:		
_____	_____	_____
_____	_____	_____
_____	_____	_____
_____	_____	_____
_____	_____	_____

CHILD SUPPORT (5a + 6):   _____

Worksheet 7: Divorce File Cover Sheet

<u>Court Information:</u>

Case Number: _____

<u>Judge:</u> _____

      Name: _____

      Mailing Address: _____

      Phone: _____

      Fax: _____

      Secretary/Judicial Assistant: _____

<u>Court Clerk:</u> _____

      Mailing Address: _____

      Phone: _____

      Fax: _____

<u>Spouse:</u> _____

      Mailing Address: _____

      Phone: _____

      Fax: _____

      Email: _____

<u>Spouse's Attorney:</u> _____

      Name: _____

      Mailing Address: _____

      Phone: _____

      Fax: _____

      Email: _____

      Attorney or State Bar Number: _____

Worksheet 8: Divorce File Document Index

Doc. #	Document Title	Date
_____	_____	_____
_____	_____	_____
_____	_____	_____
_____	_____	_____
_____	_____	_____
_____	_____	_____
_____	_____	_____
_____	_____	_____
_____	_____	_____
_____	_____	_____
_____	_____	_____
_____	_____	_____
_____	_____	_____
_____	_____	_____
_____	_____	_____
_____	_____	_____

Blank Forms

This appendix contains sample forms that are similar to those used in most states. However, because each state is different (and sometimes each county is different), you will need to do some research before using these forms. Be sure you do the following five steps.

1. Read Chapter 9 of this book regarding forms.

2. Read the information for your state in Appendix A of this book.

3. Check with your court clerk to find out if there are any official forms you can or must use. If so, use the official forms.

4. Review one or more divorce files at your court clerk's office to see how papers are prepared in your area, then use the same format.

5. Review the sample forms in Appendix B.

The following forms are found in this appendix.

form 1: Certificate of Service 245

form 2: Complaint for Divorce (or Petition for Dissolution, etc.) 247

form 3: Financial Statement 251

form 4: Marital Settlement Agreement 255

form 5: Uniform Child Custody Jurisdiction Act Affidavit 259

form 6: Answer and Waiver 261

form 7: Affidavit of Nonmilitary Service 263

form 8: Request for Certificate of Military Status 265

form 9: Notice of Hearing. 267

form 10: Motion to Enter Default 269

form 11: Final Judgment (or Decree, etc.) 271

form 12: Motion for Temporary Relief 275

form 13: Order for Temporary Relief 277

form 14: Answer. 279

_____,

CASE NO._____

_____,

CERTIFICATE OF SERVICE

I HEREBY CERTIFY that a true and correct copy of the _____

_____

WAS: ☐ mailed   ☐ hand delivered to the parties or persons listed below, this

_____ day of _____, 20_____.

Name _____   Name _____

Address _____   Address _____

_____   _____

Telephone No. _____   Telephone No. _____

_____

Signature

Name _____

Address _____

_____

Telephone No. _____

This page intentionally blank.

_____,

CASE NO. _____

_____,

_____

The _____ (hereinafter called the _____), for his/her _____ against the _____ (hereinafter called the _____), alleges and states:

1. RESIDENCE. The ❏ Husband ❏ Wife has been a resident of the State of _____ since _____, and of the County of _____ since _____, and otherwise meets all residency requirements for filing this action.

2. HUSBAND'S STATISTICAL FACTS:
   A. Name: _____
   B. Previous Names, if any: _____
   C. ❏ Current ❏ Last known Address: _____
   _____
   D. Length of Residency: _____
   E. Date of Birth: _____
   F. Social Security Number: _____
   G. Occupation: _____
   H. Employer's Name and Address: _____
   _____

3. WIFE'S STATISTICAL FACTS:
   A. Name: _____
   B. Previous Names, if any: _____
   C. ❏ Current ❏ Last known Address: _____
   _____
   D. Length of Residency: _____
   E. Date of Birth: _____
   F. Social Security Number: _____
   G. Occupation: _____
   H. Employer's Name and Address: _____
   _____

4. The parties were married on _____, at _____;
    and the marriage is registered at _____.

5. The parties were separated on _____.

6. DECLARATION REGARDING MINOR CHILDREN OF THIS MARRIAGE:
    A. ❏ There are no minor or dependent children of the parties.
    B. ❏ The wife is pregnant, with an expected delivery date of _____.
    C. ❏ The wife is not pregnant.
    D. ❏ The parties have the following minor or dependent children:

Name	Address	Birth Date	Age	Sex	Current Custody

    E. ❏ A Uniform Child Custody Jurisdiction Act Affidavit is being completed
        and filed along with this _____.

7. The ❏ Husband   ❏ Wife seeks a _____
    on the following grounds:

8. ❏ The parties have entered into the settlement agreement attached hereto, resolv-
    ing the matters of:
        ❏ Property division
        ❏ Child custody
        ❏ Child support
        ❏ Alimony
        ❏ Other:

9. The parties   ❏ DO   ❏ DO NOT have marital property to be divided.

    A. ❏ The parties have already divided their property, and each party will keep
        the property in his or her possession.
    B. ❏ The parties have entered into the attached settlement agreement, which
        provides for the division of their property.
    C. ❏ A Financial Affidavit including the parties' assets and debts is being com-
        pleted and filed along with this _____.
    D. ❏ The following are the Husband's nonmarital assets and obligations:

E.   ❏ The following are the Wife's nonmarital assets and obligations:

10.   ❏ The ❏ Husband   ❏ Wife requests that his/her name be changed/restored to: _____.

11.   This action is being filed in good faith, for the purposes and reasons set forth herein.

12.   RELIEF REQUESTED. The   ❏ Husband   ❏ Wife requests the following relief from this court:

   A.   Grant the parties a ❏ divorce from the bonds of marriage ❏ dissolution of the marriage.

   B.   ❏ Legal child custody of the child(ren) be awarded to:
           ❏ Husband   ❏ Wife
           ❏ Other:_____

   C.   ❏ Physical custody (primary residence) of the child(ren) be awarded to:
           ❏ Husband   ❏ Wife
           ❏ Other:_____

   D.   ❏ Child visitation rights be granted to the party without physical custody as follows:
           ❏ Liberal   ❏ Reasonable   ❏ Scheduled (attach schedule)
           ❏ Restricted or Supervised as follows: _____
           _____.

   E.   ❏ Child support be awarded to: ❏ Husband   ❏ Wife

   F.   ❏ Medical/dental insurance for child(ren) be provided by:
           ❏ Husband   ❏ Wife

   G.   ❏ Unusual medical/dental expenses be provided by:
           ❏ Husband   ❏ Wife

   H.   ❏ Alimony be awarded to: ❏ Husband   ❏ Wife

   I.   ❏ Property rights be determined.

J.   ❏   Wife's former name restored to: _____

K.   Any other injunctive or other orders as may be proper.

L.   ❏   Other specific relief:

DATED: _____   _____

                                                 Signature

                                                 Name _____

                                                 Address _____

                                                 _____

                                                 Telephone No. _____

I DECLARE UNDER PENALTY OF PERJURY, that the facts stated herein are true and correct.

                                                 _____

                                                 Signature

       SWORN TO AND subscribed before me on _____, 20_____, by _____, who ❏ is personally known to me ❏ produced _____ as identification.

_____

NOTARY PUBLIC
My Commission Expires:

_____,

CASE NO. _____

_____,

FINANCIAL STATEMENT

STATE OF   )
COUNTY OF   )

    BEFORE ME, this day personally appeared _____,
who being duly sworn, deposes and says that the following information is true and correct
according to his/her best knowledge and belief:

ITEM 1: EMPLOYMENT AND INCOME

OCCUPATION: _____
EMPLOYED BY: _____
ADDRESS: _____
                   _____
SOC. SEC. #:   _____
PAY PERIOD: _____
RATE OF PAY: _____

AVERAGE GROSS MONTHLY INCOME FROM EMPLOYMENT $_____

Bonuses, commissions, allowances, overtime, tips and similar payments   _____
Business Income from sources such as self-employment, partnership,
      close corporations, and/or independent contracts (gross receipts
      minus ordinary and necessary expenses required to produce income)   _____
Disability benefits   _____
Workers' compensation   _____
Unemployment compensation   _____
Pension, retirement, or annuity payments   _____
Social Security benefits   _____
Spousal support received from previous marriage   _____
Interest and dividends   _____
Rental income (gross receipts minus ordinary and necessary expenses
      required to produce income)   _____
Income from royalties, trusts, or estates   _____
Reimbursed expenses and in kind payments to the extent that they
      reduce personal living expenses   _____
Gains derived from dealing in property (not including nonrecurring gains)   _____
Itemize any other income of a recurring nature   _____
TOTAL MONTHLY GROSS INCOME $_____
LESS DEDUCTIONS:

Federal, state, and local income taxes (corrected for filing
   status and actual number of withholding allowances) $_____

FICA or self-employment tax (annualized)   _____

Mandatory union dues   _____

Mandatory retirement   _____

Health insurance payments   _____

Court ordered support payments for the children actually paid   _____

TOTAL DEDUCTIONS $_____

TOTAL NET INCOME $_____

ITEM 2: AVERAGE MONTHLY EXPENSES

HOUSEHOLD:

Mtg. or rent payments   _____
Property taxes & insurance   _____
Electricity   _____
Water, garbage, & sewer   _____
Telephone   _____
Fuel oil or natural gas   _____
Repairs and maintenance   _____
Lawn and pool care   _____
Pest control   _____
Misc. household   _____
Food and grocery items   _____
Meals outside home   _____
Other:

_____   _____
_____   _____

AUTOMOBILE:

Gasoline and oil   _____
Repairs   _____
Auto tags and license   _____
Insurance   _____
Other:

_____
_____   _____

CHILDREN'S EXPENSES:

Nursery or baby-sitting   _____
School tuition   _____
School supplies   _____
Lunch money   _____
Allowance   _____
Clothing   _____
Medical, dental, prescriptions   _____
Vitamins   _____
Barber/beauty parlor   _____
Cosmetics/toiletries   _____
Gifts for special holidays   _____
Other expenses:

_____   _____
_____   _____

INSURANCES:

Health   _____
Life   _____
Other Insurance:

_____   _____
_____   _____

OTHER EXPENSES NOT LISTED ABOVE:

Dry cleaning and laundry   _____
Affiant's clothing   _____
Affiant's medical, dental,   _____
  prescriptions
Affiant's beauty salon/barber   _____
Affiant's gifts (special holidays)   _____

Pets:
  Grooming   _____
  Veterinarian   _____

Membership Dues:
  Professional dues   _____
  Social dues   _____

Entertainment   _____
Vacations   _____
Publications   _____
Religious organizations   _____
Charities   _____

Miscellaneous   _____
OTHER EXPENSES:

_____   _____
_____   _____
_____   _____

TOTAL ABOVE EXPENSES $_____

PAYMENTS TO CREDITORS:

TO WHOM:	BALANCE DUE:	MONTHLY PAYMENTS:
_____	_____	_____
_____	_____	_____
_____	_____	_____
_____	_____	_____
_____	_____	_____
_____	_____	_____
_____	_____	_____
_____	_____	_____
_____	_____	_____

TOTAL MONTHLY PAYMENTS TO CREDITORS: $_____

TOTAL MONTHLY EXPENSES: $_____

ITEM 3: ASSETS (OWNERSHIP: IF JOINT, ALLOCATE EQUITY)

Description	Value	Husband	Wife
Cash (on hand or in banks)	_____	_____	_____
Stocks/bonds/notes	_____	_____	_____
Real Estate:			
Home:	_____	_____	_____
_____	_____	_____	_____
_____	_____	_____	_____
_____	_____	_____	_____
Automobiles:			
_____	_____	_____	_____
_____	_____	_____	_____
_____	_____	_____	_____
Other personal property:			
Contents of home	_____	_____	_____
Jewelry	_____	_____	_____
Life Ins./cash surrender value	_____	_____	_____
Other Assets:			
_____	_____	_____	_____
_____	_____	_____	_____
_____	_____	_____	_____
TOTAL ASSETS:	$_____	$_____	$_____

ITEM 4: LIABILITIES

Creditor	Security	Balance	Husband	Wife
_____	_____	_____	_____	_____
_____	_____	_____	_____	_____
_____	_____	_____	_____	_____
_____	_____	_____	_____	_____
_____	_____	_____	_____	_____
_____	_____	_____	_____	_____
_____	_____	_____	_____	_____
_____	_____	_____	_____	_____
TOTAL LIABILITIES:	_____	$_____	$_____	$_____

_____
Affiant

SWORN TO AND subscribed before me on _____,
20_____, by _____,
who ❏ is personally known to me ❏ produced _____ as identification.

_____
NOTARY PUBLIC
My Commission Expires:

CERTIFICATE OF SERVICE

I HEREBY CERTIFY that a true and correct copy of the above Financial Statement has been furnished by mail this _____ day of _____, 20_____, to: _____
_____.

_____
Signature

_____,

CASE NO. _____

_____,

MARITAL SETTLEMENT AGREEMENT

We, _____, and _____, were married on _____. We desire to terminate our marriage, and we have made this agreement to settle once and for all the matters set forth below. Each of us states that we have honestly disclosed our property, debts, and income to each other, and each of us states that we believe the other one has been open and honest in preparing this agreement. Each of us agrees to sign and exchange any papers that might be needed to complete this agreement. This agreement is based upon our current circumstances as indicated in the financial affidavits filed in this case.

CHILD CUSTODY

❑   We will share in parenting responsibilities; however, physical custody of the minor child(ren), _____ shall be awarded to the Husband; and the Wife shall have reasonable and liberal visitation rights.

❑   We will share in parenting responsibilities; however, physical custody of the minor child(ren), _____ shall be awarded to the Wife; and the Husband shall have reasonable and liberal visitation rights.

❑   Other:

CHILD SUPPORT

❑   The   ❑ Husband   ❑ Wife agrees to pay the sum of $_____ per _____ as support and maintenance for the minor child(ren) in the physical custody of the other parent.

❑   The   ❑ Husband   ❑ Wife agrees to maintain health insurance coverage for the minor child/children as long as such insurance is available at a reasonable group rate.

❑   Other:

DIVISION OF PROPERTY

We shall each keep our own personal clothing and effects, unless otherwise indicated below. We divide our property as follows:

1.   Husband transfers to Wife as her sole and separate property:

A.

B.

C.

D.

E.

F.

G.

❏ Continued on Additional Sheet.

2.   Wife transfers to Husband as his sole and separate property:

A.

B.

C.

D.

E.

F.

G.

❏ Continued on Additional Sheet.

DIVISION OF DEBTS

We divide responsibility for payment of our debts as follows:

3.   Husband shall pay the following debts and will not at any time hold Wife responsible for them:

A.

B.

C.

D.

E.

F.

G.

❏ Continued on Additional Sheet.

4.   Wife shall pay the following debts and will not at any time hold Husband responsible for them:

A.

B.

C.

D.

E.

F.

G.

❏ Continued on Additional Sheet.

ALIMONY

❏   No alimony shall be awarded to either party.

❏   The   ❏ Husband   ❏ Wife shall pay alimony to the other party in the sum of

     $_____ per _____, for a period of _____;

     or until the   ❏ Husband   ❏ Wife dies or remarries, whichever occurs first.

❏   Other:

DATED: _____   DATED: _____

_____   _____

Husband's signature   Wife's signature

Name _____   Name _____

Address _____   Address _____

_____   _____

Telephone No. _____   Telephone No. _____

     SWORN TO AND subscribed before me on _____, 20_____,

by _____, who   ❏ is personally

known to me   ❏ produced _____ as identification.

_____

NOTARY PUBLIC

My Commission Expires:

This page intentionally blank.

_____ ,

CASE NO. _____

_____ ,

UNIFORM CHILD CUSTODY JURISDICTION ACT AFFIDAVIT

1.   The name and present address of each child (under 18) in this case is:

2.   The places where the child(ren) has/have lived within the last 5 years are:

3.   The name(s) and present address(es) of custodians with whom the child(ren) has/have lived within the past 5 years are:

4.   I do not know of, and have not participated (as a party, witness, or in any other capacity) in, any other court decision, order, or proceeding (including divorce, separate maintenance, child neglect, dependency, or guardianship) concerning the custody or visitation of the child(ren) in this state or any other state, except: [specify case name and number and court's name and address]

5.   I do not have information of any pending proceeding (including divorce, separate maintenance, child neglect, dependency, or guardianship) concerning the custody or visitation of the child(ren), in this state or any other state except: [specify case name and number and court's name and address]

    That proceeding _____ is continuing _____ has been stayed by the court.

    _____ Temporary action by this court is necessary to protect the child(ren) because the child(ren) has/have been subjected to or threatened with mistreatment or abuse or is/are otherwise neglected or dependent.
Attach explanation.

6.   I do not know of any person who is not already a party to this proceeding who has physical custody of, or who claims to have custody or visitation rights with, the child(ren), except: [state name(s) and address(es)]

7.   The child(ren)'s "home state" is _____. ["Home State" means the state in which the child(ren) immediately preceding the time involved lived with his or her parents, a parent, or a person acting as a parent, for at least 6 consecutive months, and, in the case of a child less than 6 months old, the state in which the child lived from birth with any of the persons mentioned. Periods of temporary absence of the named persons are counted as a part of the 6 month or other period.]

I acknowledge a continuing duty to advise this court of any custody or visitation proceeding (including dissolution of marriage, separate maintenance, child neglect, or dependency) concerning the child(ren) in this state or any other state about which information is obtained during this proceeding.

DATED: _____

_____
Signature of Affiant

Name _____

Address _____

_____

Telephone No. _____

    SWORN TO AND subscribed before me on _____,
20_____, by _____, who ❑ is personally known to me ❑ produced _____ as identification.

_____
NOTARY PUBLIC
My Commission Expires:

_____,

CASE NO. _____

_____,

ANSWER AND WAIVER

The _____, _____, answers the _____ as follows:

1. The _____ admits all of the allegations contained in the _____, and agrees to all relief requested therein.

2. The _____ waives appearance at the final hearing.

3. The _____ requests that a copy of the final judgment entered in this case be forwarded to him/her at the address below.

_____
Signature of Affiant

Name _____

Address _____

_____

Telephone No. _____

SWORN TO AND subscribed before me on _____, 20____, by _____, who ❑ is personally known to me ❑ produced _____ as identification.

_____

NOTARY PUBLIC
My Commission Expires:

This page intentionally blank.

_____,

CASE NO. _____

_____,

AFFIDAVIT OF NONMILITARY SERVICE

STATE OF   )
COUNTY OF   )

_____, being first duly sworn, states under penalty of perjury:

_____   1.   That I know of my own personal knowledge that the _____ is not in the Armed Forces of the United States.

_____   2.   That I have inquired of the Armed Forces of the United States and the U.S. Public Health Service to determine whether the _____ is a member of the armed services and am attaching certificates stating that the _____ is not now in the Armed Forces.

DATED:_____

                                        _____
                                        Signature of Affiant

                                        Name _____
                                        Address _____

                                        _____
                                        Telephone No . _____

        SWORN TO AND subscribed before me on _____, 20_____, by _____, who ❑ is personally known to me   ❑ produced _____ as identification.

_____
NOTARY PUBLIC
My Commission Expires:

This page intentionally blank.

——————————————————————,

CASE NO. _____

——————————————————————,

REQUEST FOR CERTIFICATE OF MILITARY STATUS

TO: Commandant, U.S. Coast Guard, Headquarters, Room 4616, 2100
            2nd St., S.W., Washington, DC 22059-0001

        Military Personnel Records Center (AFPMCA), N.E. Office Pl,
            9504-IH 35 No., San Antonio, TX 78233-6635

        Department of Navy, Bureau of Navy Personnel, U.S. Navy,
            Washington, DC 20300

        Commandant of Marine Corps (CODE DGK-7), Headquarters,
            U.S. Marine Corps, Washington, DC 20350

        Surgeon General, U.S. Public Health Service, Div. of Comm.,
            Off. Personnel, 5600 Fishers Lane, Rockville, MD 20857

        Personnel Records Div., Ofc. U. S. Army Enlisted Records Center,
            Fort Benjamin Harrison, IN 46249

RE: _____   _____
            [Party]   [Soc. Sec. #]

    This case involves a divorce/dissolution of marriage. It is imperative that a determi-
nation be made whether the above named individual, who has an interest in these
proceedings, is presently in the military service of the United States, and the date of induc-
tion and discharge, if any. This information is necessary to comply with §601 of the Soldier's
and Sailor's Civil Relief Act of 1940, as amended. Please supply a certification of verifica-
tion as soon as possible. My check is enclosed for your search fees. A self-addressed stamped
envelope is enclosed.

DATED: _____   _____
                                                    Signature

                                                    Requesting Party
                                                    Name _____
                                                    Address _____

                                                    _____
                                                    Telephone No. _____

This page intentionally blank.

_____,

                    CASE NO. _____

_____,

NOTICE OF HEARING

TO:

    PLEASE TAKE NOTICE that the _____

will be called for hearing on _____, the _____ day of _____,

20___, at _____ ___. M., before the Honorable _____,

Judge of the above-titled court, _____   _____

_____.

                              _____

                              Signature

                              Name _____

                              Address _____

                              _____

                              Telephone No. _____

This page intentionally blank.

_____,

        CASE NO. _____

_____,

MOTION TO ENTER DEFAULT

The _____ hereby moves for the entry of a default against the _____ for failure to serve or file a timely response to the _____ as required by law.

DATED: _____

_____
Signature

Name _____

Address _____

_____

Telephone No. _____

DEFAULT

A default is entered in this action against the _____ for failure to serve or file a response as required by law.

DATED: _____

CLERK OF COURT

By: _____

This page intentionally blank.

_____,

                                        CASE NO. _____

_____,

_____

This action was heard before the Court. On the evidence presented,

IT IS ADJUDGED that the bonds of marriage between the Husband, _____and the Wife, _____, are dissolved.

IT IS FURTHER ADJUDGED that:

❏   1.   The settlement agreement between the parties filed in this action was executed voluntarily after full disclosure and is approved and incorporated in this judgment by reference, and the parties are ordered to comply with it.

❏   2.   The Wife's former name is restored and she shall hereafter be known as: _____.

❏   3.   The parties shall share parenting responsibilities; however, physical custody of the minor child(ren) of the parties shall be awarded to the party designated below:

Name of Child	Child's Birthdate	Custody Awarded to:

Each party shall have the right to visit any child not in his or her physical custody at reasonable times and places after reasonable notice to the custodial party.

❏   4.   The ❏ Husband ❏ Wife shall pay child support to the other party in the sum of $_____ per _____, beginning _____, 20_____.

❏   5.   The ❏ Husband ❏ Wife shall provide health insurance coverage for the minor child(ren) whenever such insurance is reasonably available.

❏ 6. The ❏ Husband ❏ Wife shall pay alimony to the other party in the sum of $_____ per _____, beginning _____, 20_____, to terminate:

    ❏ On _____, 20_____, or on the death or remarriage of said other party, whichever occurs first.

    ❏ Upon the death or remarriage of the other party.

    ❏ Alimony is   ❏ Awarded   ❏ Not Awarded   pursuant to the request and agreement of the parties.

    ❏ Alimony is   ❏ Awarded   ❏ Not Awarded   based upon the following reasons:

❏ 7. The ❏ Husband ❏ Wife shall pay the other party's attorney's fees, set at $_____ (to be paid to _____), and court costs, taxed at $_____, both of which shall be paid within _____ days of the date of this judgment.

❏ 8. The Husband shall transfer to the Wife as her sole and separate property:

❏ 9. The Wife shall transfer to the Husband as his sole and separate property:

❏ 10. The Husband shall pay the following debts and shall not at any time hold the Wife responsible for them:

❏   11.   The Wife shall pay the following debts and shall not at any time hold the Husband responsible for them:

❏   12.   The parties' nonmarital assets and debts shall be distributed as follows:

❏   13.   Other Provisions:

ORDERED at _____, _____, on this _____ day of _____, 20_____.

_____
Judge

This page intentionally blank.

_____,

CASE NO. _____

_____,

MOTION FOR TEMPORARY RELIEF

The Plaintiff/Petitioner moves this Court to enter an order granting Plaintiff/Petitioner the following temporary relief pending the entry of a final order in this action:

[ ]   Granting temporary custody of the minor child(ren) of the parties to the Plaintiff/Petitioner.

[ ]   Ordering the Defendant/Respondent to pay reasonable child support to the Plaintiff/Petitioner.

[ ]   Ordering the Defendant/Respondent to pay temporary alimony to the Plaintiff/Petitioner.

[ ]   Other:

[ ]   It is requested that this motion be heard ex parte for the following reasons:

    This motion is based upon the pleadings filed in this action and any exhibits attached hereto.

DATED: _____

_____
Signature

Name _____

Address _____

_____

Telephone No . _____

This page intentionally blank.

_____,

CASE NO. _____

_____,

ORDER FOR TEMPORARY RELIEF

Upon consideration of the Plaintiff's/Petitioner's motion, and the Court being fully advised in the premises:

IT IS ORDERED that:

❏   Temporary custody of the minor child(ren) of the parties shall be awarded to the Plaintiff/Petitioner, and the Defendant/Respondent shall have reasonable visitation rights.

❏   The Defendant/Respondent shall pay the sum of $_____ per _____ for the temporary support of the minor child(ren).

❏   The Defendant/Respondent shall pay the sum of $_____ per _____ as temporary alimony to the Plaintiff/Petitioner.

❏   Other:

This order shall remain in effect until the entry of the final judgment of dissolution of marriage, or until further order of this Court.

ORDERED at _____, _____, on this _____ day of _____, 20_____.

_____
Judge

This page intentionally blank.

_____,

CASE NO. _____

_____,

ANSWER

The _____, _____, answers the
_____ as follows:

1. The _____ admits the allegations contained in paragraph(s)
_____ of the _____.

2. The _____ denies the allegations contained in paragraph(s)
_____ of the _____.

3. The _____ is without knowledge as to the allegations contained
in paragraph(s) _____ of the _____, and therefore
neither admits nor denies said allegations.

WHEREFORE, the _____ requests this Court to:

1. Take jurisdiction over the parties and the marriage, and determine any
issues the parties may not agree upon.

2. Enter its _____.

_____
Signature of Affiant

Name _____

Address _____

_____

Telephone No. _____

SWORN TO AND subscribed before me on _____,
20_____, by _____, who ❏ is personally
known to me ❏ produced _____ as identification.

_____
NOTARY PUBLIC
My Commission Expires:

Index

A

ABO Test, 59
acceptance, 6
adultery, 30, 112, 121
Affidavit of Nonmilitary Service, 83, 84
alcoholism, 29, 31
alimony, 77, 86, 87, 90, 98, 99, 107, 121, 122,
    127, 128, 133, 135, 138, 139, 142, 144
    calculating, 49
    duration of, 49
    qualifications for, 48
    tax considerations, 52
    types of, 48
alternatives to divorce, 7
anger, 6, 7, 15
annulment, 4
Answer, 78, 83, 84, 85, 101, 102, 107, 108,
    109, 110, 112, 113, 139
Answer and Waiver, 78, 83, 84, 101, 109
appliances, 41
approved for legal announcements, 106
attorneys, 4, 19, 20, 21, 22, 23, 24, 25, 26, 27,
    33, 34, 43, 45, 54, 60, 70, 85, 86, 89, 91,
    93, 96, 103, 104, 116, 121, 123, 124, 135

advantages, 20
evaluating, 22
fees, 26
finding, 22
firing, 27
referral service, 22
selecting, 21
working with, 24

B

bigamy, 4
bill of particulars, 110, 112, 113
blue book, 40, 41

C

case law, 17
case reporters, 18
case style, 70, 71, 72, 73, 80, 82, 83, 84, 85,
    86, 96, 99, 103, 104, 108, 110, 134
Certificate of Service, 70, 81, 100, 103,
    121, 136

child abuse, 77, 124, 126
child custody, 2, 3, 4, 5, 6, 12, 13, 14, 31,
    32, 51, 55, 56, 57, 58, 59, 60, 61, 66, 67,
    75, 79, 81, 82, 86, 88, 112, 116, 123,
    126, 133, 138
    factors, 57
    paternity issues, 58
child support, 80, 86, 88, 89, 90, 92, 98, 99,
    122, 123, 127, 133, 135, 137, 138, 142
    calculating, 63
    combined income method, 65
    percentage of income method, 64
    tax considerations, 66
Child Support Worksheet—Combined
    Income Method, 66
Child Support Worksheet—Percentage of
    Income Method, 64
children, 1, 2, 3, 5, 6, 7, 13, 14, 32, 35, 37,
    51, 56, 58, 60, 61, 62, 64, 65, 67, 75, 81,
    82, 83, 86, 91, 95, 96, 97, 98, 99, 107,
    112, 118, 122, 123, 135, 138
    special needs, 58
code, 16, 17, 39, 44, 52, 53, 58, 60, 66
community property, 37, 38
Complaint, 70, 72, 73, 75, 76, 78, 79, 83,
    89, 98, 101, 102, 103, 104, 107, 108,
    109, 110, 111, 112, 113, 133, 134, 140,
    143, 144
Complaint for Divorce, 72, 73, 83, 109,
    110, 111, 112, 113, 133
consent divorce, 31
contempt of court, 91, 95, 96, 137
contested divorce, 19, 31, 32, 115, 116,
    117, 119, 121, 123, 126
counseling, 7, 8, 9, 45, 58, 90, 91
counterclaim, 107, 109, 112
court clerk, 14, 69, 70, 71, 72, 73, 78, 79,
    84, 85, 87, 89, 90, 91, 92, 95, 96, 100,
    101, 102, 103, 104, 106, 108, 109, 110,
    116, 121, 125, 126, 129, 144
court hearings, 116, 124
court rules, 17

courtroom manners, 129
cross-claim, 107
cruelty, 2, 29, 31, 38
custodial parent, 49, 51, 55, 56, 61
custody. *See child custody*

D

dating, 6
Debt Inventory, 43, 81, 117
debts, 2, 5, 35, 37, 39, 41, 43, 44, 45, 76,
    87, 116, 135, 136, 138
default, 108, 109
denial, 6
desertion, 29, 31
digests, 17
dissolution of marriage, 2, 17
Divorce File Cover Sheet, 70
divorce from bed and board, 4
divorce law, 11, 13, 15, 17, 55
divorce procedure, 14
DNA Test, 58, 59, 60
Document Checklist, 37
domestic violence, 96
drug abuse, 31, 56
duress, 4

E

equitable distribution, 37, 38
evidence, 131

F

fees, 15, 20, 26, 27, 45, 54
filing, 69, 71, 73, 75, 77, 78, 79, 81, 83, 84,
    85, 87, 89, 90, 91, 93, 96, 101, 102, 105
    fees, 90

Final Judgment, 98, 116, 120, 121, 123, 134, 136, 140, 141
final offer, 88
financial divorce, 6
Financial Statement, 79, 80, 81, 91, 92, 93, 98, 99, 107
Form 1040, 45, 54
Form 8332, 61
fraud, 4
furniture, 41

G

grandparents, 61
grief, 6
guilt, 6, 7

H

hearsay, 131, 132
Human Leukocite Antigen (HLA) Test, 59

I

illegal drug use, 124
immoral sexual conduct, 124
impotence, 29, 31
imprisonment, 31
incest, 4
insanity, 31
interrogatories, 93
irretrievably broken, 2, 30

J

jewelry, 41
judges, 12, 14, 17, 20, 21, 50, 56, 57, 61, 70, 82, 88, 89, 90, 91, 92, 93, 96, 97, 98, 100, 101, 103, 104, 107, 112, 113, 115, 116, 117, 118, 120, 121, 123, 125, 126, 128, 129, 130, 131, 133, 134, 135, 136, 137, 142
judge's secretary, 14
judgment, 76, 86, 98, 107, 111, 116, 120, 121, 123, 132, 134, 135, 136, 137, 138, 140, 141

K

kidnap, 97

L

lack of companionship, 5
law library, 92, 95, 96, 99, 102, 103, 104, 126, 129
lawyers *See attorneys*
legal announcements, 106
legal bonds, 5
legal encyclopedias, 18
legal forms
    form 1, 100, 103, 121, 136
    form 2, 73, 75
    form 3, 79, 91, 98, 100
    form 4, 75, 76, 84, 86, 101, 108, 109
    form 5, 75
    form 6, 78, 83, 84, 101, 109, 111
    form 7, 83, 84, 85
    form 8, 85
    form 9, 103, 126
    form 10, 84, 106, 108
    form 11, 116, 120, 123, 134

form 12, 99
form 13, 99, 100
form 14, 110, 111
legal research, 15
legal separation, 4

M

marital property, 37, 38, 42
Marital Settlement Agreement, 75–76, 83, 84, 86, 101, 108, 109
marriage, 1, 2, 3, 4, 5, 6, 7, 8, 9, 13, 17, 29, 30, 37, 38, 48, 49, 50, 51, 58, 69, 73, 74, 75, 76, 83, 1, 110, 118, 119, 120, 122, 131, 138, 139, 140, 141, 142
mediation, 58, 90, 91
military, 33
Motion for a More Definite Statement, 110, 112
Motion for Bill of Particulars, 110, 112
Motion for Relief Pendente Lite, 99
Motion for Service by Publication, 105
Motion for Temporary Relief, 99, 100, 125
Motion to Dismiss, 109, 112
Motion to Enter Default, 84, 106, 108
Motion to Issue Subpoena, 93

N

negotiating, 87, 88, 118
no-fault divorce, 2, 4, 29, 30
noncustodial parent, 55, 56, 61, 63, 64, 65, 137
nondeductible expenses, 45
nonmarital property, 37, 38, 39, 42, 43, 76, 107, 117, 118-119, 133, 142
Notice of Action, 105, 106
Notice of Filing the Complaint, 101
Notice of Hearing, 103, 104, 126
Notice of Production from Non-Party, 92, 93

O

Order for Temporary Relief, 99, 100

P

paper size, 70
parenting classes, 90, 91
parties, 72
paternity tests, 58, 59, 60
permanent alimony, 48, 49
Personal Information, 35
personal service, 101, 104, 105, 143
petition, 70, 72, 73, 75, 76, 78, 83, 89, 101, 110, 111, 139, 140, 143
Petition for Divorce, 70, 72, 75
premarital agreement, 138, 143
property, 37, 38, 39, 40, 41
Property Inventory, 81, 87, 117
protecting your children, 97
protecting your property, 97
protecting yourself, 96
proving grounds for divorce, 30

R

rehabilitative alimony, 48, 49
real estate, 40
Red Cell Series, 59
Release of Claim to Exemption for Child of Divorced or Separated Parents, 61
representing yourself, 21
Request for Certificate of Military Status, 85
restraining order, 96, 98

S

secretary, 93, 100, 125, 126, 136

separation and residency requirements, 3

service by publication, 104, 105, 143

Servicemembers Civil Relief Act (SCRA), 34

setting a court date, 125

settlement agreement, 75, 76, 83, 84, 85, 86, 101, 108, 109, 134, 135, 136, 137, 141

sheriff, 70, 90, 93, 101, 102, 104, 105, 108, 127, 128, 143

simplified procedures, 78, 126

social and emotional divorce

Soldier's and Sailor's Civil Relief Act (SSCRA), 34

statutes, 16, 17, 18, 58, 65

stocks and bonds, 41

subpoena, 91, 92, 93, 115, 124, 128, 129, 143, 144

subpoena duces tecum, 129, 144

summons, 70, 101, 102, 109, 143, 144

T

temporary alimony, 98, 99, 135

trial separation, 9

U

uncontested divorce, 19, 31, 32, 82, 115, 126

Uniform Child Custody Jurisdiction Act, 75, 79, 81, 82

Uniform Child Custody Jurisdiction Act Affidavit, 75, 81, 82

Uniformed Services Former Spouse's Protection Act (USFSPA), 34

V

vehicles, 40

visitation, 2, 7, 55, 57, 58, 59, 61, 62, 77, 82, 90, 123, 126, 137, 138

W

witnesses, 126

    examining, 132

    expert witness, 128

    notifying, 128

    questioning, 129

Worksheet 1, 35

Worksheet 2, 37

Worksheet 3, 39

Worksheet 4, 43

Worksheet 5, 64, 65, 66

Worksheet 6, 64, 66

Worksheet 7, 70

Worksheet 8, 70

Y

Yellow Pages, 22

SPHINX LEGAL

TAKING THE MYSTERY OUT OF THE LAW™

Find divorce information for your specific state.

how to **File** for **Divorce** in **California**

ISBN 1-57248-489-6

how to **File** for **Divorce** in **Florida**

ISBN 1-57248-396-2

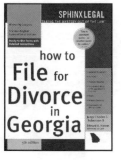

how to **File** for **Divorce** in **Georgia**

ISBN 1-57248-492-6

File for Divorce in Illinois

ISBN 1-57248-510-8

File for Divorce in Maryland, Virginia or the District of Columbia

ISBN 1-57248-536-1

how to **File** for **Divorce** in **Michigan**

ISBN 1-57248-467-5

how to **FILE** for **DIVORCE** in **MINNESOTA**

ISBN 1-57248-142-0

File for Divorce in New Jersey

ISBN 1-57248-512-4

File for Divorce in New York

ISBN 1-57248-351-2

File for Divorce in North Carolina

ISBN 1-57248-508-6

how to **File** for **Divorce** in **Ohio**

ISBN 1-57248-503-5

how to **File** for **Divorce** in **Pennsylvania**

ISBN 1-57248-495-0

how to **File** for **Divorce** in **Texas**

ISBN 1-57248-399-7

File for Divorce in Washington

ISBN 1-57248-522-1

See the order form for purchase information.